Giving Teaching
Back to Teachers

By the same author:
Language and Thought (University of Western Ontario 1982)
Injustice, Inequality and Ethics (Wheatsheaf 1982)
The Philosophy of Schooling (Wheatsheaf 1981)
Happiness (Martin Robertson 1980)
Radical Education (Martin Robertson 1978)
The Canadian Curriculum: a personal view (University of Western Ontario 1978)
Common Sense and the Curriculum (George Allen & Unwin 1976)
Plato and Education (Routledge & Kegan Paul 1976)
Moral Philosophy for Education (George Allen & Unwin 1975)
Plato, Utilitarianism and Education (Routledge & Kegan Paul 1975)
An Introduction to the Philosophy of Education, with R.G. Woods (Methuen 1974; 2nd edn 1982)
Plato's Apology (University of St Andrews 1978)
Greek and Roman Education (Macmillan 1976)
Athenian Democracy (Macmillan 1973; 2nd edn 1976)
Sparta (George Allen & Unwin 1975)

Giving Teaching Back to Teachers

A Critical Introduction to Curriculum Theory

Robin Barrow

Professor of Curriculum Theory
Simon Fraser University

WHEATSHEAF BOOKS · SUSSEX
BARNES & NOBLE BOOKS · NEW JERSEY

First published in Great Britain in 1984 by
WHEATSHEAF BOOKS LTD
A MEMBER OF THE HARVESTER PRESS GROUP
16 Ship Street, Brighton, Sussex

and in the USA by
BARNES & NOBLE BOOKS
81 Adams Drive, Totowa, New Jersey 07512

British Library Cataloguing in Publication Data
Barrow, Robin
   Giving teaching back to teachers.
   1. Curriculum planning
   I. Title
   375'.001   B1570

   ISBN 0-7108-0269-2
   ISBN 0-7108-0274-9 Pbk

Library of Congress Cataloging in Publication Data

Barrow, Robin.
   Giving teaching back to teachers

1. Curriculum planning.   2. Curriculum evaluation.
I. Title
LB1570.B329 1984   375'.001   84-14468
ISBN 0-389-20524-9

Typeset in 10/11pt English Times by Megaron Typesetting
Printed in Great Britain by
Whitstable Litho Ltd, Whitstable, Kent

for Huw Lloyd,
Whose time it is,
and
Mike Stephens,
Whose time I hope it will never be.
But most of all for
Alexandra

By the end of the 1970s it was possible to say that curriculum design was at least on the threshold of emerging as an applied science.

(David Pratt)

A man of true science uses but few hard words and those only when none others will answer his purpose; whereas the smatterer in science . . . thinks that by mouthing hard words he understands hard things.

(Hermann Melville)

> Had he but spared his tongue and pen
> He might have rose like other men;
> But power was never in his thought,
> And wealth he valued not a groat;
> Ingratitude he often found,
> And pitied those who meant the wound;
> But kept the tenor of his mind
> To merit well of human kind;
> Nor made a sacrifice of those
> Who still were true, to please his foes.
> He laboured many a fruitless hour
> To reconcile his friends in power;
> Saw mischief by a faction brewing,
> While they pursued each other's ruin.
> But, finding vain was all his care,
> He left the Court in mere despair.
> (Jonathan Swift)

Contents

ix

Acknowledgements

I should like to thank Dianne Common, Suzanne De Castell, Kieran Egan, Cornel Hamm, Tasos Kazepides, Ron Marx and Jaap Tuinman for their help in a variety of ways (Faculty of Education, Simon Fraser University). Others in North America whose work or oral communications have helped me include: Roi Daniels, Jerry Coombs and George Tomkins (UBC), Geoff Milburn, John McPeck, Don Gutteridge, Jim Sanders, Barbara Houston, Garth Lambert, Bob Clark and Bob Gidney (UWO), David Pratt (Queen's), Ken Osborne (Manitoba), Bill Hare (Dalhousie), Louis Rubin (Illinois), Kenneth Strike (Cornell), Ira Steinberg (Oberlin), David Nyberg (Buffalo), Dennis Raphael (OISE), Pirie Mitchell (London, Ontario) and Hilda Borko (Virginia Tech).

Those working in Australia and New Zealand to whom I owe something include: Jim Gribble (New South Wales), James Marshall (Auckland), Richard Kamman (Otago), John Kleinig (Macquarie), Mike Degenhardt (Tasmania) and Ross Gilham (Timbertop). I am particularly indebted to Peter Hobson, a charming and thoughtful man (New England).

I should like to take this oportunity of formally acknowledging what I owe to many friends and colleagues in Britain; at the University of Leicester I gained a great deal from working for many years with Ron Woods, a man whose increasing disillusion obscured an acute intelligence. I also profited from contact with Geoffrey Bantock, Gerald Bernbaum and Margaret Mathieson. My thanks also, for a variety of reasons, to Paul Hirst (Cambridge), David Pears, Peter Parsons and David Lewis (Christ Church, Oxford), John Gould (Swansea), Jack Wrigley, Raymond Wilson, Antony Flew and Roger Straughan (Reading), Robert Dearden (Birmingham), David Aspin (King's, London), Richard Peters, Denis Lawton, John and Pat White and John Sharwood Smith (Institute of Education, London), David Bridges (Homerton, Cambridge), Brenda Cohen (Surrey), Ian Gregory (York), John Gingell (Nene College), Hugh Sockett (UEA), John Colbeck (Goldsmiths), Phil Snelders (Scraptoft), Glynn Phillips (Westminster College), Guy Claxton (Chelsea), Olive Stevens and

Colin Brown (Avery Hill), John Wilson (Dept of Education, Oxford), Austin Greer (Matlock), Paul Croll, who will hate this book (Bristol Polytechnic), Di Moses (NFER), Sara Delamont (Cardiff), Peter Gilroy (Sheffield), Victor Quinn (Bretton Hall), Colin Wringe (Keele) and Beverley Shaw (Durham).

To many generations of students I am, as any teacher is likely to be, indebted. I should like to mention in particular my MA Philosophy of Education class 1981-3 (Leicester), Curriculum 823 and 901, 1982-3 (SFU), Ruth Jonathan (now at Edinburgh), Nigel Blake (Open University), Christine Tubb (Homerton), Neil Richards (Bramshill), Peter Shirley and Mike Deane White.

I have much enjoyed my contacts with Hong Woo Lee (Seoul, Korea).

On a more personal note, I thank John Goodbody, Alex Marshall, Peter Fearon, Terry Johnson, Derek Layder, Michael Brown, Peter Golding, Robin McCron, Rob Colls, Paul Dimmer, Patrick Gallagher, Edward Elgar, Neill Ross, Stephen Wagg, Peter Wells, Bruce Phillips, James Watson, Ken Hughes, David Morrison and Henry Karsch.

Introduction

This time, I may have bitten off more than I can chew. But it seems worth the risk, because somebody has got to start *doing* what for years educationalists have *said* ought to be done, namely to start bringing together the interests of theory and practice and, within the former, relating the approaches and claims of the constituent disciplines to each other. The field of curriculum is the obvious place to do it, and certainly many curriculum specialists have held out such hopes for it: here, psychology, philosophy and sociology could be integrated and informed by history, as well as by work in more diffuse areas such as economics, politics and management. And here the theoretical background could be applied firmly to classroom practice. In the event, these things have scarcely happened. Some curriculum work is very practical, but appears to have no theoretical backbone; some is very theoretical and has no obvious significant implications for practice. A great deal of it is very particular, and has no obvious general significance at all. A few philosophers have addressed themselves to curriculum matters, but generally without direct reference to the mass of empirical research that otherwise dominates the field. This divorce between the disciplines is particularly noticeable in the case of some of the central psychological concepts. There has been a great deal of philosophical work on concepts such as creativity, needs and, to a lesser extent, the domain of learning/understanding/critical thinking, and no less extensive treatment of such topics in psychology. But seldom does the work in either area explicitly take note of work in the other.

In this book I attempt to bring philosophy and work in the social sciences together in an explicit way, as well as to focus on the need to relate aspects of the latter, such as psychology, sociology and more generally classroom research, more closely together. Throughout the book, while arguing for the importance of facing up to the logical links between theory and practice, I seek to point out the extent to which much educational theory has had little to say of importance for practice, either because it has been poor theory or because it has concerned itself with matters of little significance to educators.

In writing the book, I have persisted in the belief I have always adopted that there is no need to think in terms of a polarisation between introductory texts and contributions to knowledge. Many introductory texts, not only in education, seem to feel obliged to remain on the level of an uncritical summary of ideas, names, claims and, if one is lucky, arguments. They avoid arguing a particular thesis, let alone an unpopular or unfashionable one. I cannot see any particularly good reason for such a limited approach. Why should a reader not be introduced to a subject, led to appraise it critically and, if it is appropriate, forced to reckon with a specific argument about it, within the confines of a single volume? That is what I have tried to do here. It is not, I think, difficult to read, since it is written in plain English, and the argument is clearly expounded as it progresses. By the end of it, the reader should be fairly well-informed about the various elements involved in curriculum theory and a great many of the particular claims made in relation to the various aspects of the subject. However, it is a *critical* introduction and appraisal in both senses of that word: first, it raises questions about those elements and claims, and does not simply catalogue them. Secondly, in many respects, it criticises them and finds them wanting. Hence the emergence of a positive thesis, to the effect that much curriculum theory has got it all wrong in placing too much reliance on the appearance and methods of science, and not enough on the need for greater conceptual finesse and logical coherence. When attention is paid to the latter, not as an academic exercise in isolation, but in the context of curriculum research and development, a sorry state of affairs begins to emerge. It is my view, and I believe the argument of the text substantiates the view, that curriculum theory, generally speaking, is a victim of the delusion that we can establish empirically a great deal that is crucial for the practice of teaching — or worse still, that we have already done so. Recognition both that this is a delusion and that we are victims of it, may pave the way for a more coherent approach to teacher education, which in turn will contribute to a more rational approach to, and body of, curriculum theory.

Part I is concerned with the nature of curriculum theory, considered at a general level. The first chapter is straightforward enough, and introduces the terms to be encountered in the field, and explains the relationship between theory and practice. The second reviews the kinds of factor that do and/or should govern our theory and our practice; certain claims made here do not receive substantiation until Part II, as I am at pains to stress in the text. The third chapter, on design, is slightly peculiar *in* design, in that it argues that the very idea of curriculum design may be misleading and inhibiting.

I devote some time to one particular kind of approach to curriculum design, and it is therefore that particular approach that I am mainly concerned about. I do not say that there is no sense in which curriculum design could be a reasonable enterprise. But I do suggest that the notion of design as an applied science is to be resisted, that many of the specific prescriptions of designers are unwarranted, and that it is probably unhelpful to think of curriculum design as an activity that ought to be engaged in in any particular way.

Part II is, in my view, the most important part of the book. A superficial oddity about it is that, although my argument is for the crucial importance of questions about content and the relative unimportance of questions about method and organisation, Chapter 4 (on content) is rather short, while Chapter 6 (on method) is the longest in the book and is supplemented by Chapter 5 (on psychology). The reasons for this are: (i) that I have written extensively on content elsewhere (Barrow, 1975 and 1980) and do not wish to repeat myself; (ii) that I am less concerned here to answer questions about content in detail than to argue that these are the important questions to consider; and (iii) that the extensive attention paid to empirical research arises partly out of self-protection. In point of fact the argument I advance is largely about *necessary* weaknesses in empirical research into certain educational matters, and therefore does not require, and is not strengthened by, cataloguing repeated instances of such weaknesses. But experience has taught me that many people find it difficult to grasp the significance of necessary weaknesses; they tend to feel that other research might avoid the problems cited in any particular piece of research, even though that cannot be so if the defects are necessary ones. (More charitably, one might say that such people refuse to accept that they are necessary.) I have therefore decided to illustrate my contentions by reference to a fairly detailed examination of a wide range of research into aspects of classroom life. This does at least serve the purpose of strengthening the weaker thesis, that in fact prominent research has given us little reliable and useful information, should the stronger thesis, that this is inevitable, fail to convince. Similarly, the discussion of such things as learning theory, developmental theory and motivation in Chapter 5 is intended to establish and illustrate inherent difficulties in making useful and well-attested claims in such areas, rather than to criticise particular theories or claims for their contingent defects.

Part III deals with those issues relating to curriculum that, strictly speaking, should follow on the working-out or planning of a curriculum: how to implement it and how to evaluate it. One of the points I seek to make is that in practice concern with such things may interfere with the planning of curriculum, but I also argue that we know very little about implementation, and that our attitude to evaluation should not be dominated by a preoccupation with scientific procedures. The final chapter (on teacher education) though short and rather cavalier in style, since it involves drawing together points argued for in earlier chapters, is very important in the overall structure of the book; I do not believe that there is much hope for education, until teachers are themselves better educated, in the specific ways I suggest, and given more freedom to manoeuvre in respect of curriculum than some in fact are and than some views of curriculum would entail.

Any book such as this will run foul of a number of vested interests and will be accused by some of merely representing its own. As to that, I am happy to leave the verdict to those who read it and understand it. I may have overstated in places, I have no doubt made some detailed mistakes in argument, but the overall line of argument, naturally enough, seems to me to be sound. As I said at the outset, I *may* have bitten off more than I can chew; but I am not suffering from indigestion.

Part I
CURRICULUM THEORY

1 Curriculum Studies

1. THE EXTENT OF CURRICULUM STUDIES

Curriculum studies is a broad and sometimes rather confused field. At the root of the problem is the fact that the word 'curriculum'† itself is at best a broad term, and at worst used in different senses by different people. In origin the word, coming from the Latin *curriculum*, which means the course or circuit that a race is to follow, implies the path or track to be followed or the course of study to be undertaken. As far as etymology goes, therefore, the curriculum should be understood to be 'the prescribed content' for study.

For some that has remained its meaning. On this view a curriculum is not a syllabus, which rather suggests a detailed account of materials or resources to be used, nor a statement of aims, but an outline of the subject-matter to be studied. If that were generally agreed to be all that 'curriculum' means, there would not be much room for misunderstanding, and the main specifically curricular question to be asked would be 'What ought the content of the school curriculum to be?' However, the interesting thing is that that is the one question that curriculum experts tend to fight shy of. Time and again curriculum books, while conceding the importance of the question, set it aside, usually on the grounds that it is a question for philosophers rather than curriculum specialists to pursue, as if the two species were necessarily incompatible. Lawrence Stenhouse (1975), for instance, acknowledges the importance of questions that relate to what we ought to provide by way of content, but continues by saying that 'the fundamental questions on which curriculum research and development can throw light'[1] are questions of translating purpose into policy and trying to realise our aspirations, whatever they may happen to be. And many other writers on curriculum follow Stenhouse in placing emphasis on the process of teaching rather than the selection of content.

---

†In this book I shall follow the convention of using quotation marks to indicate reference to a word (e.g. 'education' has nine letters) as opposed to a concept (e.g. education is desirable).

This move away from concentration on the question of what content is desirable initially comes about for a good reason. The question of what we should teach is inextricably bound up in practice with a variety of other questions. To some extent how one teaches something materially affects the nature or shape of what one is teaching, as do various features of the context in which it is taught, such as the state of mind of the student and the state of the physical environment. What an individual pupil or student actually gains from a lesson or class, which is presumably our ultimate concern, is not simply dependent upon the teacher adopting a particular curriculum, in the sense of 'a prescribed content'. As soon as we recognise this, the door is opened to a number of further questions: about our aims (What are we actually trying to achieve?), about the backgrounds of the children in question (Does this material mean anything to them? Are they hostile to school? Do their parents encourage them?), about the development of children (Is this material suited to children of this age? Are there more appropriate ways of presenting it at this level?), about our teaching methods (Is instructing the pupils counterproductive to my aims? Would streaming the class make for better results?), and about our use of time and resources, and the layout and appearance of the classroom. All such questions are pertinent to the general question of what we are actually getting across to students when we embark upon teaching the prescribed content. If students of curriculum should be concerned with content, then surely, it is commonly felt, they should also be concerned with these other questions.

This line of reasoning has gained considerable ground since the publication of Ralph Tyler's book *Basic Principles of Curriculum and Instruction* (1949). For Tyler there were four basic questions about curriculum that needed to be answered: What educational purposes should the school seek to attain? How can learning experiences be selected which are likely to be useful in attaining these objectives? How can learning experiences be organised for effective instruction? How can the effectiveness of learning experiences be evaluated? Prior to the publication of Tyler's book, the assumption had perhaps been that the key question for curriculum purposes was his first, but, since the time that he formally drew attention to the other three, they have increasingly come to dominate curriculum studies at the expense of the first.

As a result of this shift in emphasis from concern with choosing a worthwhile content to concern with understanding extraneous factors that may make a material difference to the effect and the value of teaching that content, many new definitions of curriculum have been proposed that take account of these other factors. To describe the curriculum as 'the prescribed content' is to risk obscuring the fact that the content that is prescribed is very likely both less and more than what individual students get out of it. In some respects students will learn a great deal more than the appointed course of study encompasses (how to daydream while seeming to pay attention, or how boring history lessons can be), and in others the gain they make will be less than anticipated (they will not actually master the intricacies of Tudor politics). Since the outcome of teaching a prescribed content can vary from place to place and time to time, it has seemed important to some to define curriculum in terms of end-results. But then it has to be borne in mind that some end-results are foreseen, while others are not; some content is prescribed openly, while some is purveyed by the school more informally, sometimes even unwittingly; and some objectives may be put forward in terms of presenting content, but others might be better expressed as principles of procedure, or in terms of the provision of particular experiences. All such considerations give rise to the possibility of different definitions of curriculum.

Neagley and Evans (1967) feel that we should include in the meaning of the term 'all the planned experiences provided by the school to assist the pupils in attaining the designated learning outcomes to the best of their abilities'. David Pratt (1980) wants to extend the meaning of the word to cover intentions rather than programmes of study: 'an organised set of formal educational and/or training intentions'. Lawrence Stenhouse (1975) is unconcerned with the precise form that curriculum takes, for he defines it as any 'attempt to communicate the essential principles and features of an educational proposal in such a form that it is open to critical scrutiny and capable of effective translation into practice.' Johnson (1967), by contrast, stipulates that 'curriculum is a structured series of intended learning outcomes.' Kerr (1968) has 'all the learning which is planned and guided by the school, whether it is carried on in groups or individually, inside or outside the school', while Jenkins and Shipman (1975) offer: 'a curriculum is the formulation and implementation of an educational proposal, to be taught and learned within a school or other institution, and for which that institution accepts responsibility at three levels, its rationale, its actual implementation and its effects.' Some, such as Douglas Barnes (1976), want to define curriculum to include reference to unintended consequences, as well as unadvertised intentions. (The phrase 'hidden curriculum' is sometimes used to cover either or both of these factors.) Paul Hirst (1968), on the other hand, seeks to retain something of the pristine curriculum with 'a programme of activities (by teachers and pupils) designed so that pupils will attain as far as possible certain educational ends or objectives.'

The over-eager reader who is wondering how he is going to memorise all these different definitions can relax. There is no particular merit in being able to attribute different definitions to different people out of context. These definitions are in many cases rather cumbersome and stilted, besides being rather different from one another and, in some cases, a long way from the original meaning of 'curriculum'. What matters is a recognition of the point that various factors may impinge upon our attempts to present a particular content to students.

But we have not yet reached the end of the business of extending the range of 'curriculum'. If we are to plan curricula, we also need to consider how to get them adopted in schools, and how to evaluate them. Few people perhaps would write these considerations into the meaning of curriculum (though Stenhouse comes close to doing so with his reference to forms that are 'capable of effective translation into practice'). None the less, implementation and evaluation have become a fixed part of the domain of curriculum studies. Following that, it is but a short step to adding the icing to the enterprise: the inclusion of the business of designing curriculum itself as part of curriculum studies.

By this stage the field of curriculum has become enormous. In fact, it is more or less coextensive with the domain of educational studies, of which it is usually presumed to be an offshoot. 'Curriculum studies boils down to describing, explaining and justifying curriculum practice',[2] as Jenkins and Shipman (1975) put it, and to that broad statement we should at least add that it involves prescribing for curriculum practice. At this point, therefore, it would perhaps be helpful if the commoner phrases referring to aspects of curriculum study were introduced and briefly distinguished and explained.

Curriculum studies itself is a catch-all phrase, and under its wing may be included curriculum development, curriculum design, curriculum research, curriculum implementation and curriculum evaluation. Some of these words and phrases may be used by some authors almost interchangeably, and some of the activities run into each other and overlap. None the less, the following distinctions seem reasonable.

To be concerned with *curriculum development* is to be concerned with questions relating to 'the planning and creation of alternative curricula' (Taylor and Richards, 1979). Curriculum development at heart involves an interest in considering what changes are required where and in procedures for determining what changes are needed. It should not be confused with *curriculum implementation,* which involves concentrating on how in fact curricula come to be — or how they might in future come to be — accepted at various levels, from government to classroom. An interest in development is likely very often to lead to an interest in implementation, for there would be little joy in developing a curriculum which remained ignored by all; none the less the emphasis in development is on the production of new curricula.

Curriculum design is largely concerned with the problem of how to draw up curriculum proposals, including both the question of what to include and how to present it, in such a way as to advance the chances of the curriculum being implemented with understanding and success. Curriculum designers therefore may be interested in debating various different styles of curriculum design, as well as in producing a particular design or specific curriculum plan. Some might suggest that ideally a curriculum should be set out simply in terms of the outline of a content and a rationale for that content. Some would argue that it is important that the content should be broken down into discreet elements and presented in a more systematic manner; perhaps they might add that detailed comments on methodology should be included. Others might go so far as to include ways of evaluating and implementing the curriculum as integral parts of its design. But, whatever particular views curriculum designers subscribe to, the business essentially remains one of considering how to set out one's stall in the most appropriate and effective way. Curriculum design is not usually concerned with setting out a particular curriculum for schools, despite the fact that many people on picking up a book on curriculum design might expect that. They are more likely to get a book telling them what they would need to think about, and how they might proceed, if they were about to plan a new curriculum.

The meaning of *curriculum research* is straightforward enough, even if some of its problems are not. It should however be remembered that while most educational research is largely empirical, and the word 'research' often incorrectly treated as synonymous with 'empirical research', one can research into a number of non-empirical issues, and in the area of curriculum one will need to do so; for example, any coherent educational view will require the backing of research into such concepts as culture and knowledge, and detailed analysis of the nature of particular subjects competing for curriculum time. Curriculum research includes examination of what ought to go on in schools, as well as what does go on, why it does, and how it does.

Curriculum evaluation is a matter not of evaluating pupils' performance in relation to a curriculum but of assessing whether curricula are achieving their aims and/or can be judged to be worthwhile. There is room for confusion here, since some of the means of evaluating a curriculum may involve assessing pupil performance, so the distinction needs to be borne in mind.

With that much clarification I hope that the various specific aspects of curriculum studies can be examined in a relatively clear and straightforward way.

2. THE DEFINITION OF CURRICULUM

After referring to a number of different accounts of 'curriculum', Kelly (1977) remarks that 'the problems of definition are thus serious and complex and it may be that they are best avoided by not attempting to define it [curriculum] too closely'.[3] That, I'm afraid, won't do at all. One might as well begin a peace conference by setting aside the problem of what counts as peace. If we intend to make claims about how to implement, how to evaluate and how to design curricula, then we must have a clear and consistent definition of curriculum, so that we know what we are talking about and are able to judge the sense of the claims we make as we go along. What could I possibly say to the suggestion that curriculum is best developed by practising teachers, rather than non-teaching research experts, if I don't know what counts as curriculum? If curriculum is defined in terms that do not go beyond teachers' knowledge and experience, then the idea makes sense. But, if curriculum is defined in ways that bring in reference to expertise that teachers may lack, it does not seem so plausible.

Nor is there any particular problem about definition, provided that we understand what we are doing when we ask a question of the form: What is curriculum?[4] We might be concerned with the purely verbal question: 'What is the meaning of the English word "curriculum"?' If we are, there are two obvious strategies open to us: we can look in the dictionary, or we can study usage for ourselves. But it is already clear, from the varying accounts of the word given above, that the dictionary definition and usage have parted company, as well as that usage itself is all over the place.

The question therefore is how we are to set about choosing between various different senses of the word or distinct conceptions. Are there any criteria whereby we can judge one definition of curriculum to be superior to another? In the abstract the answer to that question might be no; but given that we have a particular purpose, namely to study curriculum, the answer is yes. People may use the word in different ways, all of them being to a greater or lesser extent consistent with the broad dictionary definition 'a prescribed course of study, training'. What is important for us is to maintain the same use all the time, to have a clear grasp of that use, and to choose one that helps us to think clearly about the topic. A definition that will help us to study curriculum in a manageable and coherent way is what is required, and to that end we need a clear, consistent and relatively specific concept of curriculum.

The need for clarity, coherence and consistency is obvious enough. Ideas that are vague, incoherent or muddled do not help to advance either thinking or good practice. So whatever we do we must know, for example, whether our conception of curriculum does or does not include content that teachers put across unintentionally; and we cannot afford to define the curriculum in terms of outcomes, if we then inconsistently proceed to treat the content prescribed as the essence of the curriculum. But we must also resist any temptation to broaden the concept. In general, broad definitions are less helpful than relatively specific ones, because they lump together distinct elements which it may be to our advantage to separate. Labels such as 'socialist', 'traditionalist' and 'capitalist' seldom serve a particularly useful function since the similarities between individual members of each group are often less marked than those between some members of the group and some outside it. Some traditionalist teachers have more in common with some non-traditionalist teachers than they do with certain other traditionalists. Some socialists have less of significance in common with other socialists than they do with various non-socialists. The broad label capitalist may obscure a variety of crucial differences between individual capitalists. Classifying people in this broad way, which we might call 'package-deal thinking' since it invites us to see people as necessarily exhibiting all or none of a number of characteristics, tempts us to react to them in a limited set of routine ways, and to refrain from noticing particular distinguishing features.

There is, of course, a place for broad definitions; there are occasions on which it is convenient to have the broad concept of animal, so that we can refer to animals without having to list all the separate species. And there are, by definition, some things that are true of all animals. But, if we could only think in terms of the broad concept animal, there would be many things that we could not say or even perceive, because they are not true of all animals. When we begin to think to think in more specific terms, about human animals, snakes, hedgehogs and so forth, we are able to make many more illuminating claims. What is true of all mankind is not as interesting or important for many purposes as what is true of particular people; what we can say of all cars is less revealing than what is true of one particular model. If 'curriculum' is taken to refer to everything that impinges on the child, whether planned or unplanned by teachers, whether the effects are intended or unintended, whether observers are aware or unaware of what is happening, then it is going to be difficult to find much to say that is both true and useful about curriculum as such. Furthermore, we may miss important truths about certain aspects of curriculum, because we do not concentrate on a particular dimension, as we would if our conception was more specific.

As against this, it might be argued that if we operate with a relatively narrow or specific conception we may ignore or fail to see dimensions of curriculum that would be covered by a broader definition. But this is a groundless fear. Thinking in terms of snakes and dogs does not prevent one from focusing on wider issues relating to animals in general, nor from raising the question of what is common to them such that both are species of animal. Similarly, the fact that a definition of curriculum does not include reference to the unintended consequences of teaching particular things does not mean that we couldn't or shouldn't talk about these unintended consequences; no more does the fact that 'school' does not include in its meaning reference to other sources of instruction, such as television, prevent us from considering television as an agency of education in a discussion of schooling. It is easier to recognise that a curriculum, defined relatively narrowly in terms of content, may have unintended consequences, and then to explore that issue, than it is to be alert to all the conceivable ramifications of a broad conception. If we wish to engage in discriminatory thinking, showing awareness for fine distinctions, we need to operate with relatively specific concepts.[5]

We require, then, a conception that is clear, coherent, consistent and relatively specific. For that reason we do not want to include reference to the hidden curriculum in our definition of curriculum itself. Rather, we should make a positive distinction between the curriculum, which refers to what we deliberately and overtly provide, and the hidden curriculum which refers to what is unknowingly and/or covertly put across. Things that may be true and important about putting French in the curriculum, may very well not be true of the fact that a school subtly preaches patriotism through the hidden curriculum. It would also be advisable to exclude reference to the consequences that actually arise from our practice from our definition of curriculum. We shall certainly want to talk about both what we teach and what students learn, but that does not require that the word 'curriculum' should be taken to cover both. Indeed, to define the word in such a way may serve to obscure the distinction between the two.

I shall therefore use the word curriculum to refer only to prescribed content, leaving open the question of the manner in which content should be prescribed. The prescription might take the form of naming subjects, naming activities to engage in, or simply outlining situations for children to experience. In so far as we are concerned with an educational curriculum, the prescribed content must obviously relate to educational ends, just as the more specialised curriculum of a ballet school must incorporate content (exercise, activities, etc) that pertains to ballet. But a school curriculum may in fact legitimately serve more than merely educational aims, as I shall argue below,[6] so the content of the school curriculum overall may be designed to meet other ends besides educational ones.

In order to avoid adding yet another definition of 'curriculum' to the many that have already been proposed, I intend, in the light of what has been said, to modify Hirst's (1968) definition very slightly and to see the curriculum as 'a programme of activities (by teachers and pupils) designed so that pupils will attain so far as possible certain educational and other schooling ends or objectives.'

Having established this relatively specific definition of curriculum, we shall not ignore various extraneous factors that may have important repercussions on the nature, efficiency and value of curriculum. We need to consider, for example, whether anything useful can be said about teaching methods, given that they may conceivably affect the nature of what is taught. But we do not therefore need to write some reference to methodology into the definition of curriculum. That would be to begin the process of turning 'curriculum' into little more than a synonym for 'education' or 'schooling', thereby making the term both redundant and relatively useless for our purposes.

3. CURRICULUM THEORY

Curriculum theory is theory related to curriculum and closely relevant matters.[7] It is centrally related to the prescribed content of schooling, but it must also concern itself with closely connected issues such as the unintended consequences of teaching a curriculum, the problem of establishing whether one is achieving one's object, and the methods suitable for imparting it. An important question that needs to be dealt with here is that of the relationship between theory and practice, for, although this issue is fairly straightforward, some people continue to make the mistake of believing that theory and practice are not only distinct, but actually at odds with one another. Theory and practice are distinct in the sense that they are theoretically distinguishable, just as love and lust or the constituent parts of water are theoretically distinguishable. But it is another matter to try and separate lust from love in practice, or to try to physically separate the elements contained in a glass of water. In the same way to imagine that one can in fact separate practice from theory is absurd.

To 'theorise' originally meant no more than to 'speculate' or 'conceive in the abstract' ('speculate' here lacking the connotations of wild guesswork nowadays sometimes associated with it). Over the centuries, and very largely as a result of such speculation slowly having given rise to systematic abstract bodies of understanding, such as science, mathematics and moral philosophy, 'theory' has come to suggest a set of explanatory principles. Some bodies of theory have been fairly thoroughly and rigorously worked out, as is the case with mathematics. Slightly rougher at the edges, but still remarkably robust, is theory in the realm of the natural sciences. Towards the other extreme, theory in the domain of art is some way from presenting a clearly agreed set of basic principles. And in some areas the question of the soundness of the theoretical base is itself a contentious issue: for instance, it is a matter for argument as to how sound a body of theory has been built up in the social sciences.

But in every case the relationship between the body of theory, however tentative, and practice in the area is the same: the theory represents understanding of the practice. The practice logically presupposes the theory, even if nobody has yet worked out or grasped the theory, for the theory *is* the explanation or account of the practice. The theoretical explanation of a volcanic eruption was always the same and there to be appreciated even before it was understood by man. The fact that volcanoes continue to erupt, while man is ignorant of the reasons why, shows only that practices can continue when people lack theoretical understanding; it does not show that theory is in fact divorced from practice.

In every case, in so far as the theory is good, that means that it does explain or offer a true account of what is the case. So whatever the status of theory in, say, the social sciences, it is still possible in principle to offer good theory in that area: people may be cautious about social science theory, but there must none the less be a sound theoretical explanation of phenomena in the social sciences.

What gets theory a poor name is poor theory. Somebody offers an account of the nation's economic workings that looks implausible and in the event leads to chaos, and then people ridicule the account as 'mere theory'. What it should be dismissed as, however, is bad theory. The fact that economic theorists fail to establish the basic principles of the way in which economic forces operate shows only that we have not yet developed a sound body of economic theory, indeed may never do so; it does not show that there is no account to be given. There must in principle be such an account to be given, for economic forces do operate. Good economic theory would, by definition, tell us how economic factors do operate.

As far as education goes, those who talk of practice being more important than theory or who seek to set the two at odds with one another, are guilty of considerable confusion. Of course it is possible to practise teaching without any theoretical understanding of one's practice, and to do it very well, just as it is possible to love without any psychological understanding of human emotions, or to build bridges or paint beautiful pictures without much theoretical understanding of either. But no amount of multiplying such examples of the divorce between acting and understanding will alter the fact that good practice logically presupposes theory, as a good bridge presupposes scientific theory and a good painting theory of art, in the sense that the goodness in question is a matter of the bridge or painting matching up to theoretical requirements.

Recognising that one's teaching, bridge-building or painting is good even more obviously requires theoretical understanding, for it is the theory that provides the standards by which quality is judged. And, again, any rational attempts to improve practice will necessarily involve theoretical understanding, since one cannot see what needs to be done to improve bridge design without some grasp of the explanation of the various facets of bridge performance. To have theoretical understanding of bridge-building is to understand why your bridge functions as it does, and why it should be accounted a good one, and the same is true of painting and education. The only things that need to be stressed are that, as the subject-matter changes, our understanding may differ in its degree of certainty, and we may need to ask different kinds of question. Thus, the theory behind the bridge is largely technical, since there is little disagreement about the purpose of bridges and hence about how to judge their quality. When we turn to painting, however, understanding that the 'Mona Lisa' is a great painting is less a matter of understanding technical details and more a matter of having some coherent grasp of what constitutes art. Education clearly incorporates both technical and evaluative elements: recognising good teaching requires both knowing what the teacher is doing and to what effect, and having a clear view of what effects are desirable and why.

Curriculum theory, then, will primarily address itself to questions about the prescribed content of the school curriculum, on the grounds that a good theoretical grasp of what we are teaching and why, and what we should teach and why, is essential to judging our practice, carrying it out, and improving it. But in order to clarify our ideas about curriculum, we need first to have a clear idea of what schooling and education are all about. We also want to pursue the questions of what we know about the effects of different teaching methods, what factors may affect the manner and success of our teaching, and what we can do by way of evaluating the progress that we are making in teaching a particular curriculum, for those are questions that have a direct bearing on prescribing a particular content. The issue of the politics of getting a curriculum proposal accepted is less directly related to that of prescribing the content, but it too should be considered, if only because even the most soundly based curriculum proposal is of little immediate use, if it is generally ignored.

These are the questions that will be pursued in the following chapters.

2 Influences on the Curriculum

Curriculum theory involves both descriptive and prescriptive work. It is necessary to understand and describe what does go on when we try to teach different people different things in various ways, why it goes on, and what it seems likely would happen if we did something new (*descriptive theory*). But there is also a need to explore and offer some kind of informed answers to questions of value and priority, such as whether we are prepared to accept certain consequences of a particular practice and what we ought to be trying to achieve (*prescriptive theory*). This duality in curriculum theory arises out of the fact that, while the business of schooling is generally agreed to be valuable, there is a lot of disagreement about what it is that is valuable; it is thrown into relief when it comes to considering what is sometimes called the context of curriculum — that is to say, when we attempt to assess what factors may impinge upon curriculum. We need to know not only what kinds of influence may or do affect the curriculum, but also what we regard as acceptable influences. We also need to distinguish between influences on what does happen in curriculum practice and influences on theoretical accounts of what does and should happen.

This chapter will concentrate exclusively on making general points about possible influences on curriculum and some of the problems involved in researching those influences. I shall not refer to any specific examples, but the general points will be taken up and illustrated by reference to particular curricular claims and pieces of research in subsequent chapters.

1. WHAT SHOULD INFLUENCE PRACTICE?

There can be no doubt about what should be the essential influence on curriculum practice, and that is sound curriculum theory. For that is to say no more than that what we teach in schools should be based upon a thorough understanding of what effects various procedures may have, what changes might be brought about by different strategies, and what there is good reason to regard as desirable. Such understanding constitutes sound theory. As has already been conceded, it is possible to have sound practice without conscious theoretical understanding. Boats may be made to float before anyone has worked out what makes them float. But if the practice is sound, then there must in principle be an explanation of why this practice is sound and another is not, just as there must in principle be an explanation of why this lump of metal floats and that does not. Furthermore, in the case of teaching, since what makes good practice is not self-evident in the way that it is self-evident that good boats must float, there is need for further theoretical understanding in order to determine that particular practices are indeed sound.

This simple truth is seldom stated in curriculum textbooks. Most writing on curriculum context and implementation concentrates on evident, but avoidable, influences as if they must necessarily be accepted and circumvented, rather than simply crushed. They tend, for example, to stress the need to get politically powerful groups or senior officials in the educational hierarchy on one's side, rather than the need to ignore them and concentrate on sound theory. And it has been argued that, since teachers are by and large little impressed by research, they should be won over by involving them in the research rather than that they should be educated to understand the significance of research. Such strategies are not necessarily objectionable in themselves, but why do we assume that curriculum practice has to be arrived at by coming to understand the workings of power rather than through reason?[1]

The answer in general terms very likely has something to do with the anti-theoretical stance of many teachers and the political importance of the educational system. More specifically, the answer is partly that as a matter of fact curriculum studies expertise tends to lack the philosophical dimension; it is usually acknowledged as being important, but then set aside for philosophers to deal with. It is also partly that curriculum experts are serving two masters in trying to write for students of curriculum who are also, very often, practising teachers. Curriculum practice *should* be based on sound theory, and one might reasonably be expected to insist as much to other students of curriculum. But, if one is addressing practising teachers, it may not be very realistic to say as much; they are likely to be more interested in how to get whatever they want to do going, than in re-opening the debate about the value of what they want to do. They may also reasonably enough observe that they are not necessarily free to do whatever there seems good reason to do. Yet a third part of the answer is that North American curriculum writing, which forms the bulk of curriculum writing, has deliberately eschewed the problem of values, and built up a body of curriculum theory on the pattern of engineering, a subject the ends or objectives of which are relatively uncontentious.

This is rather serious. One sympathises with the widespread desire on the part of teachers to get on with teaching rather than theorising about what to teach, but surely one must insist that there be some good reasons to get on with whatever they want to get on with, and probably that they should have some understanding of those reasons. Nor is the emphasis on getting round practical and political obstacles entirely acceptable. Many curriculum writers appear to believe that any change is for the better; but that is not so, and therefore outflanking or winning over potential opposition to change is not necessarily desirable. Rather than seeing curriculum theory as a body of technical knowledge to be thrust on the schools through political *savoir-faire*, we should think of actual influences on curriculum as constraints on past and present practice that need to be understood, very often in order to be challenged. This will help us to appreciate that much of what is going on is a product of circumstance rather than reason. We must also avoid the common mistake of confusing explanation and justification. The fact that we can explain why the curriculum takes a particular form in terms of, say, historical accident, leaves untouched the question of whether there is or is not good reason for it. To understand the power of circumstance is one thing; to bow down to it as a determinant of future practice is another.

We need to become aware of the non-rational factors that have influenced current practice and theorising, so that we are enabled, not to manipulate them to good advantage, but to avoid them — so that our practice may be based upon sound theory rather than chance circumstances, and our theory on sound examination of the matter and argument.

I have deliberately used the word 'influence', and avoided terms such as 'determine', because it is not self-evident that anything is inescapably determined in the sense of 'unavoidable, given certain antecedent facts'. It may well be that to some extent the curriculum in the form we have it arises as a consequence of the economic structure of society, but, even if that is so, it does not follow that it was inevitable that it should have done. It is necessary therefore to distinguish between the view that certain factors have influenced curriculum practice and the view that they necessarily must continue to do so. The latter kind of view is exceedingly difficult to substantiate, and I am not aware of any obviously convincing theories about factors that necessarily predetermine the nature of curriculum. It is plausible to say that the economic base has influenced and very likely will continue to influence curriculum; it is not plausible to say that it necessarily shapes it in predictable ways. Too often in curriculum theory a claim to the effect that X caused Y is treated as an inescapable law to the effect that X always and necessarily causes Y. In this chapter we are concerned not with an attempt to formulate laws of curriculum change, but with noting the factors that may have some effect on curriculum, so that we can be alert to them.

2. WHAT INFLUENCES THEORY?

If theory ideally ought to influence practice, what are the possible influences on theory itself? What factors other than the disinterested pursuit of truth may shape the theoretical position one adopts? The most obvious ones are fixed opinions or prejudices previously acquired through one's background and upbringing; these may have been casually acquired through peer group, systematically instilled by family, learned at school, or acquired in a variety of other ways. Thus one person may develop a theory of intelligence which is heavily influenced by a long-held, but not necessarily closely examined, belief that intelligences differ innately; some people's interpretation of a Darwinian account of evolution may be considerably influenced by their fundamentalist religious convictions. Sometimes firmly-held opinions that affect one's subsequent theorising may themselves have been acquired neither by chance nor through non-rational influences, but through wrong or partial understanding of other facts or principles. No doubt, for example, many people's theorising about the merits or demerits of the European Economic Community is hampered by misinformation or misunderstanding, rather than simply by ignorance or prejudice. Further factors that may influence one's theoretical view include concern for approval, acceptance or advancement, professional constraints on the type of research that is encouraged, and commitment to some ideological position.

Many more instances could be given of these general, more or less psychological, factors that may affect the purity of one's theorising. Less obvious and more interesting are certain problems inherent in much research which may make our descriptive theory very much less sound than we appreciate, despite our best endeavours. There are a number of weaknesses which, though avoidable in principle, are in fact very difficult to avoid.

One such weakness is that empirical research in education tends to draw on very small samples: only a few classrooms are observed; only a small number of students studied, or a small number of teachers consulted. There are some understandable reasons why this should be so (to do with time, cost and manageability), but it remains an obvious shortcoming. To draw conclusions from a study of twenty schools is less convincing than to draw them from a study of eighty. A more critical problem, since it strikes at the heart of the scientific method supposedly employed, is a distressingly widespread lack of control of variables, exemplified by research into teaching effectiveness that fails to allow for or control for such things as the varying experience of teachers, the differing backgrounds of children, and the different types of school involved in the study. Again, one appreciates the difficulty of carrying out research in a way that succeeds in minimising the significance of, or in allowing for, such differences. None the less, we must face up to the implications: when such variables are not controlled, they, rather than the factors our research is focused upon, may be the cause or partial cause of different outcomes. (Examples of these and other weaknesses to be noted will be found in the following chapters, especially Chapter 6).[2]

The most serious of avoidable but widespread weaknesses is the conceptual vapidness of most research. If one is going to research into creativity, effective teaching methods, or children with learning difficulties, one needs to operate with very clear and specific conceptions. One needs to be precise in categorising this piece of work as creative and that as uncreative, in classifying a particular teacher as progressive or traditional, or in judging whether that child is or is not paying attention. Almost everybody will formally agree that we need to define our terms; that however is not quite good enough. A word may be correctly defined, but the definition may still be unclear, incoherent or very general, all of which could be severe shortcomings, as I suggested when considering how to define curriculum.

Take, for example, this definition of 'existentialism': 'a theory that holds that existence precedes essence.' That is not only a genuine definition, it is also an accurate one. However, it is not very useful because it doesn't mean anything to most people; despite being couched in plain and simple English, the definition remains obscure to those who are not already immersed in the philosophy in question.

Consider next the definition of a 'creative act' as 'one that occasions a feeling of effective surprise'.[3] In this instance there are two more, slightly different, problems, which again render a seemingly straightforward definition practically useless for the purposes of research and inquiry. First, although in this case we know what the definition means to some extent, in a way that we did not with the definition of existentialism, we none the less do not know what counts as a feeling of effective surprise. Should I be on the look-out for the sort of feeling I get when I run across an old friend, when I see my wife with another man, when I gaze at a beautiful sunset, when I win an unexpected prize, or what? Until this feeling of effective surprise is more sharply characterised, we are in no position to recognise it, even when we experience it. Secondly, if we hope to recognise it in other people, then the definition must be such as to lend itself to some means of recognition. How am I supposed to know whether others are experiencing 'a feeling of effective surprise', even supposing we have determined more exactly what it means? And here we should note that sometimes clarity of definition may be bought at too high a price: it might be suggested that we define 'a feeling of effective surprise' in terms of the person in question 'giving a yelp'. This has the advantage of being tolerably clear and of being observable, but it has the disadvantage of being less than adequate as a definition: giving a yelp is neither a necessary nor a sufficient condition of experiencing a feeling of effective surprise.[4]

The need for specific concepts is no less important than the need for clear ones, as was pointed out in Chapter 1. It is particularly important not to confuse the two in the context of empirical research. A general concept may be relatively clear or unclear, as may a more specific one. Both the general concept vegetable and the more specific concept carrot are, or may be, reasonably clear; on the other hand, the general concept of love and the more specific concept of loyalty are for most of us rather unclear. Empirical research, if it is to be productive, must make extensive use of relatively specific concepts, for they have the capacity to yield more illuminating and reliable information. If one seeks to examine the difference between two broad and general categories such as traditional and progressive teaching styles, or instructional and discovery methods of teaching, there are three immediate problems: first, the very generality of the concepts makes the initial classification of people very hazardous: it is much easier to classify somebody in respect of something specific, such as the use of the cane, than something more general such as being a disciplinarian. This means that, using broad concepts, some researchers might classify the objects of their study quite differently from others, which would play havoc with the conclusions drawn: imagine that, out of our pool of thirty teachers, ten of those whom one person would classify as traditional might be classified by another as progressive, and then think how different their conclusions would be, based on the same data. Secondly, it also follows from the use of broad categories that locating precise causes for observed effects is relatively difficult. If the only difference between teachers who achieve X and those who don't is that those who do have blue eyes, then we can relatively confidently ascribe the achievement of X to the possession of blue eyes. But, if we are operating with some broad concept such as that of a traditional teacher, then it is not clear which aspect or aspects of the many that make up the package-deal 'traditional teacher' can be accounted the cause of the observed consequences. We are somewhat in the position of medical science when it knows that a particular disease only befalls males, but doesn't know what it is about being male that leads to the disease. Thirdly, although general concepts are not the same thing as unclear ones, there is in fact a danger that use of general concepts will lead to uncertainty, simply because broad concepts, by definition, cover a wide area and thereby increase the scope for lack of clarity. What, for instance, counts as part of instruction? Is telling a child a story instructing him? Is answering a question to count as a form of instruction? Is setting an example part of instruction? Increased specificity is certainly not necessarily a sufficient solution, as we shall see in Chapter 6, but general concepts are prone to vagueness in education.[5]

We shall need to return to this issue of conceptual weaknesses in empirical research several times in subsequent chapters. For the moment we are concerned with the general point that sound empirical research must be based upon clear and specific concepts. If you want to research into whether students of history are more intelligent than students of science, you need a clear conception of intelligence. A mere definition, such as 'mental sharpness', won't do, for that does not provide us with a clear idea of what we are looking for. Not only must an account be given that clarifies the idea, it must also be given in terms that indicate how it can be recognised if we are going to monitor it, and it must be given in those terms without grossly distorting it: it is no good defining 'intelligence' in terms of size of vocabulary, just because that is a relatively assessable matter, if that is not in fact a necessary or sufficient indication of intelligence. And finally, if we hope to find out something useful, we require a definition of intelligence that is not so general as to cover all exigencies. Intelligence conceived of as 'competent thinking or sensible behaviour in many of the various possible aspects of life', for instance, would not be readily researchable with reference to gaining important knowledge about the relative merits of different courses of study.[6]

In principle, difficult as it may be in practice, the conceptual shortcomings of much research can be put right. Some difficulties in empirical research in education however are, to all intents and purposes, unavoidable. Sometimes, we are trying to find out about things that simply are not directly observable, and any attempt to depict them in ways that make them observable distorts them beyond recognition. Research into the development of aesthetic sensitivity, for example, is always going to be hampered by the fact that that sensitivity itself cannot be adequately characterised in observable terms. Generalising, we may say that one of the unavoidable constraints on our educational theory is that many of the things we are most concerned with, such as development of understanding, intelligence, critical thought and creative imagination, do not lend themselves to direct observation or measurement. The tests of achievement relating to such things therefore do not directly test them. If they have any value, it can only be through indirect validity, which is to say if they can independently be shown to correlate with intelligence, critical thinking or whatever, as assessed in some other reliable way. Since the development of such tests generally arises precisely because we *don't* know how else to assess the quality in question, it is difficult to see how such indirect validity is going to be convincingly established. Intelligence tests, for instance, are popularly supposed to have indirect validity, but in fact this assumption is based largely on evidence that people who do well on IQ tests tend to do well academically and to achieve high socio-economic status. Quite apart from problems about interpreting the relationship between these findings, it is far from clear that either of those achievements are necessarily related to intelligence.[7]

There are also undeniable ethical restraints on what we can do by way of empirical research with human beings. There are a number of matters on which we *could* become a great deal better informed, if we were willing to conduct experiments on children that involved depriving a control group of any education or any parental love. But, for obvious reasons, these are not practices we allow ourselves to engage in, and therefore yet again our research is inevitably less thorough and reliable than we could wish.

The above are factors that do, whether we like it or not, materially affect the quality, and therefore the reliability, of our theory. One should perhaps add that the research that lies behind descriptive theory is subject to inevitable further distortion through individual interpretation. Whatever definition of 'a creative act' we produce, individual judgements as to whether a child is being creative according to that definition at a given moment may differ. It is also the case that researchers, being human, are fallible enough to fail to observe what they are looking out for on occasion, to confuse their figures and so forth, and finally that, anyway, the conclusions to be drawn from empirical research are at best tentative generalisations, rather than general laws.

Add all these points together — the avoidable, the unavoidable, the serious, the trivial, the difficult and the easy to remedy — and it can hardly be denied that we ought to be very cautious indeed, far more so than we are, about the conclusions of empirical research, particularly when we are merely drawing on or referring to summaries of the research of others. Curriculum textbooks very often state that 'X is the cause of Y', and refer to Smith and Smith (1902), or some such research, in a bracket. Most readers will take that to mean that Smith and Smith have proved that X is the cause of Y. But were it to be the case, as well it might, that Smith and Smith had fallen foul of even one of the possible shortcomings referred to, the question of whether X is actually the cause of Y would be as open as it was prior to their research, and their conclusions would be quite simply unfounded, even if by chance correct. It is, I think, scarcely surprising that educationalists today increasingly admit that as a matter of fact there is very little that we can say we know: many of our empirically researched conclusions are contradictory, and many others have to be treated with considerable scepticism.[8]

I have emphasised the weaknesses endemic in much educational research, partly because it is a truth too seldom uttered, but partly because sometimes when the point is acknowledged it is presented in a curiously disarming manner — as if candidly to admit shortcomings made them less consequential. But the sort of limitations noted here, ranging from reliance on small samples to gross conceptual inadequacy, cannot, where they exist, be glossed over or confessed away. They make our theory poor theory and that, in turn, may support or lead to poor practice.[9]

3. WHAT DOES INFLUENCE PRACTICE?

When we turn to the question of what actually does influence practice in curriculum, it is probably true to say that the least directly influential factor is theory. It is rare indeed that a school adopts a curriculum as the direct result of some theoretical argument establishing its quality and its advantages. However, we should perhaps beware of drawing too gloomy a conclusion from this. It obviously does not follow that theory does not affect practice to some degree, still less that it doesn't affect it at all. Throughout history theoretical arguments of people such as Plato and Rousseau, Durkheim and Marx, Piaget and Freud, and Burt and Jensen, regardless of their soundness, have had considerable effect on what actually happens in the world.[10] But they have tended to influence indirectly rather than directly, and often only over a long period of time. Furthermore, the nature or direction of the influence is not necessarily that which the authors might have wished.

Plato made some interesting and percipient remarks about play and young children, but it is most unlikely that he would have been pleased to be saluted as an inspiration for a play-way style of education, as he has been on occasions.[11] The British tripartite system of schooling (now largely replaced by comprehensivisation) undoubtedly owed a great deal to Plato's theorising, but the manner of this influence was indirect and very often not formally articulated or reasoned, and it is not necessarily the case that Plato himself would have supported the system he inspired. On the other hand, Plato's views of the nature of knowledge and reality have had profound effects in a way that he might well have approved. Likewise many other historical and contemporary theorists, John Dewey, Paul Hirst, Richard Peters and Ivan Illich, for example, have had considerable influence, sometimes as they might have wished, sometimes not, and usually indirectly, mainly through the particular activities of teachers who at one time or another have picked something up from their work. Hirst, for instance, has explicitly been invoked as a justification for maintaining subject divisions in the school curriculum, a view which he himself has never explicitly endorsed. And Dewey's complex views on democratic education have frequently been misrepresented, and yet have had impact.[12]

In considering some of the factors that may influence curriculum practice, it is helpful to distinguish between what influences curriculum as such (i.e. curriculum content), and what may influence the effect that the curriculum has on individual students — so called 'learning outcomes'.

So far as the curriculum itself goes it is clear that tradition ranks high as an influence. Regardless of how it originated, a lot of what goes on in schools, both at the level of broad subject-matter and that of choice of materials, is there, or done, because it is there. That in turn is often the consequence of fairly obvious factors such as limitation of resources, limitation of parental expectations, constraints produced by various features of the system, control exercised by publishers who have material they intend to sell, and the conservatism of teachers. This last factor might, in turn, be caused by teachers finding it hard to break away from the tradition in which they were raised, perhaps because they are prone to laziness or feel more secure with the familiar, perhaps because of the difficulty of persuading parents of the desirability of some newfangled course. Such things surely explain some of our curriculum practice, at least as much as any commitment, reasoned or otherwise, to the courses in question.

The prevailing fashions of society, especially as mediated through popular newspapers, television, cinema and radio, likewise obviously serve to sustain a particular kind of curriculum. Emphasis on technology is clearly nurtured by a general media preoccupation with the technological side of life, just as at other periods of history an arts-dominated curriculum has gained support from the arts-centred ethos of journals and newspapers. We should not forget, however, that the fact that these are not in themselves good reasons for doing anything does not mean that there might not be good reason to support a curriculum that actually owes its survival to tradition, current fashion or even professional laziness.

Although such general phenomena undoubtedly do affect what happens in practice, there are also a variety of institutions and individuals who may more directly influence curriculum. In Britain, headteachers exercise considerable power in shaping the individual school curriculum, and they are at liberty to do so in view of the very limited statutory demands made on the school curriculum by government (though there are currently signs that central government would like to exercise more control). In France and Sweden central government is already very influential, while in the United States and Canada there is control from both federal and state or provincial government, the latter usually exercising itself through school boards. (Such school boards may be roughly compared to Britain's local education authorities.) Beyond that, in all countries, but particularly in Britain, there are a number of more specialised and more or less autonomous agencies which may influence curriculum, such as the Schools Council, the Nuffield and Gulbenkian Foundations, and the National Federation for Educational Research. Her Majesty's Inspectors occupy a particular and distinctive role in Britain, influencing through their *auctoritas* as much as anything (the personal authority they carry as a result of their reputation built up in the public role).

Besides individuals and formal institutions, pressures and pulls may be exerted by systems of public examination and the demands of universities and industry. And finally there is the consumer, the citizen body itself, which may seek to bring pressure to bear on the curriculum either directly or through parent-teacher associations, or by active participation in school government.

This is not the place to attempt a comprehensive list of agencies, nor to pursue detailed examination of what each one tries to, might try to, or does achieve.[13] What is of immediate importance is to understand that what lies behind the curriculum currently adopted in our schools, the subjects we teach, is not only, if at all, a divinely inspired piece of pure reasoning, but the impact of a number of competing agencies. What we have is to some extent a compromise arising out of political struggle (or, in some cases, political domination). Given that, the detached observer might sometimes be surprised and thankful that the situation is not considerably worse than it is.

The school curriculum, then, generally tends to be the product of various competing individuals and groups adopting, accepting or changing what they can of the tradition they inherit, in the light of ideas they have acquired. That, crudely, accounts for what we present to students. But what about what they get out of it? What, besides the nature of what we present, may affect what they receive? Here we encounter some less obvious and probably more potent influences. We are referring essentially to a host of sociological and psychological claims, evidence relating to individual differences, differences in backgrounds of groups, and the effects of various kinds of institutional arrangement on people; seldom, if ever, does the experience in one classroom, let alone of one individual, match another exactly, even when the same curriculum is presented.

Possibly the single most important variable is the individual personality of the teacher, by which I mean to refer not to personality as categorised in a range of stereotypes such as cheerful, introvert, extrovert, shy or boisterous, but more generally the overall make-up, including all the traits, foibles, habits, mannerisms and moods of the individual. I refer not to the significance of the teacher being of a certain broad type, but to the significance of his being precisely the person he is. I am not therefore suggesting that we can, at any rate yet, usefully categorise good teaching personalities, but rather that a vital factor in what actually results in the classroom is the unclassifiable individual personality of the teacher.

The reason that I am not supporting the idea that we need to classify teachers in terms of such distinctive traits as anxiety, aggression or cheerfulness is that we know, and are likely to continue to know, very little indeed about the effects of anxious, cheerful or any other type of teacher on children, except that which is true by definition. (Aggressive teachers being defined, amongst other things, as people who engage in threatening behaviour, we can be confident that such teachers will cause children to experience some fears.) Indeed, it is quite possible that a particular type of teacher personality will have quite different effects on different students. What I am endorsing is the less readily researchable, but probably truer, views of those such as the Inspectorate that 'personality, character and commitment are as important as the specific knowledge and skills that are used in the day-to-day tasks of teaching' (*Quality of Teaching,* 1983). This is given some slight support by McNamara's (1977) claim that different types of institutional setting have far less effect on the perception and reception of the BEd degree by students than do the differences between the individuals concerned with teaching it.

But it seems highly likely that, though our individual personalities will always have important effects on other people, we shall never be in a position to pinpoint cause and effect in any coherent way. We must therefore bear in mind that one of the most important factors relating to what children get out of a curriculum may be not what is in it, not what use is made of it, not how it is taught in terms of techniques of instruction, not how the instruction is organised, but who is teaching it. This point is of crucial importance not just because it is often ignored by curriculum theorists, but because giving it due weight throws yet more doubt upon the conclusions of such research as we do carry out: for here is one possibly very significant variable that can never be adequately accounted for or controlled. It follows that any observed difference between, for the sake of example, a class taught through lectures and a class taught through seminars might have nothing at all to do with the manner of instruction, and everything to do with the personalities of the individuals involved.

This leads us directly into the question of teaching methods. It may seem that how we teach the curriculum is likely to be the single most important factor in what we achieve. But the research that has been conducted in this area is not particularly impressive and yields few clear conclusions.[14] The problems that beset it should by now be becoming obvious. First, there is the problem of how to characterise and pinpoint various teaching styles. The objections to dealing in broad categories have already been referred to, but there are also difficulties in seeking to break down classroom transactions into a series of discrete observable units. The very idea of seeing the teacher-class interaction as a finite number of distinguishable activities, rather than seeing the whole as being altogether greater and more complex than the sum of its parts, may strike some as questionable, and such itemisation does not do away with the difficulties of providing adequate conceptualisation, distinguishing between items in practice, and individual observer judgement, as we shall see.[15]

Attempts to avoid these problems, either by adopting informal research techniques such as what are sometimes referred to as ethnographic studies or participant-observation, both of which imply relying on the unstructured observations of observers, sometimes openly taking part in the lessons being observed, create new problems of their own. Such research presents us only with individual perceptions and interpretations of particular situations, and provides no clear account of how those judgements were arrived at. The study of Aptitude Treatment Interactions is similar, in that it seeks to observe classroom interaction as a totality, and it runs into similar difficulties in trying to generate reliable generalisations from particular, unsystematic observations. Indeed, advocates of this approach acknowledge being 'thwarted by the inconsistent findings coming from roughly similar inquiries' (Cronbach, 1975),[16] and admit that at best what they observe will be 'quite specific, limited in both time and place'. 'As work on ATIs has proceeded it has become clear that interactions, both among individual difference variables and between them and instructional conditions, can be so complex as to push generalisations beyond our grasp, practically speaking' (Snow, 1977).[17]

The upshot is that while one may continue to presume that different techniques of teaching and different behaviours in the classroom are likely to be significant in attaining different results, we do not in fact have any persuasive evidence that this is so, and certainly do not have any convincing empirical evidence that some techniques are better than others for particular purposes, still less in all circumstances. These important contentions will be fully argued for below (Chapter 6).

There seems rather more reason to accept some of the claims made about the significance of the language of instruction used by the teacher, the significance of the degree of support for school the children experience at home, and the significance of the nature of the child's background in more general terms. There is evidence to support the fairly obvious contention that differing backgrounds tend to be supportive of schooling to different degrees, and that to some extent the variation follows class or economic patterns: middle-class, relatively wealthy homes tend to prepare the child better for schooling and to continue to offer stronger support, because they enshrine and overtly strive after some of the same goals. A specific aspect of this general point is the varying extent to which different children are initiated into the sort of formal language predominantly found in the school at home. School-teaching at the secondary level tends to proceed, as children get older, increasingly in terms of abstractions and generalisations; such language is more characteristic of some homes than others, which tend to remain at the level of the concrete and particular. There is evidence to suggest that this difference too follows class and economic lines to some extent. (I am not suggesting that the work of those such as Bernstein, Labov and Barnes, who are concerned with such issues, is beyond criticism. But the general claims, as I have expressed them, seem to me to be reasonably well attested.[18])

There is also evidence to be noted emanating from psychology about individual differences, though it is easier to classify theoretical differences than to detect them in practice, or to draw conclusions about their effects on the individual child's experience of curriculum. It is a safe enough bet that the individual child's intelligence, in some sense, his capability, his personality, his moods and the circumstances of his life are likely to make some difference to what that individual child takes from the curriculum. But precisely what effects anxiety, a broken home, a low IQ, or high self-esteem may have on particular children is not easy to predict.

There are some severe problems here, beginning with the questions of what intelligence, anxiety, self-esteem and so forth are, and whether we can identify them in practice. There are indeed tests and measures of self-esteem, anxiety and intelligence, but whether they are reliable measures of what they purport to measure is another question. It is generally agreed that it is unwise to assume that IQ tests, for example, necessarily show much more than the ability to do the tests in question. They are not evidence for a capacity to engage in such things as intelligent literary criticism or intelligent scientific deduction, nor are they known to be accurate predictors of subsequent intelligent behaviour in general. It seems, therefore, considerably more useful to stress certain logical and commonsense points about intelligent thought and behaviour and particular states of mind.

The ability to understand or make anything of particular activities generally presupposes having grasped certain other things, and such requisites therefore need to be satisfied if the experience is to be worthwhile. A child won't get much out of a physics class if he can't handle numbers. Again, who would deny that children are likely to get more out of situations where they are already motivated and interested, or where they can be brought to be interested by the material or motivated by something extraneous, than where they are not motivated or interested? Although there is a sense in which some kind of motivation and interest are needed to engage successfully in an activity by definition, these are not simple truisms, and it is important to bear in mind that the experience of curriculum will vary from individual to individual, partly as a result of different motivations and interests. One might choose to say that the child needs to be ready, cognitively and emotionally, to get the most out of what is in the curriculum, but it is important not to slip into the habit of assuming that readiness is a state of grace that visits children and that can be instantly recognised by teachers. Whether somebody is ready to gain from a particular curriculum experience is a matter of judgement, and the judgement consists in assessing whether the individual has the intellectual equipment, the background and the state of mind to make something of it.[19]

There is also reason to believe that providing students with a clear understanding of what they are trying to achieve is a potent factor in improving performance (Bryan and Locke, 1967).[20]

In Chapter 5, we shall look in more detail at some of the claims made about child development, learning, intelligence and other aspects of psychology, and consider how reliable and useful for curriculum purposes such claims are. For the moment I would merely suggest, in anticipation of the argument there, that, although the individual psychology of children, their background, the methods of instruction and the nature of institutions themselves (the way they are organised, their overall ethos) all undoubtedly alter the nature of the experience children receive, we are not in a position to make any firm statements about the effects such differences may have in individual cases. This may be because we cannot research such matters adequately, or just because we haven't yet adequately researched them. But it may equally well be because there are not many hard-and-fast rules of practical significance, partly because the theoretically distinguishable factors cannot in reality be distinguished, and partly because a crucial factor in successful teaching may be the interplay between particular individuals and particular environments. That of course is the contention of those who adopt the ATI approach. But, if that is the case, it is difficult to see how we could hope to conduct illuminating research into the matter, or produce any rules for curriculum practice.

There is one final important distinction to be noted between the influences that may affect the drawing-up of a curriculum or its planning, and the various influences that may affect what the individual gets out of a curriculum. As was pointed out above, the former are clearly resistible in principle and should ideally be resisted, but the latter, those referred to here, are sometimes unavoidable, and generally have to be understood and taken account of by teachers on the level of the particular. If I am planning a curriculum and see good reason to teach English, but I am opposed by a headteacher, then by definition there is good reason to seek to resist the influence of that headteacher (even though there may be prudential reason for me to tread carefuly or even retire). But if a child does not know something that is necessary for understanding something else, or is in some other way unable to cope with the teaching provided, then the curriculum must be modified to take account of that or fail to be effective.

4. WHAT MAKES GOOD THEORY?

We have considered some of the influences that do affect theory and practice, and we have seen that some of them are to be resisted, while all of them need to be recognised and understood. We have also said that what ought to influence practice is sound theory. This leaves us with the question of what influences we ought to admit in the shaping of theory. What makes good theory?

Complete curriculum theory will involve both description and prescription. It will give an accurate description of what is going on and an accurate explanation of why it is going on, and it will also offer a rationale for doing some things rather than others and information pertaining to the necessary or best means to those ends. Good curriculum theory will therefore involve or be based upon a sound understanding of such sociological and psychological data as there are, not forgetting that understanding is not necessarily measured in certainties: our understanding may be that we cannot accurately measure individual intelligence, for example. It will be able to explain how the practice that we have has come about, what its strengths and weaknesses are, and what alternatives could realistically be tried. But it will also need to contain an account of the kind of content that can be justified and presented in ways that will take advantage of, resist, or survive the various potential influences of which we are aware. The element of justification is crucial in two respects: first, without it we are logically unable to assess the efficiency of method, for its efficiency is geared to a certain end result: a way of making a cake can only be an efficient way if, amongst other things, it makes a good cake. Secondly, in practical terms, we cannot expect support for techniques without reference to purposes. Why should one support a means of achieving an end, if no reason is given for supporting the end?

How, then, does one set about justifying curriculum content? What sort of considerations would a good theory incorporate? We shall look into this in more detail in Chapter 4, but briefly the answer lies in a proper understanding of what schooling is all about; that will furnish the essential content of the curriculum as surely as an understanding of what football is about will reveal the essence of what good footballers ought to do, or an understanding of art will reveal the essential characteristics of good painting. We do not require here a descriptive account of what does go on in schools, for what is actually going on in schools might be a travesty of what schooling is ideally all about, just as the actual behaviour of footballers often incorporates elements (dissent, professional foul, bad play) which decidedly don't have anything to do with what football is really about. What is required is an abstract account of the idea of schooling or an analysis of the concept.[21]

Consideration of the ideal nature and functions of schooling will itself involve reference to a number of other ideas such as one's view of the good life, the nature of knowledge, the role of culture and facts about human nature. Taylor and Richards (1979) have stressed how important different conceptions of such things may be for curriculum theory, though they tend to fall into the academic trap of seeing everything in terms of polar opposites. Thus we are reminded that some people see children as inherently good, others as inherently bad; that some see knowledge as absolute, others as relative. But although this may be misleading, in that very often the truth lies in some accommodation between extremes, their basic point that what one thinks about these things affects what one thinks about schooling, and hence curriculum, is correct. Any adequate curriculum theory must have something to say about such things, if only by implication.

Some would argue that it is therefore necessary to start with such considerations, and directly address such questions as whether man is God's creature, an autonomous being, or a cipher buffeted by economic forces. However, it seems more sensible to start by focusing on the idea of schooling, allowing the implications of one's conception to emerge, and, if necessary, be defined at a later stage. The alternative would take an immense amount of time and, moreover, the particular significance of schooling, as opposed to, say, parental guidance or religious instruction, may be missed. It is true that one's view of schooling is shaped to some extent by one's view of more ultimate matters, but what is immediately important for us is what we believe to be *distinctive* about schooling. Granted that a religious person may have a particular view of education that is informed by his religious convictions, so he may of marriage and of the Church; the question of interest to us is what he, or anyone else, thinks schools, as opposed to the family, the Church or whatever, should be concerned to do, in virtue of the fact that they are schools.

5. THE NATURE AND PURPOSE OF SCHOOLING
(See also Chapter 4, ss.6 and 7)

The function of schooling is to watch over, superintend and guide the development of young children into adult life, having concern both for their roles as members of society and for their individual fulfilment. It involves educating and socialising them, as well as nurturing their physical, moral and emotional development.[22] Some might wish to challenge this view. Some would say that the purpose of schooling is to produce good communists, others that it is only to initiate them into the established norms and habits of the society in question. I do not, therefore, claim a universal sanctity for my account of the functions of schooling. I propose it as a reasonable starting-point that is likely to get a wide measure of agreement. It is schooling in something like this sense that we are surely concerned with. The question is one of arguing over detailed interpretation of this definition of schooling.

Some of the elements referred to in this account of schooling are fairly straightforward and easy to understand, though not necessarily easy to carry out. For example, what is involved in *developing physical health* is relatively uncontroversial. True, we can argue about whether people who do not take any exercise and are several pounds overweight are healthy, or about whether drugs necessarily impair health, and we can certainly disagree about the best way to pursue health. I am not, therefore, suggesting that matters to do with health, fitness and diet are quite unproblematic, still less that they are trivial. But I think it fair to say that they are not contentious, in the sense of legitimately hotly disputed at the level of their contribution to curriculum. By and large, the value of health, and the contribution to health of typical programmes of physical activity in schools, would not be disputed.

Socialisation, as I use the term here, is not a technical or complex matter either. I refer simply to the business of introducing and acclimatising people to the habits, beliefs and way of life of a society, avoiding on the one hand merely offering information, and on the other indoctrination. Thus, when I go to Greece with a classical education behind me, a guidebook and some previous experience of the country, I am not really socialised; I do not participate in life as a native; I am a foreigner with some understanding of the culture. When I become a fanatic for the way of life, in act as well as thought, and totally committed to the ideology of the country, then I approach the state of being indoctrinated. But when a child or an immigrant grows into the ways of a community, he is becoming socialised. This seems to me essentially what both the man in the street and a dictionary mean by 'socialisation', but, more to the immediate point, that is what I mean by it.[23] People are socialised in so far as they are able willingly and easily to cooperate in a way of life.

Education, on the other hand, is a more complex and contentious notion. Some people regard being educated as synonymous with learning something, and are therefore inclined to see no difference between training a mechanic and developing a subtle mind; some identify it exclusively with academic know-how, others with academic credits or qualifications. Some have even been known to identify being educated with speaking in a cultured accent. None of these definitions, however, seems adequate to justify all the fuss and ballyhoo that is generally raised about education, quite apart from the fact that they seem plainly incorrect.[24]

Education, in the sense that we are concerned with, is surely essentially about developing mind. It is therefore a rather narrow or specific concept. It has nothing directly to do, for example, with developing health or moral maturity, for we recognise that people can be bad but educated, and sick but educated. Indeed, we recognise that people can be in practically any shape, spiritual, physical or emotional, without it affecting whether they are educated or not, for that is a matter of mind. But what kind of development of mind is required in order to become educated? Is it a question of gaining good academic qualifications? Surely not. We are all familiar with the idea of the academically brilliant but seemingly otherwise uneducated scientist, the narrow-minded boffin beloved of popular fiction; a man may be very clever in a specialised field, but being educated is not quite the same thing. Likewise, it is not a question of being very well informed in the manner of the quiz-show champion. That may be a laudable achievement, but it is not a sure sign of education.

Surely the essence of the educated mind is a breadth of understanding: it is a question of understanding rather than of information, and breadth of knowledge rather than brilliance or speed in a specialism. The mark of the educated mind lies in being able to disentangle complex problems and being able to recognise different kinds of question for what they are. Uneducated minds oversimplify and confuse logically distinct issues. Precocious or pedantic minds, by contrast, overcomplicate. But the educated mind observes due proportion.

However, that is not quite everything. For surely we do not think of people as educated who, while they exhibit such balance and breadth of mind, do so only within a closed system of thought that is not open to alternatives and shows no awareness of, nor respect for, other modes of explanation and other ways of looking at the world in other times and places. A sophisticated but indoctrinated Marxist or Islamic imam, or a member of an isolated tribe, wise in the ways of his tribe but unaware of a world elsewhere, would not rank as a well-educated person. And surely we expect also, not necessarily wisdom and sense, but a degree of conceptual finesse in relation to problems and matters of concern in daily life.[25] That is to say, we expect educated people to show the same kind of fine, discriminating, coherent reasoning in thinking about matters generally — by which I mean to refer to thinking about such diverse things as politics, marriage, the Henley Regatta and the latest TV soap opera — as we expect clever mathematicians to show in respect of mathematics. One might say that the educated mind has the hallmarks of the good academic mind, but displays them in a wider setting.

It must now be evident, as anticipated above, that in this particular conception of education, as in any other, there are implicit certain views as to what ideally people should be like, a view of the nature of knowledge and a view of what is characteristically human. For instance, it is presumed that there are logically distinct types of knowledge, and that human beings should develop their minds and strive to be autonomous. Those assumptions will be examined in greater detail below, but for the moment it may be observed that they are at any rate not unusual or wildly contentious assumptions. They could be questioned, but they do not seem obviously vulnerable to criticism.

Education is not synonymous with schooling, and, in saying that educating does not involve *moral* or *emotional development,* I am not saying that the latter are unimportant or not a proper part of the concern of *schooling*. Schools should indeed also seek to promote moral and emotional development. Here it is perhaps less immediately clear what is involved, but the weight of considered opinion would probably accept that the crux of moral behaviour is not so much behaviour in accordance with a particular set of rules, but seeing things in a particular sort of way. After all, animals can be trained to behave in particular ways, but we tend not to think of them as moral beings. Likewise, humans can do good things for immoral reasons, such as self-interest. We think of behaviour as moral — even when we think the wrong thing was actually done — when people freely choose to act in a particular way as a matter of principle, consistently, and showing some concern for others. These are the basic ingredients of morality: the responsibility of autonomous decision-making; concern for others; impartiality and consistency. Adherence to those formal ideals will not in itself make an action right, but it will classify it as a moral act as opposed to an economic, prudential or other kind of non-moral act.[26]

Similarly, developing emotional maturity should be distinguished from other related, but distinct, activities such as developing emotional restraint (developing a stiff upper lip), or encouraging the outward expression of emotions. These may or may not be desirable aims for schooling but either way they are not the same thing as developing emotional maturity, which certainly is a desirable aim of schooling. Emotions are sensations tied up with particular objects and particular ways of looking at the world;[27] they are not just sensations. Jealousy, for example, is not just a certain kind of feeling. Indeed, it may not involve one particular kind of feeling at all; whether it does would be hard to determine, since I have never experienced your feelings and you have never experienced mine, and there does not appear to be any way whereby any of us could feel the sensations of others. But anyway, concepts such as jealousy involve feelings that accompany a particular kind of appraisal of what is going on; they are not just free-floating sensations of a distinctive feel. You cannot just wake up with a feeling of jealousy; you classify a feeling, whatever it feels like, as one of jealousy, when, and only when, you connect it with a particular state of affairs. It is reasonable to classify a feeling as jealousy if, and only if, the feeling can be attributed to some such perception as that your wife is flirting with another man. (Incidentally, your perception of the state of affairs may be incorrect, but the fact that your jealousy would therefore be unwarranted does not stop it being jealousy that you feel.)

Emotionally mature people are people who classify their own and others' feelings accurately and appropriately. That is to say, at the crudest level, they don't confuse a stomach pain with a broken heart. At a more sophisticated level, they read situations aright and correctly connect particular sensations with those readings: thus, an emotionally mature person recognises when the feeling of antipathy he experiences towards someone is not dislike but envy. (Possibly one should add that emotionally mature persons express their emotions with due measure, but that may be slipping into the area of training emotions and is certainly more debateable.) Essentially, emotionally mature people have true understanding of those feelings, in themselves and others, that we classify as emotions.

This brief examination of some of the main features of schooling is the sort of thing least found in books on the curriculum — the beginnings of a philosophical examination of what is involved in the whole enterprise of schooling, through consideration of its basic concepts. Yet, while being far from the only necessary activity for curriculum theorists, it is clearly a most necessary thing. For it must be obvious to anyone who thinks about it that one cannot plan a curriculum coherently without a clear idea of what it is all in aid of. A curriculum for trainee nurses differs from one for trainee policemen. Why? Because they are designed to suit different kinds of purpose. So what is the school curriculum for? That is the question that has been raised here, and the answer that I have sketched out is that it is for developing breadth of understanding at the logical level (as opposed to the level of information), particular understanding of the realm of emotions and the nature of morality, some historical and cross-cultural awareness, a degree of socialisation, and some concern for physical health.

Since it is only a sketch, such a prescription, as formulated, is open to the charge that it is only summarily presented and might be challenged in various ways at a number of points (e.g. is it really the case that schools should be concerned with promoting physical health? Is the characterisation of emotions I have offered adequate? In what way, if at all, are there logically distinct kinds of understanding?). In Chapter 4 I shall expand on the topic by suggesting something of the kind of curriculum that such a view leads to, and the reader will find a more thorough statement of this argument in *The Philosophy of Schooling* (1981). But I accept the substance of the charge as it relates to what is said here. My purpose has been to indicate the essential first step in curriculum theory, and to offer some kind of view about it, rather than to provide a comprehensive treatment of it. The student of curriculum does, I maintain, now need to pursue this question of the nature of schooling more thoroughly. But since this book is concerned with the nature of curriculum studies, the main thing is to emphasise the need for this step, and to consider the question of whether it is not of far more importance than some of the other aspects of curriculum studies that we shall consider.

3 Curriculum Design

This chapter, like the previous one, is largely concerned with general issues to do with procedure. Substantive points will be taken up, illustrated and considered in more detail in subsequent chapters.

It is necessary to consider curriculum design and development together because the distinction between them, both in theory and practice, is far from clear. Taylor and Richards (1979), for example, in a chapter entitled 'Curriculum Design', deal with more or less the same people and subject-matter that Kelly (1977) deals with in his chapter entitled 'Curriculum Development'. The former also have a short chapter on 'Curriculum Development', the latter has nothing on 'Curriculum Design' by name. Pratt (1980) entitles his book *Curriculum: Design and Development,* but explicitly says that 'both terms . . . are used frequently and to an extent interchangeably throughout this book.'[1] Such equivocation in practice is at least partly due to the fact that it is difficult, even in theory, to draw a clear line between the business of studying curriculum change and the business of studying curriculum presentation, when the former is thought to be considerably affected by the manner of the latter, and the latter is believed to be best determined by understanding the former. The fact is that most curriculum designers and developers believe that we need to establish a set of ideal steps that will both lead to coherent proposals for curriculum change and, when incorporated in the curriculum proposal, enable it to be successfully adopted. But they will differ in the emphasis that they give either to consideration of the appropriate steps for arriving at a curriculum or to consideration of the most appropriate way to lay it out. In this chapter I shall, for convenience, use the phrase 'curriculum design' to cover both aspects, allowing the particular content of my remarks to make it clear which aspect is to the fore.

Curriculum design, it will be recalled, is not directly concerned with planning a curriculum. It is concerned with plotting the steps that need to be followed in devising and/or outlining a curriculum. Books on curriculum design do not, except incidentally, argue for a particular curriculum or for setting a particular curriculum out in a certain way. They are concerned to establish general rules for the formulating and/or presentation of any curriculum. They argue that certain steps should be taken in a particular order when devising curriculum (e.g. begin by establishing broad aims, then reduce these to more specific objectives), that these steps should be taken in a particular kind of way (e.g. objectives should be specified in behavioural terms), and that the curriculum should be presented with reference to certain particular matters made in a particular kind of way (e.g. outline of objectives, statement of prerequisites and list of materials). Since, generally speaking, curriculum designers adopt very broad definitions of curriculum, the range of the rules they come up with, particularly for presenting curriculum, is very wide. They tend to suggest not only how content should be organised, but also how points about instruction, evaluation, logistics and implementation should be incorporated.

Engaging in curriculum design is therefore comparable to engaging in the task of formulating ground rules for those who want to write successful advertising copy or good novels. And we can hardly avoid the question of whether any such enterprise is not radically misconceived. Is it sensible to imagine that there *are* any firm rules that anyone who wants to write a good novel ought to follow, or that successful advertising necessarily must arise out of taking certain steps in a certain order? In the same way, is it plausible to suggest that there is a proper way to devise and present curriculum, no matter what its subject-matter may be or for whom it is intended? The field of curriculum design has thrown up many competing metaphors for the activity itself. Some see it as analogous to designing a house, some to producing a blueprint for a technological artifact such as a ship or an aeroplane, some to providing a recipe for a cake, and some to outlining a theory of art.[2] But the very existence of so many widely divergent metaphors as there are might well incline one to suspect that all are wide of the mark. And the very openness of some of them might well cause one to wonder whether curriculum design, besides not being directly comparable to anything else, might not be a field in which there are a number of equally sensible ways of proceeding, perhaps some ways being more suited to particular situations. One might suggest, for example, that although curriculum design is not analogous to producing manuals on the composing of symphonies, they have in common the fact that there is no single correct way to do it.

I shall argue that there is no proper way to set about formulating new curricula or presenting them in general, that there are no good grounds for presuming that *any* curriculum should be set out in one particular kind of way, and that, in any case, one cannot hope to formulate rules for curriculum design, or to judge whether proposed rules are good ones, without reference to the question of what schooling and education are all about, as many curriculum designers seek to do.

1. NEEDS

(See also Chapter 4, s.3.)

I shall begin by looking at David Pratt's book *Curriculum: Design and Development* (1980), treating it as a case-study. Since many of my comments will be critical, I wish to make it clear at the outset that I regard this book as being good of its kind. It is clear, sensible, comprehensive, imaginatively laid out and well articulated. It is also, I believe, representative of its kind, which is important for my purposes, since my objection is to the kind itself, rather than to this particular example of it. Pratt is one of those who explicitly suggests that curriculum design should be treated as an applied science, which is, I shall argue, one of the sources of many troubles in curriculum studies. It is no accident that, while in the previous chapter I have already begun referring to such things as autonomy and emotional maturity, Pratt, by the end of his book, has, with very rare exceptions, talked only in terms of courses in first aid, mechanics, typing, survival in the wilderness, nutrition and other such practical and technical matters. Our different attitudes to curriculum design are in part related to our different conceptions of schooling and education, and in part to our different views about the desirability of seeing 'curriculum design as an applied science'.[3]

According to Pratt, the steps through which curriculum design should proceed are first, assess the needs of children; second, consider the restraints of time, money, personnel, etc. that have to be faced; third, having devised the curriculum content by reference to needs, set out one's plan in an appealing way, specifying aims, objectives and criteria of performance. In addition, the curriculum plan should include a statement of entrance requirements for the course and details relating to instructional procedures; the latter should allow for differences of aptitude in pupils and make explicit reference to good materials that are readily available. Finally, Pratt advises that, if one wishes to see one's curriculum implemented, one will need to be diplomatic and tactful in one's dealings with various people. This bare outline, since it does not contain reference to Pratt's detailed views about such matters as instruction and implementation, would for the most part probably be acceptable to many curriculum designers. The exception to this is the claim that the curriculum should be based on needs, but even that view would be supported by a number of other curriculum designers, and it is to consideration of that view that I shall first turn.

Since Pratt believes that the fundamental requirement is to base the curriculum on needs, one might expect either an attempt to pinpoint an exhaustive, or at any rate a substantial, list of cruicial needs that schools are particularly well placed to meet, or some discussion or consideration of how in principle one sets about determining important needs. In the latter case one would expect some attempt to be made to distinguish between the needs of different people and groups, between pressing needs and less urgent ones, between presumed needs and actual needs, and between strong and weak needs. What in fact we are treated to is a resumé of ways in which one might gather various people's opinions about needs.[4] We are informed about the mechanics, the ways, of collecting opinions, on the assumption, apparently, that truth is the product of a large sample. This is misleading. What truth there is in the view that opinion about needs should be widely canvassed lies in the point that a broad sample is of course preferable to a narrow one; but even a large sample may be an inaccurate measure of opinion, and at best it is only that — a measure of opinion. It is not a measure of the wisdom or correctness of that opinion. To be fair, Pratt himself notes 'a tendency to overlook distinctions between objective and subjective data', and the need to distinguish 'unsupported opinions gathered in surveys' from truth, but he never explains what this distinction is or how one should in practice make it.[5] Nor do his examples help to clarify the matter or reassure the reader.

Take, for instance, his illustration of curriculum design in the context of nutrition. His concern is to establish as a starting-point that malnutrition exists. Pratt's approach — and we should remember that this is the kind of approach that he is advocating in general — is to solicit the opinions of all kinds of people, even whilst acknowledging that many people consulted do not know what they are talking about, that we cannot be sure that the opinions they give are sincerely held and, in general, that the questionnaires such research involves have been shown to be of 'doubtful veracity'.[6] We are none the less, abjured to solicit these various opinions, supplementing them by making telephone calls to the famous, by holding public hearings to gather impressionistic opinions, which it is also conceded may have doubtful validity, by observing what adolescents do in their free time, by engaging in some reading around the subject, and finally, by 'brainstorming'.[7] We are to solicit all these opinions because, even if they are ignorant, unhelpful and misleading, virtually everybody has a reason to expect his opinion to be taken into account. Parents, we are told, deserve to have their opinions taken into account because they have 'authenticity' (presumably this refers to a sincere interest in getting at the truth. If so, it is not necessarily the case that they have it, and not necessarily the case that having it will help them get at the truth). Political groups deserve to be listened to because they have the power to rock the boat; students deserve to be listened to because they have 'a keen appreciation'; teachers deserve to be listened to because they have some experience; employers deserve to be listened to because they have knowledge of what they want. Even drop-outs deserve to be listened to since they have 'a detailed critique' to offer.[8] One wonders why Pratt stops there: surely the CIA should be listened to, since they have a vested interest in such matters, and the various Churches and feminist groups, and homosexual groups, and scuba-diving associations. . . .

One thus arrives at the extraordinary conclusion that the school curriculum is to be based on a *confessedly* grossly fallible and confused system of collecting the opinions of people who do not necessarily know what they are talking about as to whether children may or may not need something.

The example cited by Pratt, being relatively simple and unproblematic, makes the procedure look less ridiculous than it might have done. There will be fairly widespread agreement that malnutrition is a bad thing and some agreement on what constitute at any rate extreme cases of it. But imagine applying this approach to all curriculum planning. Imagine basing our English curriculum on a survey of public opinion about the need to be an adept reader of literature. The only thing that is immediately clear is that whether children do have that need or not, this is not the way to set about finding out. Many of those consulted, not being adept readers of literature, would be in no position to comment, and the rest would undoubtedly have different conceptions of being adept, different experiences of the consequences of being adept, and different views of life and schooling, such that their opinions on this putative need would bear no relation to one another. In general, the more complex and educationally interesting claims about needs become, the more manifest does it become that assessing them cannot be a matter of opinion-gathering, no matter how sophisticated or all-embracing the means of gathering opinions may be.

The fundamental objection to Pratt's approach to needs is that it is too mechanistic. It treats the question of what needs people may have as a matter of straightforward observable fact, and therefore proposes empirical surveys of various sorts to establish what children's needs are. There are two things seriously wrong with this approach.

First, what a person needs is not a straightforward matter of observable fact. One does not simply perceive that someone needs something as one perceives that he is six feet tall. To say that somebody needs something is to say that without it he will not attain some further desirable objective. Strictly speaking, to say that I need something does not even necessarily imply that I lack it (I need the air that I breathe no less because it is there), though for the most part we talk about needs that we feel are not being met. But any needs claim necessarily implies reference to some objective. I only need air on the assumption that I intend to go on living. I only need penicillin if I am sick and want to get well. I only need a certain book if my objective is to read it. Since we happen to hold many objectives in common there are a number of needs on which we can readily agree. Most of us accept that children need love, shelter and sustenance, because we share the view that they should survive comfortably, and we recognise that those things are necessary to that end. But this agreement disappears as soon as we pass beyond such basic needs, the sort of needs outlined by psychologists, and these basic needs are of very little use for curriculum purposes, since the school curriculum can scarcely be adequately conceived as primarily or exclusively concerned with, say, Maslow's (1954) five classes of human need: physiological needs, need for safety, social needs, need for esteem, and the very obscurely conceptualised need for self-actualisation. ('What a man can be, he must be. This need we may call self-actualisation' Maslow, 1954.) We do not necessarily agree that children need to study a foreign language, need to study English grammar, need to pursue courses in nutrition, need to be taught how to survive in the wilderness, because we do not necessarily share the same objectives. Any discussion about what children need therefore presupposes discussion about our objectives.

Secondly, if we are talking about the school curriculum, we specifically require agreement on educational and other schooling objectives. The question is not what are our needs, but what are our educational needs. There may, for example, be widespread agreement that people need secure homes, both physically and emotionally, without it being felt that this has much to do with schools.[9]

Pratt's needs-based approach to curriculum is therefore vulnerable on several counts. First, asking people for their opinions even about matters of fact, such as whether malnutrition exists on a wide scale or whether there is widespread ignorance about nutrition, is a very poor way of getting at the truth. In this respect Pratt does also refer to the value of social, economic and demographic indices, but these too are imperfect so long as there is no clear, consistent and publicly articulated account of what constitutes what we are looking for. (Even something as basic as malnutrition is defined differently on different indices.) The only way to establish the extent of malnutrition is to define it clearly and to look for it. Secondly, establishing that there is a degree of malnutrition and a degree of ignorance about nutrition, does not establish that there is a need for doing anything about it, any more than establishing that there is widespread ignorance about opera establishes that we need to do anything about that. To establish what people need, we have also to establish what matters, and that requires close argument rather than empirical inquiry. Thirdly, agreement on the question of what people need does not necessarily lead to agreement on what to do about it. If we established that people need to develop their self-esteem, it would still require separate argument to establish that the best way to deal with the issue would be to lay on courses designed to develop it. This is a step largely ignored by Pratt. Fourthly, agreement that people need something is not the same thing as agreement that this is an educational need, or a need in some other way of direct concern to schools. Many people would quite reasonably question whether trying to combat malnutrition is a proper concern of the school curriculum. The curriculum cannot be expected to cater for every conceivable social need, so even if we were to agree that children need a stable home, a religious faith, the ability to brush their teeth and to control their sexual desires, it would not automatically follow that all these things should be catered for in the school curriculum.

Pratt remarks that 'the fact that a need is being largely met by other agencies does not preclude the school from responsibility. Eighty per cent of the students may learn to swim in the local pool, but the school may legitimately assume responsibility for the other 20 per cent.'[10] But this does not reveal whether he thinks it *should* assume such responsibility, nor how we are supposed to decide. And when he does consider the question of whether schools should meet the alleged need for courses in malnutrition, he confines himself to logistic matters, such as whether it might be more economic and efficient to rely on outside agencies or visiting speakers than for the school to run such courses itself. He does not directly address himself to the question of whether this is the sort of thing that schools ought to be concerned with at all. Unfortunately almost all his other examples (avoiding and handling unwanted pregnancy, consideration of the role of nuclear power stations, juvenile alcoholism, learning driving skills) are similarly relatively easy to define and recognise, but arguably not specifically educational concerns. What is whatever mysterious process of reasoning he intends to employ to determine whether the school should take on certain responsibilities going to lead him to say about conceivably more central curriculum questions such as whether children need to study history, literature or a foreign language?

It will be appreciated that my argument is not designed to suggest that malnutrition doesn't exist or doesn't matter, or even necessarily that courses in nutrition are a bad thing. My concern is to make the more general point that the idea that curriculum design should start with needs assessment in this form, is one particular general rule that should be rejected. This is not the way to start planning a curriculum.

2. OBJECTIVES

(See also Chapter 5, s.5.)

Now that some idea of the content of curriculum has been delineated to his satisfaction, Pratt turns to the question of how to present the curriculum; what to exclude, what to include, and in what form. Aims, we are told, should be stated. As should now be clear, this is not a reference to the aims of education, but the aims of the course. We are being advised to produce a statement of what we aim to do in our nutrition course, rather than what we aim to achieve by it (although the two might sometimes happen to coincide). It is said that a properly drawn-up curriculum should state its aims in a form that is concise, exact and complete. That is a general rule that we might be inclined to accept. But then, besides being on the level of a commonsense truism, it is not a rule of any practical use, unless we know what makes a statement of aims concise, exact and complete. This is not considered by Pratt, as indeed it cannot be, since whether an aim is set out concisely, exactly and completely must depend on what the aim is. All that he can do, therefore, is provide some examples. In the event these examples, besides remaining on the level of relatively concrete matters for the most part, could be argued to not meet the criteria in particular ways. But even if they were successful and appropriate examples, they would not enable us to formulate any general procedures for ensuring concision, exactness and completeness: providing examples of something is never an adequate way of explaining that something. Examples of kind acts, for example, do not in themselves explain what constitutes kindness. Even if it were true that 'to enable students to use an English dictionary effectively' meets all the criteria of a good aim, we would not be able to deduce automatically from the example how to present any aim in such a way as to meet the criteria.[11]

We are also told that an aim should be presented in a form that is 'acceptable'. There is a sense of 'acceptable' too in which it is a truism that specification should be acceptable. But by 'acceptable' Pratt means 'politically acceptable' and not, for instance, 'logically acceptable'. What he is concerned with is not a curriculum that is acceptable to reason, to justice or to educational aims, but one that is 'eloquent and persuasive' and appealing to the powers that be.[12] But it is at least open to question whether an aim should be deliberately couched in politically winning terms, particularly if that is allowed to override considerations of its educational acceptability, for curriculum designers surely have some educational, if not moral, responsibility to the community.

The statement of aims, it is next said, should both specify one's intentions and identify significant expected changes in the learner. But is it necessarily true that a curriculum should specify significant expected changes in the learner? At first blush it may seem self-evident that it should, but is there anything necessarily wrong with specifying situations into which one wishes to place people, without any preconceived idea of what they will get out of it? Is it necessarily objectionable to propose reading Shakespeare's *Hamlet* in the expectation that some valuable things may be got out of it, without specifying what they may be, indeed without knowing what they may be? By the same line of argument one might question the need for the teacher's intentions to be specified in the detailed kind of way that Pratt and other curriculum designers require. No doubt a teacher ought to have some overall idea of what he is aiming at — indeed I am arguing that that is above all what he should have — but it does not follow that he needs to have specific preformulated intentions relating to every step in the programme.

As is not atypical of curriculum designers, Pratt is rather demanding about the way in which intentions are to be expressed. We should not describe 'what will happen during instruction', but what will happen 'as a result of it'.[13] Therefore, it is all right to aim 'to enhance students' enjoyment of poetry', but not (as I proposed to do above) merely to introduce them to a poem. Other examples of statements of aims approved by Pratt include: 'to develop in students ease and confidence in speech and movement', and 'the student will be able to express feelings and communicate ideas creatively and effectively through writing.'[14] It is noticeable that these are the only examples in the entire book that relate to non-technical areas, and they immediately reveal the limitations of this approach in stark detail. Perhaps if we are facing a class learning some technical skill, such as stripping an automobile engine, it makes sense to design the lesson in this rigid way. But in the case of poetry there is no reason to suppose that it does. These are well-presented aims, argues Pratt. But are they aims worth presenting? And why is it necessary, or even desirable, that they be written down as part of a curriculum, or written in this particular manner?

Nor is it clear that they *are* well-presented aims. We encounter here the problem that was present, but less obviously and less damagingly, with the proposed course on nutrition, namely that if we express aims firmly like this, we must know what we are talking about. But do we? Concise, exact, comprehensive statements are not necessarily clear and unequivocal. And I, for one, should be inclined to respond to the third aim cited by asking what is meant by 'communicating ideas creatively and effectively through writing'. Unlike Pratt, I think that that is a very poor statement of aims, for the simple reason that I don't know what it means, and that I therefore wouldn't know what I was trying to do.

Pratt's intentions here are laudable enough. He wants to ensure that the aims of a curriculum are properly understood so that they can be more easily achieved. Having stated an aim, such as that of making people happy, he wants to make it easier for teachers to reach this goal by giving a more tangible or recognisable account of it. But in addition to the inevitable distortion that this approach sometimes involves, the desire to make the whole business look like a technology leads Pratt to suggest further that there is a unitary skill of breaking down generalities into specifics, as there is a skill of breaking tiles cleanly. This skill, it is presumed, is one that curriculum experts should have. However, this is a most implausible idea. There may be a *disposition* on the part of some people to engage in the task of breaking down generalities whenever and wherever encountered, and there may be one or two *specific skills* possessed by some of which use can be made in this business, but the business of breaking down generalities *as such* is no more a unitary skill than critical or imaginative thinking are. Like these latter, the business of breaking down generalities is context-bound to a large extent, so that my ability to break down a general concept, such as happiness, tells you little about my ability to break down a political concept, such as proportional representation, or an aesthetic concept. (See also Chapter 4,s.5.)

More reasonable than the notion of a skill of breaking down generalities and than the desire for definitions in observable terms, is the view that emerges later from Pratt's text to the effect that there are a number of different factors that need to be taken into account, if and when one is trying to offer relatively specific objectives. For example, one wants to have some estimate of the learning time required for an objective to be met, a view of the relative importance of the objective, and an idea of the sort of equipment that might be needed. But the importance of those sorts of consideration seems rather obvious, and it is not clear why the curriculum should actually specify them, nor by what means one is supposed to be able to determine substantive recommendations in these respects.

It is not clear, then, that a detailed statement of objectives can be made without distortion, that it can be done at all in some cases, that we have anything useful to say about how in general it should be done, or that it is necessarily worth doing. Not for the first time we find Pratt reverting to relatively concrete examples, such as surviving in the wilderness, and backing away from his isolated reference to the enjoyment of poetry. The explanation of this might simply be that it is more difficult to deal with such things as appreciation of art in this manner, but it might also be that it would be time wasted, partly because it would be sufficient to specify merely the idea of introducing children to the enjoyment of poetry, whilst leaving individual teachers to devise ways of handling that idea in ways appropriate to their situations, and partly because one distorts if one seeks to characterise enjoyment in terms of specifiable learner behaviour. At this point one begins to question not so much Pratt's specific design, but any insistence on a general pattern of design. Why on earth should one expect the specification for a course on survival in the wilderness to be set out in the same way as the specification for a course in the classics? The differing subject-matter, the individuality of the teacher, the state of mind of the child, and a number of other things are *prima facie* more than likely to make different approaches to curriculum outline suit different occasions and different people. Certainly the case has not been made for the need to specify objectives in general, nor for a way of specifying them in particular.

3. EVALUATION

(See also Chapter 8.)

At any rate Pratt's design now has its objectives. The next item on the

list is evaluation. It is a well-worn cliché of curriculum that you have
to build evaluation into the design. Pratt himself remarks that an
educational programme with no specific assessment procedures
written in is comparable to a hospital operating at the level of asking
patients how they feel.[15] This seems a questionable analogy for a
number of reasons. Asking patients how they feel is certainly inferior
as a mechanism for testing health to using technical apparatus such as
the thermometer (although in straitened circumstances it is still not an
absurd method). But the parallel is far from exact, for nobody is
arguing for bad or even avowedly inferior methods of assessing
curriculum. The question is whether evaluative procedures must
necessarily be written into the design. It would be fairer to ask
whether doctors in presenting treatment or performing surgery need
always to evaluate their progress as they go along. And the answer to
that is clearly 'not always'.

More importantly, the analogy is misleading because it is at least an
open question as to what methods of assessment in the school context
are as reliable as the thermometer in the hospital context, and whether
an informal judgement made by a teacher in school is on the same
level of inadequacy as the patient's view of his own state of health.
Equally suspicious is Pratt's assertion that what some would regard as
intangible or unmeasurable concepts are just inadequately defined,
and that 99% of our objectives could probably be measured if we set
our minds to it.[16] The explanation of this dogmatism seems to lie in
confusion: first, Pratt fails to appreciate that whether that is true or
not is not a simple matter of fact, but a matter of judgement or
ideology, since whether one regards it as true depends upon whether
one regards behavioural definitions as necessarily adequate in all
cases. There is no doubt that one could provide accounts of 99% of
concepts, or indeed all concepts, in behavioural terms, but most of us
regard many purely behavioural accounts as plainly inadequate
accounts of the concepts in question. The question is not whether one
could define happiness or creativity in behavioural terms, but
whether, if one did, the definitions would provide an adequate
characterisation of the concepts.

There then seems to be a further confusion between evaluating and
measuring. Measuring may be taken to be 'the assignment of
numerals to entities according to rules', if we follow a well-known
definition of Stufflebeam's, quoted by Pratt.[17] Possibly it is true that,
being what it is, the enterprise of schooling necessarily requires some
kind of assessment. (I certainly think that it is.) But it is not
necessarily the case that everything that we wish to assess can be
measured, for the simple reason that so long as the conceptual work

remains undone, the rules referred to in Stufflebeam's definition are not agreed in relation to education. We are not in a position to measure performance in poetry writing, so long as we are not agreed on the criteria of quality in this sphere. Clearly, so long as assessment has to take the form of appraisal it cannot be systematically written into the curriculum design as procedures for measurement can be, even if we wanted it to be. Once again, a case has not been made either for the general rule that evaluation procedures ought necessarily to be stated in a curriculum outline or for more particular rules about how they should be presented. And we can already see that there are some reasons for objecting to any such assumptions. We shall return to a more detailed consideration of evaluation techniques in Chapter 8.

4. ASPECTS OF CURRICULUM DESIGN

Pratt offers one particular example of an approach to curriculum design. His attempt to ground curriculum in the needs of children, and more particularly his view on how to assess those needs, are not features of all curriculum design. His particular views on objectives and evaluation are likewise not shared by all curriculum designers but most designers would agree that some reference must be made to these matters in a curriculum plan. The most obvious feature of his approach is that it presumes that a curriculum should be laid out beforehand in terms of a fairly detailed specification of its objectives, the performance criteria to be assessed in respect of knowledge, skills and dispositions, the necessary prerequisites for embarking on the curriculum, strategies of instruction, and means of evaluation and implementation. This presumption is common to all approaches to curriculum that are sometimes loosely classified together as rational-planning or means-ends models of design, even though they may exhibit considerable variation.

At one extreme are proponents of what has been called the Grand Design approach, which suggests that we should start by laying down detailed specifications of the general aims of schooling and the requirements of society, before proceeding to formulate precise schooling objectives in the light of them and in the light of our knowledge of such things as the nature of children and the psychology of learning. We thus arrive at a utopian blueprint for schooling. Such a view may perhaps be attributed to Wiseman and Pidgeon (1970). It is certainly the kind of approach adopted in the past by many educational thinkers, such as Plato, Rousseau and Comenius.[18] These men offered markedly different educational proposals, but they had in common this tendency to specify a particular kind of curriculum to suit their ideals of human nature, society and education.

Sockett (1976) suggests that Tyler (1949) should also be classified as a Grand Designer, but this, I think, obscures an important distinction between those who believe that broad questions about educational and social aims have to be addressed, and those who believe that a curriculum has to contain precise specification of these and more immediate aims. Tyler's approach is in fact more fluid and flexible than many people's, since he emphasises the need to consider our broad aims, as well as to select appropriate learning experiences by reference to them, and to organise and evaluate those experiences; but he does not emphasise an order in which those steps should be followed. Since he recognises the interplay between them, he is relatively open about the form that objectives should take and, above all, he is not primarily interested in arguing that a curriculum should contain detailed specification of our view of these matters. His point is that there are all kinds of questions that need to be answered if our curriculum is to be rationally based, rather than that a curriculum plan should be designed in this way.

By contrast with both the Grand Design and Tyler, such people as Bloom (1956), Mager (1962), Gronlund (1970), and Popham (1977) stress the importance of clearly establishing curriculum objectives and of doing so by presenting them as behavioural objectives so that they can be clearly and readily monitored. Goodlad and Richter (1966) and Wheeler (1967) all have a similarly firm view of the importance of precise objectives but, while stopping short of the Grand Design, they seek to relate these to wider educational aims. Taylor (1970) has argued that, though objectives should be 'integrated with full weight into (the) total scheme', this does not mean that they should 'necessarily be the starting-point' for curriculum design.[19] He suggests that the starting-point should be the selection of content and some general idea of the appropriate methodology, followed by a consideration of the pupils' interests and attitudes, which may lead to modification of the original proposals. Then, from consideration of what has been arrived at, statements of aims and objectives can be developed.

Then there are those who, by implication at least, argue against any such means-end approach with the stress on objectives. Prominent among these is Stenhouse (1975), who advocated what has been called a 'process model' of curriculum design. Having rightly seen that a major problem is the gap between what a curriculum is supposed to achieve and what it actually does achieve, he argued that the way to improve practice was to approach it through improvement of teaching and learning. He therefore proposed to specify content and principles of procedure rather than objectives and intentions. Malcolm Skilbeck (1976), with his 'situational model', took the theory one step further, making the starting-point critical appraisal of an actual situation on the grounds that 'school-based curriculum development is the most effective way of promoting genuine change at school level.'[20] One feature of Skilbeck's approach is that it commits itself to no particular model of design, arguing rather that the important thing is to conduct one's inquiry into goals, content selection, evaluation and implementation with an awareness of the various internal and external factors that are relevant in the context of particular situations. Sockett (1976) is perhaps even more open and flexible, arguing that curriculum design has to be slow and piecemeal, and that the focus should be on designing particular curricula for particular situations. On this view we should think not in terms of a curriculum design, but in terms of designing, for example, a science curriculum for a particular age group, and begin by analysing the present curriculum situation in that regard.

Various objections could be raised to each of these, as well as to other examples of curriculum design that I have not referred to. A Grand Design is likely to show little awareness of the needs and problems of particular situations. Specifying objectives, particularly in behavioural form, has all sorts of difficulties, which will be discussed in Chapter 5. Focusing on the present curriculum experience of children as a starting-point may blind one to unthought of possibilities, and incline one to accept restrictions that ought ideally to be removed. But more significant is the fact that the range of approaches to curriculum design is so broad as to make one wonder whether the idea of curriculum design itself is very profitable: the difference between the views of Wheeler and Sockett seems sufficiently marked for it to be rather misleading to think of them as offering alternative accounts of the same thing. And indeed the very idea of curriculum design seems to be being stretched almost beyond recognition by those such as Skilbeck and Sockett, for the very openness and flexibility of their approach is almost a negation of the idea of a design, in the sense of an outline of the way in which a curriculum should be planned and set out. It is certainly the case that it is inaccurate to see all of these as alternative models of curriculum design, since Skilbeck, for example, far from offering an alternative to the process or objectives approach, argues that either is compatible with his emphasis on the school context and, similarly, Sockett's approach is compatible with several others.

Many of the differences between proposed curriculum designs arise out of the fact that their proponents are talking about not simply different but different kinds of things. Tyler, I have suggested, is primarily interested in establishing what sort of questions a well-planned curriculum ought to have an answer to; Popham is concerned to argue that a curriculum ought to be framed in terms of specific behavioural objectives; Wheeler wants to remind us that objectives have to be selected in the light of some educational aims; Skilbeck draws our attention to the importance of understanding the context in which we are operating. To think of these as competing designs ignores the fact that some of them are not designs at all, the fact that some are mutually compatible, and the fact that some are concerned with stating the sorts of question we need to answer, some with stating a particular answer to some of those questions, and some with establishing the order in which we ought to approach the questions. Beyond that, they offer different and not always very clear views about the extent to which a curriculum plan should, in its final form, incorporate statements relating to these specific elements. Much of the seeming disparity between curriculum designs arises out of a basic confusion between talking about what is logically involved in a well-thought-out curriculum proposal, and what is practically effective or necessary in outlining a proposal. Stenhouse and Skilbeck, for example, are very likely right that curriculum work centred on the classroom will be more popular with teachers (more in tune with their practice, anyhow) and hence perhaps more acceptable to them, but that simply ignores the question of what the school curriculum ought to look like and how it should ideally be designed. Similarly, a lot of argument about objectives fails to distinguish different types of objective, and the difference between having objectives in mind and teaching according to a pre-specification of them in practice. The truth is that any rational curriculum must have objectives; it must, by definition, if it is rational, be doing some things rather than others in order to achieve certain ends. But it is a further question whether those objectives necessarily have to be specified and, if so, in how much detail and in what terms.

Given these points, we can hardly avoid facing directly the question of whether we actually need to have a design, either in the sense of a pattern for the setting-out, or in the sense of a pattern for the formulating, of curricula. Is there any warrant for the assumption of most of these approaches that we need to set out all curricula in a particular way that specifies the kinds of thing we have been considering. Is there good reason to suppose that all curriculum planning should proceed in one or other of these ways? It is my view that the answer is no, essentially because curriculum cannot sensibly be looked upon as an applied science as many of these approaches explicitly or implicitly suggest. If it were such, if there were a body of uncontested theory concerning means to uncontentious ends, and putting forward a curriculum was like putting forward a bridge design, it would follow that would-be curriculum designers would need to know how to set about their task as would-be bridge designers need to know how to set about theirs. But it is *not* like that. Every curriculum proposal is grounded in arguable views of human nature, of the purpose of schooling, of the scope of the proposed subject, and so forth, and supported by very little solid evidence about the effects of various means to those disputed ends. In such circumstances it seems evident that what is required is not a ground plan for designing curricula, but a recognition of the varous sorts of questions that will require some answers, albeit different answers on different occasions, whatever the curriculum put forward. I shall return to this issue in the final section of this chapter. First, it is necessary to comment on certain features of the style in which writing about curriculum design is conducted.

5. THE STYLE OF CURRICULUM DESIGN WRITING: MODELS, DIAGRAMS AND VOCABULARY

Curriculum books and articles have a tendency, as we have seen, to talk in terms of models. They are also prone to make use of diagrams, and to revert to a certain amount of quasi-technical jargon. Most of this dressing-up is irrelevant to the fundamental business of planning and justifying curricula, but it may serve to support a misleading impression of the nature of curriculum theory. .

We are told that there are a number of models of curriculum dissemination (the social-interactive model, the centre-periphery model, the proliferation of centres model, the learning-systems network), as we are told that there are various models of teaching, models of classroom organisation, models of toilet-training, and so forth, as well as models of curriculum design.[21] Reference to a model carries with it connotations of the precise, mechanistic world of physics or engineering, the suggestion of distinct alternatives, each specific and inflexible in itself, though exchangeable for another model. Is there any justification for using such a term in situations where all that is being referred to are some few examples out of a multitude of subtly varied ways of proceeding? As we have seen, the so-called models of curriculum design are often no such thing. They are not necessarily representations of the structure of an ideal or desirable curriculum plan, in the manner of an architect's drawing, or a three-dimensional model. When they come near to being true models, as in the case of Pratt, they are open to the objection that in this complex field it is inappropriate to reduce matters to a schematic and inflexible pattern of requirements or procedure. Models of classroom organisation either illegitimately suggest that there is a limited number of precisely classifiable and distinct modes of organisation, or else they are not truly models. So-called models of curriculum dissemination are merely artificial attempts to fossilise in a series of rigid alternatives the perception that one might attempt to spread knowledge and information about a proposed curriculum in many various ways, ranging from attempts at autocratic imposition through to democratic participation, and that the effectiveness of these ways may vary, largely in ways and to degrees that we do not have much understanding or control of.

Perhaps it is not in itself a crime of major significance to talk of 'models', but it is misleading in that it implies clear distinctions and straightforward limited alternatives where they do not exist. Furthermore, this is merely one example of a more general tendency to create an aura of mechanistic and technical knowledge, implying precision and expertise, by using a language that is highly misleading. To think of the business of teaching in terms of even a dozen or so models is to distort and impoverish one's conception of teaching.[22] For teaching is not reducible to, or adequately characterised in terms of, some limited number of alternative, precisely specified packages of activity. Teaching may take one of a million forms so subtly distinguished and interrelated that it would be fruitless to clarify them, even if one had time, as a million models.

The too easy use of diagrams serves likewise to reinforce the idea that we are dealing with a relatively precise domain comparable to that of the natural sciences. Again there is nothing inherently wrong with a diagram, but, at least for most people, a diagram cannot convey more than can be conveyed in words, and is generally less subtle than verbal formulations. When a diagram is subtle, it is correspondingly incomprehensible to most people, simply because, as most people do their articulate thinking in words, in order to be understood it has to be explained. Diagrams, in short, in the context of education and other similarly complex areas, tend to be either pointless, because they merely present pictorially what is readily comprehensible, or misleading because they oversimplify or stand in need of verbal explanation before they can be understood. But the main objection to them in curriculum is that they may unwarrantably

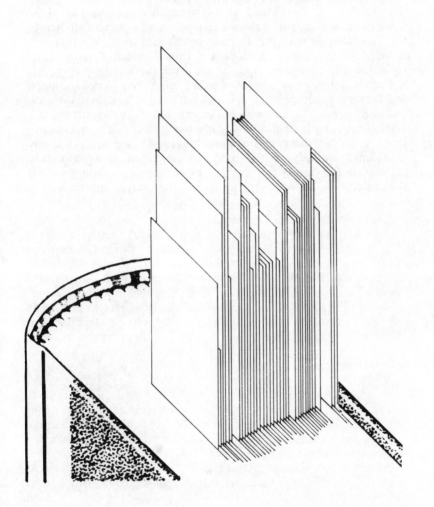

Figure 3.1

imply something of the certainty and precision of the natural sciences or technology, where they naturally find their home.

Diagrams have their place essentially in situations where they help us to visualise what is at rock-bottom a matter of seeing something that is there to be looked at — something that has a spatial dimension. A diagram of the water-pipes in a house usefully serves this function, as does the diagram of the interior of a house in a murder story. But now compare this diagram (Figure 3.1), reproduced from a recent book on the art of the detective story. It is not immediately clear what it is telling us. When I explain that it represents the pattern of suspense engendered in a particular novel, and shows that 'the suspense builds gradually', it remains unclear what presenting it diagrammatically has added to the occasion.[23] Prior to the explanation it meant nothing; following it, it is scarcely necessary. Similarly, in the field of curriculum, straightforward accounts of the various factors that may effect a curriculum plan, and the interplay between them, are commonly represented in

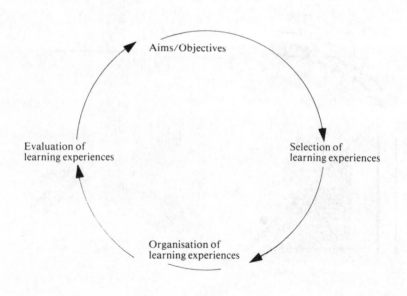

Figure 3.2: *The Tyler model for curriculum planning*

diagrammatic form ranging from the banal to the visually incomprehensible. This diagram of Tyler's 'model' (Figure 3.2) adds nothing to what has been said in the text, while the diagram in Figure 3.3. is, as it stands, incomprehensible.[24] At best, even a simple diagram such as Tyler's can only be understood when the accompanying text is understood, for as yet the conventions of diagrammatic language are not sophisticated enough to rule out misinterpretation even of something so simple. It is not, for example, *wrong* to interpret A→ B→ C as A follows B follows C, although experience suggests it is more likely to mean A leads to B leads to C, or perhaps A causes B causes C. But, at worst, diagrams may seriously mislead by wrongly suggesting that the interplay and connections they depict have some kind of mechanical inevitability. When a diagram is appropriate, for the wiring circuit of a hi-fi perhaps, for depicting human veins, or for an automobile engine, it offers a very accurate pictorial representation. To use a diagram to

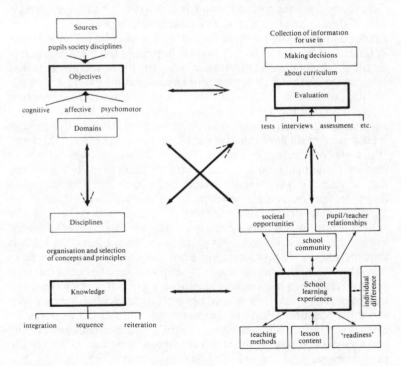

Figure 3.3: *A model for curriculum theory*

summarise one's interpretation of T.S. Eliot's *The Waste Land*, besides being almost certainly inadequate, is to suggest that a poem can profitably be treated like the cross-section of a motorbike engine.

Some of the vocabulary of curriculum development, indeed of education generally, is also a contributory factor to the impression that hard information is being conveyed when in reality we have only tentative or commonplace assumptions. A phrase such as 'teacher-input' may seem inoffensive enough, but its usage in the context of education being a metaphorical extension, it may carry over from its proper home potentially misleading connotations. 'Input' belongs to the world of electrical circuitry: teaching a child to understand something is not necessarily, if at all, like plugging in a current of power. Note, too, that the particular use of some words in *educanto*, as this educational jargon has been termed, reveals a basic ignorance: one may, of course, defend particular cases of extending or even changing the meaning of words, but one can hardly defend the practice of misusing the word 'parameter' as if it were a synonym of 'boundary', as many educationalists do, when it has a very precise and different meaning. Granted, language is flexible and does develop; but that can no more excuse the person who initiates misuse in ignorance by, for example, saying 'hopefully the plane will arrive on time' (which means, *per impossibile*, 'the plane will arrive full of hope on time') than such a plea could excuse calling a dog a cat.[25]

Much of the new vocabulary appears to have no further function than to enhance the mystique of curriculum theory. 'Brainstorming', for example, means no more than 'unstructured thinking',[26] though it misleadingly suggests that it is a skill, or particular kind of thinking. When we come across or devise a truly new concept (which is to say idea or thought), then it is important to mark it with a new and distinct name. But there is no obvious point in calling what the pupils learn 'learner-outcome', or referring to the various influences on curriculum as 'curriculum context', beyond that of giving the spurious impression that the study of curriculum involves specialist knowledge of various concepts peculiar to the subject. The truth is that there are very few worthwhile and original concepts that have been thrown up by curriculum designers, and very few concepts that are not familiar to most educated people, a point that the plethora of new phrases, or new uses for old phrases, in curriculum writing only serves to obscure. Why call the business of looking into potential difficulties before one sets about planning one's curriculum 'front-end analysis'? It has the merit of brevity certainly, as do many of the new coinages; but the value of brevity is lost when, being a new phrase, it needs to be explained. More serious an objection is the fact that this brief phrase, like 'brainstorming', misleadingly gives the impression that what it refers to is a skill, the province of experts, and a technical matter. The suggestion that curriculum planners should consider possible long-term consequences seems sensible enough, but in calling that activity 'engaging in impact analysis' we improperly suggest that there is a specialism akin, say, to psychoanalysis that some are trained to perform.

Some may feel that this issue of vocabulary, models and diagrams is a small one in itself. I doubt that: these are the 'clothes' that are disguising the Emperor's nakedness. Besides being aesthetically displeasing, inaccurate and unnecessary, such stylistic features are a sign that the world of curriculum design, perhaps like the world of fashion design, often has more pretention than precision, more scenary than science.

If we used plain English and resisted the tendency to hide behind models and diagrams, we would surely be less inclined to see educational issues in mechanical and technological terms, less inclined to think in terms of precise alternative procedures, and less inclined to reduce the matter to one of devising specific and rigid means to unquestioned ends. As I shall argue in subsequent chapters, we are in no position to treat education in this way and, in any case, to do so is to fundamentally misrepresent the nature of the educational enterprise. The phrase 'curriculum design' itself gives a wholly misleading impression of what arguing for, planning and outlining a curriculum involves. It suggests, particularly when it has recourse to models, diagrams and jargon, that we are dealing with an applied science. And that, I shall now suggest, is quite inappropriate.

6. CURRICULUM DESIGN AS AN APPLIED SCIENCE

If curriculum design is to be correctly categorised as an applied science, as Pratt and others explicitly want it to be, and others implicitly suggest, then there must be some science or sciences on which it draws substantially. There are unquestionably some scientific truths, even laws, that lie behind and relate to schooling. For example, research suggests (Seymour, 1937) that dark writing on a light background is easier to read than a blackboard, and there are other specific, but limited, truths of like order of relevance to teaching of which we know. There are, besides, many more general laws of science that obviously have application in the sphere of schooling, as they do in most spheres of life. For example, a freezing temperature is not conducive to successful teaching, or many other things. But, beyond the level of commonplace, if far from inherently unimportant, scientific principles which naturally have to be taken account of by educationalists as by everyone else, the bulk of the science that lies behind curriculum theory comes not from the natural but from the social sciences.

It is a truth that the student of curriculum might be forgiven for forgetting, despite the fact that it is formally acknowledged by most curriculum theorists, including Pratt, and regardless of whether they would like to treat curriculum design as a scientific enterprise or not, that we do not know very much about the business of learning, or the particular effects of differing situations and various psychological and sociological factors on the effectiveness of teaching. (See Chapters 5 and 6.) Despite the impressive number of references to research to be encountered in any respectable curriculum book, nobody can point to any evidence that overwhelmingly establishes anything about the overall superiority of any method of teaching, ranging from standing before massed silent ranks and lecturing them to standing back and leaving students to proceed as they see fit. Nor do we have much in the way of sure information about the effects of particular practices in particular situations, or about the effects of such things as working with pre-specified objectives as opposed to working without them, about the effects of various evaluation techniques, about what will happen if we present curriculum in one way rather than another, or about most of the other issues involved in curriculum design. (The argument to support such a claim will be found in subsequent chapters.) Well may Taylor and Richards (1979) quietly observe that as things are ' "scientific" curriculum theory has little or no predictive power'.[27] The scientifically established data here are very limited. This being the case there is not very much that a curriculum design can legitimately specify about instruction, evaluation and so forth, even if it were agreed that that is what curriculum design should do.

But now we come to an even more important point. The view that curriculum design is an applied science can only be maintained if we not only exaggerate the number of scientifically attested facts that we have to draw on, but also ignore the crucial role of non-scientific problems in curricula, in particular the conceptual and evaluative issues that permeate the business. The natural sciences work with very precise and clear concepts and relatively unquestioned values and procedural assumptions; that is why they can proceed as they do. They are precise areas of inquiry, finely honed by time and tradition, working within agreed and sharply delineated boundaries. That is why they give rise to the sort of certainty we think of as 'scientific'. It is true that within the natural sciences, particularly in areas such as genetics and astronomy, some claims that we take to be true are not empirically attested and are by no means incontrovertibly established. It is a mistake to distinguish between the natural and the social sciences purely in terms of the former yielding unequivocally established truths and the latter merely poorly attested probabilities. However, it is the case that the natural sciences proceed without the degree of conceptual and procedural equivocation that plagues the social sciences in general, and their application to education in particular. Schooling is an area of discourse clogged with unclear and general concepts, and one that is marked by intense rivalry as to its ends, purposes and legitimate means, none of which is the case in, say, physics or chemistry. As was pointed out above, the very variety of analogies that curriculum designers have produced for their activity indicates that it cannot reasonably be asserted that it is clearly one particular kind of activity, let alone a specifically scientific one. To make the assumption that it is an applied science is comparable to assuming that marriage guidance is an applied science.

One could initiate courses in, and write books about, 'marriage design', meaning the business of writing out blueprints for married life, and one could treat the enterprise scientifically. But if you do, you miss rather a lot. You ignore the controversial issue of what marriage is supposed to be. You ignore questions such as whether it is the quality rather than the appearance of behaviours and responses that matters, and you unreasonably take it for granted that there is only one, or a limited number of ways, of setting about married life. Beyond that, your recommendations, being based on unproven claims about human psychology and social interaction, might be agonisingly poor. (Indeed it is arguable that many people's lives have been wrecked by taking too seriously the presumed scientifically established truths of marriage guidance experts.) The stark fact is that there are many things about marriage that we might in principle but do not as yet know, and there are other crucial things that by their very nature are not amenable to scientific research. But if one recognises that marriage cannot be treated scientifically, then the notion of marriage design as a professional activity, the idea of expertise in setting out the format(s) for a good marriage, to be distinguished from the idea of particular individuals trying to understand and plan their particular marriages, becomes very suspect.

What is crucially missing from almost all curriculum designs is a recognition that the whole operation can only make sense, let alone be successfully carried out, in the light of a clear articulation of the

central educational concepts. (There are exceptions to this, as we have
seen. People such as Wiseman, Pidgeon and Wheeler do recognise the
need to formulate aims, although their work is still imbued with the
idea that everything has to be done in a certain order, and organised
schematically and in detailed precision, so that we still end up with an
invariant pattern of procedure for planning and writing up
curriculum.) It can be seen from the outline of Pratt's approach,
given above, that he nowhere deals directly with the question of what
what we are doing is all for, or what it is all about. He does not ask
what the curriculum is needed for in the first place, nor explore the
question of what our values and our ideas of education may be. He
does recognise that there are questions to be raised about such things,
but he is willing to comment on them only to the extent of pushing
them aside to the philosophers' hinterland. In one page on curriculum
rationale which contains all he has to say in 500-odd pages about the
basic justification of the school curriculum, he is exclusively
concerned not with what does justify a curriculum decision, but with
how to present a rationale that will carry people with it. The rationale
put forward should be 'eloquent and persuasive'; it 'should be written
with a view to convincing everyone who will read the curriculum, but
especially those who have the power to prevent or intervene in its
implementation.' 'It will often be an advantage to adduce "extrinsic"
arguments.'[28] Good Machiavellian stuff this, but not a word about
what makes a rationale rationally defensible.

Pratt is concerned, as the title of one of his sections indicates, with
aims *in* education, not with the aims *of* education. He sees the
curriculum designer's job as being to organise learning experiences,
given a set of values or desired ends. The designer takes the ultimate
ends for granted and breaks them down for curriculum purposes into
manageable aims. But he is not to trouble himself about the ends
themselves. If they are not taken trustingly from wise philosophers,
they may perhaps be taken from a consensus among the populace on
the grounds that in a democracy aims and ideals should be decided by
the people, while appropriate materials of instruction should be
technical questions.[29]

But a curriculum designer cannot sensibly and legitimately take for
granted fundamental questions about the purpose of the enterprise,
as the bridge designer may reasonably take it for granted that his
bridge should be able to stay up and take loads. There are indeed
principles for designing bridges that cannot be ignored, whatever
your personal values, so long as it is a bridge you want to build and
not, say, a folly. But then all bridges, whatever their distinctive
features, have certain clear, overriding purposes that are the same.

Different curricula, by contrast, may have quite different purposes, and for that reason they may require quite different kinds of design. Furthermore, the aims of any curriculum are more contentious than the ends that bridges are designed to serve. Part of the problem is therefore that this divorce between ends and means, or purposes and techniques, so simple in the case of bridge-building, cannot easily be made in respect of schooling, where what are to count as the criteria of success is part of what the argument is about. We cannot begin to judge the efficacy of means so long as what constitute *successful* means remains obscure, as it must so long as the question of the purpose and nature of education is hived off and ignored. The notion that there are certain specific principles of curriculum design that can be formulated without explicit reference to particular educational ends simply doesn't make sense.

But now, assuming that we did reach agreement on our ends, is there any reason to suppose even then that any particular form of curriculum design would be more conducive to realising them than another, or that there are any principles of design that make a material difference to the successful teaching of curriculum in terms of attaining our ends? Pratt believes so and, in common with other curriculum theorists, refers to Soviet success in launching the first Sputnik satellite as an impetus towards redesigning curriculum in the United States, presumably on the grounds that the Soviet achievement was to be attributed to superior curriculum design.[30] But there is surely no secret or mystery about how the Soviets achieved their triumph. That leap forward in the space race was obviously *not* achieved because the Soviets had perfected better curricula in some technical sense, still less because they were in advance in curriculum design. It was achieved because they had been more committed to space exploration in terms of money and resolution, no doubt aided by some individual insights and luck. The idea that the Soviets had discovered a new science of instruction or better techniques of teaching, in the abstract, or that the Americans with better language programmes would have been more likely to read technical articles in the Soviet press, and hence to keep up with the competition, is faintly ridiculous. The difference was more likely one of conceptions of schooling than programmes of teaching. In just the same way, the Spartans in Classical Greece beat the Athenians in war not because they had a better methodology for teaching military training, but because they devoted themselves to military training. It was a political and evaluative decision that made the difference rather than a technical one.

It is still unclear, then, either why we should presume that general principles of curriculum design can be formulated and would lead to improved curriculum practice, or in the light of what aims such principles would be established.

Pratt, reasonably enough, goes on the offensive against the tendency of my argument by questioning the value of 'armchair' theorising.[31] 'Armchair theory', if it simply means one man's thoughts as he lounges in his chair and knocks back a whisky, is indeed no better than pseudo-science. But it is a mistake to confuse formality of procedure with objectivity in the sense of truth, duly determined by public procedures. An armchair theorist may hit upon the truth as readily as a questionnaire, or the systematic researcher. Furthermore, the relative value of armchair, questionnaire and observational research depends very much upon the questions being asked. How many people there are in Marks & Spencer in Granville Street on Monday 12 July at 2.00 pm is best researched by some observers armed with counting machines. What people in general feel about Marks & Spencer might best be left to questionnaires. But if we wish to inquire into the value of a store such as Marks & Spencer, then, in so far as we need opinions and observations to be collected at all, we need to hand the data we obtain over to the armchair theorist to *think* about. Even more obviously, questions such as how happy people are, how educated they are, what kinds of thing can be known in principle, and what the nature of moral upbringing is, are questions that will necessitate armchair theorising, and matters where it may be positively misleading to rely on observation.

It is true that the *test* of success in curriculum matters must lie in some kind of observation. The main value of tightly controlled empirical observation is to confirm or refute the hypotheses of armchair theory where possible. We may, for example, legitimately reject a curriculum design if we see that it consistently leads to results agreed to be disastrous. But even in an extreme case such as that, we should not be in a position from observation alone to know why the curriculum produces disastrous results, and we could not draw conclusions without agreement on what constitutes disaster. More to the point, there is very little either within particular curriculum designs or about the nature of curriculum design in general that ever has been put to the test.

We must, therefore, criticise any conception of design that fails to take account of the justification of schooling in general, and the evaluative and conceptual issues that arise in curriculum in particular, and that fails to see that without these everything else is necessarily merely an account of how to market and sell a package. Quite simply, we are in no position to treat curriculum design as an applied science.

7. SETTING ASIDE CURRICULUM DESIGN

I have also tried to suggest that curriculum design is an otiose notion: we don't want curriculum designers in the sense of people adept at telling us formally how curricula should be set out, or laying down an invariant order of steps to be taken in formulating a curriculum. We want people to design particular curricula in intelligent ways. Much of the divergence between designers and between theories of curriculum design is essentially irrelevant, since it boils down to quibbling about how best to start tackling the problem, and how best to make an impact, rather than arguing about what a coherent curriculum proposal *should* involve. If it is said that that is so because curriculum design is a practical business, I reply that in this sense of 'practical business' it shouldn't be. Maybe it is all right to sell soap, even life insurance, but it is not all right to sell education. Education should be thought about, explained and understood. Furthermore, I suggest that the very determination to have a design is an impediment to clear thinking about schooling in general, for people trained to worry about the technicalities of design rather than the nature of the enterprise worry more about whether they can cut their cloth to the rules of their design, than about whether the cloth is worth designing.

The design bandwagon gains a lot of mileage from the idea that being a curriculum designer is a specific kind of job, like being an engineer. Thus Franklin Bobbitt wrote in 1918: 'It is more important that our profession agree upon a *method* of curriculum discovery than that we agree upon the details of curriculum content'; and Goodlad in 1958 called for 'a conceptual system to guide decision-making . . . in the field of curriculum'.[32] The time has come to say that this approach is entirely ill-founded. There is no 'method' of curriculum discovery, any more than there is a method of exploring the jungle or falling in love. There is just understanding something about jungles, love and school curricula, and the use of a motley collection of skills, disciplines of thought and ideas to make progress in them. There is no 'conceptual system' to guide decision-making. (At least, I don't think there is. I'm not sure what a conceptual system to guide decision-making looks like. If Goodlad meant that we need some new ideas around which to organise our thinking, some new categorial concepts perhaps, it is far from evident that we do; if he meant that we need a new vocabulary, which is all he got in the event, he is mistaken.)

Planning a curriculum — and now I deliberately avoid the word 'design' which has connotations of precision, agreed procedures, and standards that are misleading and unwarranted in this context — is a complicated business, requiring primarily such tentative understanding of children as we can muster, both in general and particular, a well-thought-out and coherent view of human life in a social context, coupled with awareness of other competing views, such knowledge of what actions, beliefs and procedures produce or inhibit what results as may be possible, and, most important of all, understanding of the nature and purpose of schooling and all that that entails. There is no 'way' of doing it, no 'way' of designing curricula. Curricula are formulated and presented in a hundred ways, and may legitimately be so, provided that their authors understand the intricacies in the sphere in which they are operating.

Setting aside the idea of curriculum design on the grounds that it is a confused and unhelpful concept does not in any way militate against the importance of curriculum studies. Curriculum theory does not disappear, nor does the need for it diminish, because the idea of a proper manner of designing curricula disappears. (Nor incidentally does the good sense to be found in various curriculum designers' work disappear because of the weakness of the overall approach.) But rather than deploying various designs we should surely be addressing these fundamental questions: What kind of curriculum provision should we make for children, and what different kinds of question need to be raised in order to determine the answer? Beyond that we need to consider how best to approach and present particular curriculum proposals by reference to particular situations. The emphasis in curriculum work should fall less on procedures or styles of operation, and more on establishing a sound theoretical base for such prescriptions as we feel we may legitimately make. What we must have is a coherent argument for our overall curriculum aims and a convincing case for particular curriculum recommendations, rather than strategies for devising, outlining and successfully implementing them. Once we have that, we can turn our attention to convincing people of the wisdom of our proposals. But there is no merit whatsoever in successful curriculum change unless the changes are inherently desirable in terms of schooling and education. Therefore we need, first, to consider what is desirable in the context of schools — not what people say they desire, but what is coherently defensible as desirable. That means that we must go back to theory, for inquiring into what is educationally worthwhile just is a theoretical pursuit.

A more flexible approach to curriculum is required than is suggested by the phrase curriculum design itself, simply because curriculum theory is necessarily a multidisciplinary exercise. We have to sort out not only and not primarily techniques and procedures of teaching and class organisation, but questions about our priorities and our ideas. We would be well-advised to approach this by thinking in terms of questions rather than strategies or tasks. Perhaps we might go back to something like Tyler's approach, asking ourselves what educational purposes the school should seek to attain, how the learning experiences that are likely to be useful are best selected, how they can be organised, and how we can evaluate them. But this time we need to recognise that the first three questions are written out in their order of importance, that the second and third cannot be answered without reference to the first, and that the answers to the second and third are probably a great deal more open than some might anticipate.

More simply we want to deal thoroughly with these questions: What should we teach and why? How should we teach it? How should we organise it? What can we do to evaluate our progress and monitor and, if needs be, modify our practice? How, given that we have a good case, can we best see our curriculum implemented? What is required is not so much the misleading appearance of science in the form of diagrams, schemata, jargon and empirical procedures of inquiry, as a better idea of what is going on and what ought to be going on; a better idea is assessed not so much by the amount of information it purveys, or the manner of its acquisition, as by the quality of the thinking brought to bear on that information.

Those who are strongly wedded to the idea of curriculum design, especially if they also persist in seeing it as an applied science, may respond: 'That might give us a curriculum, but surely we need to present the curriculum to teachers in such a way that they will and can adopt it. Therefore we must have an account of how we should set it all out.' The reply to this is that we do indeed want teachers to be able and willing to adopt curricula that we have convincingly argued there is good reason to adopt. But there is a proper and honourable way to approach that, namely, to proceed in the same way with introducing proposals to teachers as we did in arriving at our curriculum proposals: by reason. Car salesmen need to sell cars, but it does not follow that they have to resort to the tricks they do, albeit they are very effective. If they had a good car to sell, the best way to sell it would be to educate people in the ways of automobile structure and performance. A good car then sells itself. In the same way the best way to sell a curriculum, or to present it so that it is not misapplied, is to give teachers a clear idea of what they are being asked to do, why they are being asked to do it, and why they should be doing it. Teachers don't need books of rules or tips about curriculum design

('Remember to remember that the temperature of the room may affect concentration'; 'Remember not to forget the structure of knowledge.') They might reasonably feel somewhat offended that it is assumed they need to be reminded of the sorts of factor that may affect what is going on. What they do need, and may have to develop, is understanding of these factors, their significance, their implications, their interrelationships, and so forth, in respect of the nature and purposes of schooling and education. Teachers, like anybody else interested in education, should be given the opportunity not to memorise patterns of ways to draw up curriculum proposals, but to think about and increase their understanding of the justification for some curriculum proposals rather than others. In the final event they will, and they will only, successfully implement what they thoroughly understand.

Part II:
CURRICULUM

4 Curriculum Content

A curriculum theorist needs to have an answer to the questions of what sort of content the curriculum should provide, and why it should do so. The word 'content' does not have to be interpreted in advance in any particular way. It need not, for example, necessarily imply reference to formal subjects; indeed, at this stage it need not even commit us to a specifiable content, since the answer to the question 'what content?' might be 'whatever turns the individual child on'. But some answer to the question 'what content?' is required.

It should be clear from Part I that preoccupation with establishing a justifiable content does not imply that one assumes that what is presented to the student is always what the student gets out of it. None the less, in order to distinguish so-called 'learner-outcome' from 'teacher-input', and in order to make sensible observations about the gap between them, one does need to have a clear idea of what in principle one is trying to get across. And in order to arrive at a justifiable content, one needs to have a clear idea of how to set about determining whether content is justified.

A variety of approaches to the question of determining a worthwhile curriculum have been suggested by curriculum theorists at one time or another. Plato *(Republic)* derived his curriculum from a particular view of knowledge coupled with a particular conception of man; Rousseau *(Emile)* tried to base his curriculum on the demands of nature; the Russian educationalist Makarenko (See, Bowen, 1962) wanted the curriculum to be justified in terms of state ideology. In this chapter I shall review the main theories that still have some support today, and I shall conclude by sketching an account of what seems to be essential to the establishment of a sound and worthwhile curriculum in the light of the preceding argument.

1. INTRINSIC VALUE

How does one set about choosing a worthwhile curriculum? How does one justify the value of teaching one thing rather than another? One deceptively simple tradition has it that the answer is to select intrinsically worthwhile activities or subject-matter, and to build one's curriculum out of that. For instance, Peters (1966) has argued for the inherent value of certain truth-seeking activities, such as the established disciplines of science, mathematics and history. Another tradition emphasises the intrinsic worth of a cultural tradition containing great works of art. No doubt a good many schoolteachers, too, see the teaching of their subject, whatever it may be, justified in terms of it being a non-trivial, inherently valuable pursuit.

This view has sometimes been dismissed purely on the grounds that it is élitist, as if any concern for distinguishing good from bad were somehow objectionable and undemocratic. But without doubt some activities *are* in themselves more trivial than others, some are less useful, some are less demanding, some are less authentically satisfying, and so forth. Furthermore, the established disciplines have been refined and developed precisely because of this manifest value, and subjects such as history, the study of literature and science are more worthwhile in a number of specifiable ways (more illuminating, more mind-stretching, more enduring, for example) than a number of other activities such as learning to type, playing cricket or collecting records. What precisely the charge of élitism is supposed to mean is not always clear. But neither the fact that not everybody can be equally successful in relation to these worthwhile pursuits, which is one possible implication, nor the claim that the values inherent in the disciplines in question are somehow peculiar to a dominant social group, nor even the blunt assertion that no type of activity can be accounted superior to another, are very plausible objections.[1]

However, there are certain problems with this approach. First, to agree intuitively that some things are more worthwhile than others is not the same thing as being able to establish that they are, or even to explain why one believes that they are. One of the problems is that it is not even clear what is meant by the phrase 'intrinsically worthwhile' (or 'inherently valuable'/'valuable in itself'). Some argue that to call something 'intrinsically worthwhile' is no more than a way of saying 'I value this, and that's all there is to it.' Others point out that very often when people say that something is intrinsically worthwhile, they don't actually mean that; they mean rather that it is valuable for some immediate, but none the less further or extrinsic purpose, such as providing better understanding of the human condition. There is not even agreement on what is involved in valuing something. Some think that value is just a matter of taste (what I value is what I have a taste for), while some link it to happiness, seeing worth in whatever promotes happiness, and others regard it as a unique quality, comparable in its logic to the quality of beauty that is thought to reside in the object or activity itself. And there are many other possible views about the nature of the worthwhile.[2]

But the immediate conclusion to be drawn is that although particular readers might, for instance, hold the view that studying science is worthwhile but that studying music is not, it is quite likely that different people would mean different things by the claim, and it is very unlikely that they would either find universal support for their view or be able to establish the truth of that view sufficiently incontrovertibly to silence dissent. This may not make any practical difference in a community where there happens to be widespread agreement, but we, living in a relatively open and pluralistic society, can hardly ignore the fact that many people sincerely and strongly question the alleged inherent value of subjects that others regard as self-evidently worthwhile.

A second objection to this approach is that it is not clear that the school curriculum *should* be simply or primarily concerned with the promotion of intrinsically worthwhile activities, even if we knew or agreed what they were. Schools should be concerned with what is worthwhile in terms of the various functions and purposes of schooling. The school curriculum should therefore be concerned with what is educationally worthwhile or with what is socially desirable, which may not be the same thing as what is simply inherently worthwhile. Suppose we agree that opera and ballet are worthwhile pursuits; it surely doesn't follow automatically that it would be right to include them in the school curriculum. Conversely, some things that nobody regards as intrinsically worthwhile, however extrinsically useful they may be, may none the less be thought to have great educational value or worth in the school curriculum: for example, understanding something about the handling of money, or mastering the mechanics of writing.[3]

A third objection is that specific arguments put forward to support views about the intrinsic worth of certain activities, such as Peters' transcendental argument, which seeks to show that anyone committed to the value of having good reasons for actions is thereby committed to seeing the value of certain truth-seeking and reason-providing pursuits such as science, can be and have been criticised as inadequate. It has been said of Peters' argument, for example, that, though it may show that a certain kind of person must see *a* value in such pursuits as science, it does not show either that one ought to be such a person, or that such a person ought to agree on the value of *people in general studying* the subject in question.[4]

These three different kinds of objection, particularly when taken together, seem quite sufficient to suggest that this is not a satisfactory way to approach the drawing-up of a worthwhile curriculum. We are not necessarily disassociating ourselves either from the view that such things as history, science and literature are in some sense inherently worthwhile, or from the view that they ought to be on the curriculum. All that is being claimed is that this line of justification seems unlikely to succeed.

2. USE, RELEVANCE AND REALITY

A view that will not die, although it has been killed more often than it knows, is that the solution to the problem of establishing a worthwhile curriculum lies in seeking out content that is useful or relevant.[5] This view has sometimes gained new impetus in the western world from the complaints of both industry and government that schooling has tended to become irrelevant and too impractical. Complaints from such sources should perhaps forewarn us: irrelevant to whom and for what? Impractical in what sense, and in what respects? These are the crucial questions. What concerns industry is what is relevant to industry. A complaint from this source to the effect that schooling is irrelevant or not teaching useful lessons presumably indicates that industry is not getting the skilled technicians, the cooperative labour force or the presentable management it wants. Government may be harder to pin down, but one imagines that when ministers or departments criticise schooling for a lack of realism, or the impractical and irrelevant nature of its curriculum, they are thinking partly in terms of meeting industry's demands and partly in terms of producing compliant, orderly and industrious citizens.

But such complaints from such sources must give rise to the important question of whether schools were, or should be, set up simply to feed industry or serve government. As we have already indicated (Chapter 2, s.5), schools are there to do a number of things, one very notable one of which is to educate, which is not at all the same thing as, and may not be easily compatible with, preparing people for skilled positions or promoting political docility.

There are two issues here. The first is a general one: to argue that the curriculum should be relevant or useful is effectively useless in itself, because we need to know whom it should be useful to, what purpose it should be useful for, and in whose judgement it should be useful. Similarly with relevance. Activities do not possess or lack relevance in the abstract. They have or lack relevance to particular people, for particular purposes, in particular circumstances. Therefore, to agree on the relevance of something presupposes some agreement on priorities, perspectives and purposes. Since different people will answer questions about to whom and for what purposes things should be useful and relevant in different ways, what we inevitably end up doing, if we take this approach, is arguing about something else — namely, about our varying views as to what schools ought to be doing. That being the case, appeals to relevance or usefulness, which sound well enough and have an air of honest practicality about them, are in fact just wasting time, and they certainly don't provide a criterion of content selection.

The second issue is more particular: so long as these over-worked words won't lie down, we need to watch very carefully to ensure that they are not appropriated by any particular faction and given a specific substantive meaning. This is particularly to be guarded against in the case of relevance. Studying the operation of a lathe is in itself no more relevant a pursuit than studying Chinese poetry. The relative relevance of the two can only emerge in particular contexts and for particular people. That being the case, it is very important actively to resist attempts, conscious or otherwise, by government, industry or any other special-interest group, to equate usefulness or relevance with usefulness or relevance in terms of their ideals and concerns. It may be that some people believe that schools should act as trainee establishments for industry, but that viewpoint needs to be argued for like any other. What has to be resisted is the assumption that 'useful' *means* something like 'useful in economic terms', or that 'relevance' *means* 'relevant to immediate profitability'. It is very disturbing to see that in Britain the Manpower Services Commission, supposedly an agency concerned with employment, has been given certain powers over the school curriculum (without so much as a warning, let alone public discussion). The assumption is, presumably, that a school curriculum designed to fit in with the poor employment prospects of a substantial number of school-leavers would obviously be a useful curriculum and one that is relevant to society's needs. But whether that is desirable for the school curriculum or not, it is a mistake to think that such a curriculum (courses in immediately marketable skills) is relevant in some abstract, inherent way. It is only useful and relevant for those limited purposes and in the eyes of those who wish to subserve those limited purposes.

Another problem with this approach is that, in practice, appeals to relevance are sometimes interpreted as appeals to what the child regards as relevant. This view leaves less room for argument about what is relevant, but on the other hand it seems even more obviously a view to be resisted. No doubt in various ways, to varying degrees, the individual student's perceptions of relevance should influence what goes on in curriculum, but that does not mean that they should serve as the principle of selection, or as the arbiter of content. The mere fact that a student regards a pursuit as relevant to his purpose is not a sufficient condition for making that pursuit part of his curriculum. There are some things that we can rationally demonstrate ought to figure on the school curriculum, essentially because of what schools are and what they are for, and, given that, one could not possibly accept that the sole criterion of curriculum selection should be what the child sees as relevant, regardless of its triviality, undesirability or irrelevance to education.

There are similar problems with the word 'reality'. The demand is sometimes made that education should be for the real world, and that may be unexceptionable as an ideal. The problem is that although 'real' means 'actually existing' people have very selective views of reality. In particular, people seem prone to associate reality with the dour and the unavoidable, and to ignore the joyous, light-hearted and chance events of life. Thus education for the real world is interpreted by many as an education for the *grim* realities of life: an education aimed at securing a job, fitting in with contemporary conventions of sexual behaviour, or being a dutiful citizen. But why should we agree to that particular slant on reality? My reality includes daydreaming, casual sexual encounters and listening to music, perhaps. Therefore, in so far as I want an education for the real world, I want an education that caters to those interests too. An additional difficulty with using reality as a criterion for judging curriculum content is that to some extent future reality is a product of our choices and actions now. If, in the name of reality, we train people as computer operators and clerks today, that will have a significant bearing on the future reality of our society. If by contrast we were to produce poets, we would have a rather different reality. Consequently reality, like relevance and usefulness, though it sounds such a practical notion, is in fact of very little use as a guideline for establishing a curriculum. A curriculum that is relevant to the educational goal of promoting critical thought as judged by educationalists will look rather different from a curriculum regarded as relevant by the local supermarket personnel manager. A curriculum that is judged realistic by one person will not necessarily be by another.

The argument is not that we do not want a realistic curriculum, a curriculum for the real world, or a relevant and useful one. (We certainly do not want an irrelevant, unrealistic or useless curriculum.) The argument is that these are all formal notions, which everybody is in favour of, but that to give them substance it is necessary to relate them to one's ideals and to one's views of society and schooling. That being the case, this approach offers no solution, no short-cut; it merely draws our attention to the need to argue about our more fundamental assumptions. Perhaps the point to be stressed most is that we must beware of seeing useful, relevant, realistic curriculum in terms of a curriculum geared directly to economic demands. One may concede that we cannot ignore economic demands, and in some circumstances, such as war-torn Vietnam, it might be quite unreasonable to insist on education having priority over basic economic needs. But in the western democracies as they are, for all their differences and all their faults, there is no excuse for treating reality as coextensive with economic demands. More generally, we do not want any vested interest appropriating any of these terms and thereby effectively impoverishing our conceptions of education. Education itself is part of reality and has relevance and use in relation to certain ideals of human life.

3. NEEDS

(See also Chapter 3, s.1.)

At this point some would revert to needs. 'Surely', it may be said, 'the curriculum would be justified if it met people's needs?' Possibly it would be, but appealing to the criterion of needs will not solve any problem in practice, for the logic of needs is not unlike the logic of relevance, and deciding whether somebody needs something is as much a matter of individual judgement and perspective as judging the relevance of an activity. (The following paragraphs repeat and elaborate some points made in Chapter 3,s.1.)

Needs are not simply things that one lacks, or things that are absent. I don't have cancer, and I don't need it. I don't have an expensive car, and I don't need that either. Conversely, some things that I do have might be classified as needs: I have love, and I need it. A need is something that, if it were to be missing, one would want to have replaced. But it is more than that, since it is not simply a desire or want. It is something that is necessary to some desired end or objective agreed to be desirable.

Since people are different and have different values and priorities, as well as because they are in different circumstances, what they need may vary. Perhaps you do need a fast car, even though I don't, to assuage your macho self-image or to travel long distances as rapidly as possible. Who then is to judge what people, especially children, do need? The agent is not necessarily the best judge of his own needs, partly because he may lack empirical knowledge, partly because he may literally not know his own mind in respect of priorities, and partly because he may not be sufficiently conceptually alert to the distinction between needs and wants. I might need penicillin but not realise as much because I am ignorant as to the state of my body, or ignorant of the powers of penicillin. I might need to leave my wife, in as much as it would be better for all concerned if I did, but not know that I need to because I do not appreciate that fact. I might want a drink and, unaware that drinking is killing me, wrongly claim that I need it to keep going. But experts don't necessarily know what other people need either. A doctor could usually tell me whether or not I need penicillin. It is far from clear that a psychiatrist could say for certain whether I need to leave my wife.

Determining what someone needs is partly a matter of determining or knowing what their objectives are, and partly of knowing what is in fact necessary to meet those ends. When it comes to schooling, the experts do not agree on what students need for the simple reason that they have different views on the ends of schooling. Even in quite simple cases there is widespread disagreement. Whether a child needs to be toilet-trained, to learn to read, or to study physics, for example, depends partly on one's views of the facts of the matter, and partly on one's views of what children and the world are like, and partly on one's values. It is at this point that Pratt, it will be recalled,[6] aware of diversity of opinion about needs, tried to assess them by gathering opinions in a systematic and comprehensive way; but that misses the point. The point is not that no one knows better than anyone else what a given person needs (which, if it were true, might certainly be used as an argument to justify some kind of democratic compromise to determine needs), but that what a person needs, although it may be quite determinate and specific, is geared to what is determined as a desirable end-state for that individual. Where, as in the case of young children, the individual doesn't have a coherently formulated view on desirable end-states, the matter is further complicated, and what he needs has to be seen as what someone else says he ought to have.

Although the above can hardly be disputed, it is often pointed out that there are some basic needs that would generally be agreed upon. Thus Pratt (1980) has offered a categorisation of physiological needs based on Maslow's (1954) classification: the need for meaning, aesthetic need, survival needs, social needs, and the need for self-actualisation. The problem with such schemata is that they contain items which are either admittedly uncontroversial and straightforward, but lacking in significant curriculum implications, or else, while possibly having curricular implications, are very vague and possibly contentious.

We could readily agree upon a number of survival needs. We agree that people should survive, and we agree that in order to do so they need to learn how to cross the road, about the dangers of boiling water, about electrical plugs, and about the dangers of drugs. But, as Pratt himself says, 'Water safety and drownproofing, home safety, much of first aid, fire emergency procedures, pedestrian safety and defensive driving can each be learned in a few hours.'[7] And, we might add, in some cases can be, and are readily, learned out of school. In other words, granted that there are certain agreed survival needs, there is not much here for a school curriculum to be built out of.

On the other hand, the view that we need to develop aesthetic awareness, besides being very unclear in its curricular implications, would not be universally or even widely recognised as an undisputed human need. By no means everybody would agree that 'lives that lack the aesthetic dimension . . . are . . . impoverished.'[8] We are not saying that it couldn't or shouldn't be argued that they *are* impoverished, whatever some people may think, but that simply to assert the need, to say that it is a need, is to beg the question and therefore not a helpful procedure. To establish that it is a need one would have to convince people that all students ought to have their aesthetic side developed. Since that has to be done, it is more clear, useful and straightforward to get on with doing that than to argue about basing a curriculum on needs, as if a statement of needs would give us the final step in discussion rather than the first.

When we turn to the needs for self-actualisation and meaning, the main problem is clearly one of meaning itself. What is actually involved in self-actualisation, and what is meant by a need for meaning? Nor would the curricular implications of these needs be very clear, even if we had a clear conception of them. Suppose we agree that people need to know who they are, and how to get on socially. How does one construct a curriculum on that basis? What does acknowledging a need for self-actualisation tell us about the school curriculum? Some would argue that if we were to break down those needs into aims, and then into rather more specific objectives, we would arrive at some clear curriculum prescriptions. But that cannot be done without a better grasp of what 'knowing who I am' and all the other phrases in question mean, and a better knowledge than we have of how to cater for such needs. Of course, one could produce a set of clear objectives relating to self-knowledge, but if they are that easy to produce they are likely to trivialise the concept, as is the case if we list as elements in knowing who I am such things as 'can respond to his own name'. If, on the other hand, we are thinking of something like Socratic self-knowledge, then its obscurity and complexity defy reduction to discrete observable objectives. (On objectives, see also Chapter 5.)

A further problem for the idea of a needs-based curriculum is that, in so far as a curriculum is going to be built upon students' needs, we shall have to predict needs (unless we arbitrarily choose to cater only to present needs). As Pratt (1980) says, forecasting technical skills that will be needed by industry, even if we accepted that we should do something about them, requires a degree of sophistication that we do not appear to have at present. He continues, 'it requires rather less expertise to guess what general capabilities will be needed. They will certainly include imagination, adaptability and versatility'.[9] But a curriculum designed to meet those general needs is not of any obvious shape. Once again we are caught on the horns of a dilemma: either we have a list of uncontroversial, simple needs that lead to nothing of significance in curriculum terms, or we have needs such as these, which, whilst they may be agreed to be needs, are none the less so general and vague that more or less anything might be done in curriculum terms in allegedly serving those needs. What does a curriculum designed to meet the needs of developing imagination look like? There is only one way to attempt to answer that question, and that is to begin by giving a comprehensive account of the notion of imagination. By the time one has finished, not everyone will remain in agreement that children necessarily need it, but, more to the immediate point, it would be this account of imagination and its importance that would lead to the formulation of a particular curriculum, and not the mere assertion of an alleged need.

4. INTERESTS

One equivocation in talk of curriculum based on needs is the exact force of a phrase such as 'based on'. There is, after all, a considerable difference between taking *some account* of needs in developing one's curriculum and using needs *exclusively* as the *criterion of selection*. The same point arises when people suggest a curriculum based on student' interests, but here there is also an ambiguity between interests in the sense of 'what interests one' and interests in the sense of 'what is in one's interests'. The two do not always march hand in hand. It interests the sadist to torture someone, but it is not necessarily in his interests to do so. It is in my interests to attend the office party, perhaps, but it doesn't necessarily interest me to do so.

Once this ambiguity is removed, the idea of establishing a curriculum on the basis of this criterion on either interpretation seems unhelpful. If the suggestion is that we should produce a curriculum that is in the interests of children then it is not self-evidently desirable, since some might set the interests of certain adults or society in general against the interests of children, and it is not a helpful guideline, since what actually is in children's interests is a matter hotly disputed, and depends upon one's views of human nature, schooling, and so forth. If we are being invited to let children do whatever interests them in the sense of whatever they feel inclined to do, the invitation seems plainly unacceptable. Schools exist for certain purposes rather than others, and those purposes must define to some extent what it is appropriate to do. We are not here discussing the empirical question of the effects in terms of motivation of placing some emphasis on what interests students, nor are we saying that their interests have no relevance at all to the question of establishing a worthwhile curriculum. But what we are saying is that since students will sometimes be interested in trivial, immoral, counterproductive, short-term and otherwise puerile interests, we cannot sensibly take their interests, whatever they may be, as the criterion of curriculum selection.[10]

The view that we should develop our curriculum out of what interests students might be based on one of two different assumptions: that as a matter of fact what interests children tends to be worthwhile, or that the criterion of worth in an activity is that people have an interest in it. The latter is a most implausible suggestion: whatever it is that makes something worthwhile, we should surely agree that the mere fact of wanting to do something doesn't make it worthwhile. (Not thus can thieves, rapists and concentration camp commandants justify themselves.) The former assertion is not backed by any convincing evidence that I know of, and could only be shown to be the case if we had prior agreement on what is worthwhile, which, as this chapter goes to show, we do not have. (For how could anyone perceive that as a matter of fact what children freely choose to do is always what is worthwhile, without having a clear idea of what constitutes worthwhileness?)

It might be suggested that the reason that children should do whatever interests them is that this will lead to greater psychological security and happiness. It is very far from clear why one should suppose this to be so (and, again, in order to investigate whether it was, we should need to get agreement on what constitutes security and happiness). It is not, as I have argued elsewhere (Barrow, 1980), a conclusion that follows even from regarding happiness as the supreme value. And it fails to take account of the cardinal point that schools are schools. Even if we agreed on the importance of happiness considerations in determining what should go on in this world, we still have to say something when determining curriculum that takes account of the fact that schools are not churches, private homes, therapy units, places of leisure, social clubs or supermarkets. Granted that everything should subserve the claims of happiness, what should the particular contribution of schools be to that general overall aim? All in all there seems no argument for and nothing to be gained from talking of basing the curriculum on interests.[11]

5. TRAINING THE MIND

(See also Chapter 3, s.2.)

Another approach that is misplaced, but for rather different reasons, is the view that curriculum content should be selected with a view to training the mind. (Similar, in terms of the problems involved, would be claims about selecting curriculum content with a view to developing critical thought, logical powers, creative thought and lateral thinking powers.) The notion that the school curriculum should develop the mind, at least among other things, has a long and distinguished pedigree, and is surely substantially correct. As we have seen, education *is* cognitive development, and since a major function of school is to educate, the school curriculum must be concerned to develop the mind. The question is on what matter and in what ways should the mind be developed.

We need to distinguish the general notion of developing the mind from the more specific idea of seeking to train the mind, the latter implying some regimen, some experience, some activity or set of procedures whereby the mind becomes a better-tuned instrument. On the whole, concern with the idea of training the mind has not been shown by those interested in an overall rationale for curriculum, so much as by those interested in defending particular subjects. Classics used to be defended by some on the grounds that it disciplined or was a good training for the mind; sometimes today mathematics or modern languages are similarly defended. That line of defence was thought by many to have taken a knock when various empirical surveys concluded that there was not much transference of training between subjects, so that the mind allegedly disciplined by classics could not be relied upon to exhibit that same discipline in mathematics, history or the day-to-day business of living.

The story of 'transfer of training' is a sad example of the all too common phenomenon in education of people solemnly looking to empirical confirmation of something that could not in fact be otherwise as a matter of simple logic. Of course one cannot automatically transpose one's disciplined mind from here to there, from one subject to another, because all disciplined (and undisciplined) activity of mind has to take place in a context. It doesn't matter how disciplined your mind is, you cannot switch to another subject and talk intelligently about it unless you have some competence within that subject.[12]

The confusion appears to have arisen out of people's tendency to see critical thinking, rigour, intelligence, and such like as skills, comparable to motor skills, such as raising one's left arm, which can of course be employed in a variety of different contexts. But whereas if I can raise my left arm I can do a number of different things that require little more than my raised left arm (e.g. hold a plate, touch the ceiling, wave), the fact that I can think critically as a historian does not mean that I can necessarily think critically in physics. Thinking critically is not comparable to raising my arm.[13] A person may have certain attitudes or dispositions, such as a willingness to look critically at evidence, or a concern to be rigorous, that are common to various intellectual activities (*not* even in this case *transferred* between them like a suitcase, but *common* to them as my genial good humour may be common to all my dealings with people), and there are some low-level skills, such as the ability to read, to use a library or a microfiche machine, that may also be common to various activities. One may say, therefore, that it is highly likely (though certainly not necessary) that one who has had a critical and rigorous turn of mind developed in one context will display it in other contexts that he regards as serious, in so far as he can. But the qualification is vital. He would only be able to display rigour and critical acumen if he could handle the content (and if he chose to do so). The notion that rigorous training of the mind in a particular context may lead to a similarly rigorous approach in other subjects has not been discredited by any empirical research, nor could it be, for empirical researchers will only be able to observe situations that involve a combination of dispositions, skill and competence. The notion that has been discredited by such research, namely that overall competence was transferable, was always absurd.

The problem, then, about using 'training of the mind' as a criterion for selecting curriculum content is not that there are no aspects of a trained mind that might be carried over from one context to another, but that such aspects of mind that can be carried over are necessary but not sufficient conditions of the educated mind, and that since the development of such dispositions and skills has to take place in a context, we still face the question of what content to select with which to take whatever steps we are able towards training the mind.

6. CULTURE AND KNOWLEDGE

At this juncture we turn towards more useful approaches to curriculum planning. Development of mind must have something to do with the acquisition of knowledge and understanding. Therefore, it must surely be relevant to our purposes to consider the nature of knowledge or what different kinds of thing can in principle be known. Closely related to the issue of the nature of knowledge, and linked through the concept of education, may be considerations of culture.

The notion of culture is more problematic than may at first appear. It sounds well enough to say that the school curriculum should introduce people to our culture or make a judicious cultural selection, but what sense of culture are we concerned with? And whose culture are we concerned with? Is a cultural content, in one sense or another, either necessary or sufficient for the school curriculum?

There are two well-established senses of culture.[14] First, there is 'culture' meaning a body of work of quality usually, but not exclusively, in the arts. Matthew Arnold *(Culture and Anarchy)* characterised culture in this sense as the best that has been thought and said. T.S. Eliot *(Notes Towards the Definition of Culture,* 1949) refers to 'high culture' in a similar sense, and G.H. Bantock (1963, 1968) has defended a curriculum interest in such cultural works.[15] Culture in this sense is, by definition, of value. There are, however, two disadvantages in using it as a means of curriculum selection. First, an obvious but very real problem: we have to agree on what works are representative of culture, and it is just a fact that increasingly people challenge each others' judgements in this respect. Secondly, we would still have to find a criterion for deciding what areas we should seek to cover. Should we, for example, seek out the best that has been produced in literature only? Should we look for the best that has been thought and said in science, in country music, in management, in ballet, or what?

The other sense of 'culture', sometimes called the sociological or anthropological sense, refers to the way of life of a specified group of people. We refer to English culture, Eskimo culture, Californian culture, drop-out culture, drug culture, or Canadian culture, in each case referring not only, if at all, to works of quality produced by the group in question, but rather to their code of living, and their overall pattern of life, including their characteristic activities, rituals and beliefs. There is a fairly straightforward sense in which the school should undoubtedly be concerned with culture in this second sense. Schools are partly concerned with socialisation, and socialisation involves initiating people into a culture. Both for their individual benefit and for the benefit of society, children have to be brought up so as to understand and be able to participate in (not necessarily approve) the ways of their community, the reference points of their fellow beings, the allusions, the humour and other features that are pervasive in and help to constitute that particular society. The main problem here is not the principle that curriculum should be based to some extent on cultural considerations, but the questions of what aspects of a culture should be emphasised, how great a part they should play in curriculum and, above all, the question of whose culture, given that we live in a multi-cultural society. Should all individuals be initiated into aspects of their parents' culture? Should they be made aware of each others' cultural heritage? Should they be initiated into the dominant culture, or what?

One commonly accepted view amongst those with a professional interest in cultural issues appears to be that we should seek a multi-cultural curriculum in the sense of one that initiates all children into aspects of all cultures significantly represented within their society. When such a view is put forward, however, it is important to consider whether the suggestion is that the children should be informed about the various distinct cultural backgrounds that different members of the community may have, or that they should in some way gain experience of, and keep alive aspects of different cultures. It is difficult to see any sound case for arguing that it should be the school's function to take active steps to preserve or promote minority cultures. There are many good reasons for seeking to preserve, say, Welsh or Indian culture. But it is not the function of a national system of schooling in Britain, Canada or anywhere else to take each individual and emphasise his personal cultural background. However, one can certainly see a case on grounds of truth and social tolerance alone for making people aware of the fact that there are other cultures besides the dominant one, stressing that these are living cultures, and providing some idea of the distinctive features of cultures that belong to immediate neighbours.

But provided that the value of promoting awareness of cultural differences has been agreed, there is a strong case to be made for the school seeking to emphasise and initiate all children into the dominant culture. (I am presuming that the culture in question is not thought to be inherently objectionable. If it were to be regarded as obnoxious, that would raise different issues.) There is nothing new about this view, either in theory or practice. Plato *(Republic)* promulgated the idea 2000 years ago, and countless societies have been melding disparate groups of immigrants together in this way for centuries, gradually weakening the original cultural ties and forging a new culture out of the mix of new and old. Cultures that are too diversified eventually cease to survive as cultures. Thanks to the autonomy and jealous rivalry of the Greek City States, as well as their ethnic and tribal distinctions, there was in the end no truly Greek culture; and then there was no Greece. Conversely, there was in the beginning no United States culture, and it only emerged as a result of a slow process of coming together, emphasising where necessary new community of spirit at the expense of old loyalties. If countries or communities are to remain culturally vibrant and rich, whilst accomodating the many immigrants in their midst, then it is important that respect and understanding of cultural differences should not lead to cultural disintegration. A curriculum that serves cultural ends should not, for instance, accept different programmes centred on the cultural differences between groups. It must both disseminate widely information about cultural differences and seek to forge a cultural homogeneity.[16]

One reason why dissemination of understanding about minority cultures should be a curriculum concern is that such knowledge is part of what an educated mind requires, for ignorance, while never the hallmark of the educated mind, is particularly to be regretted in respect of matters of social importance. More strongly, as I have argued elsewhere (Barrow, 1981; see also Chapter 2, s.5), being educated surely necessarily involves some understanding of one's society and its place in time and space. It might seem superficially that, if education is development of the mind, then ideally the educated mind should know everything. That is not quite correct. To be educated is not the same thing as to have encyclopediac knowledge. A developed mind is one that has understanding, one that can see things when they are explained rather than one that one can explain everything, one that can follow logic and detect fallacy, one that can see distinctions that are there to be seen, operate with precision and subtlety, and one that exercises this understanding particularly in relation to matters of importance. (Indeed, one might argue that the ability to see what is important is another aspect of being well-educated).[17]

If that is so, a further crucial question will be: What kinds of understanding are there? We have already seen that understanding is context-bound: that I can understand the causes of the Peloponnesian war does not indicate that I shall be able to understand how a certain chemical reaction may be obtained. That is partly a matter of a certain amount of information being a necessary condition of understanding, and partly a matter of a grasp of certain key concepts being a necessary condition of understanding. But in addition understanding is bound by a limited range of specific kinds of logic or different types of reasoning, each with its distinctively appropriate kind of step.

There have been various attempts to classify knowledge, but only one type of classification is of direct relevance to us here.[18] It is implicit in what has been said that we require a classification in terms of distinct types of reasoning. Some classifications of knowledge are divisions of subject-matter, some of distinct types of experience, some divisions of social importance, some divisions in terms of distinct media of expression. Such classifications, though they may certainly have their value for various purposes, are not to the immediate point because they do not pinpoint the aspect of understanding that enables us to avoid logical error, or misunderstanding as opposed to mere ignorance. To be ignorant of the subject-matter and business of insurance is not to lack understanding in the way that confusing a moral with an aesthetic judgement would be. To fail to recognise an aesthetic judgement for what it is is to be distinguished from lacking aesthetic awareness or appreciation itself; in the latter case, though I lack something (which might be referred to as a type of understanding), I am not thereby led into actual *mis*understanding, even though there are aspects of the world that I cannot understand in the rather specialised sense of experience. Likewise, if I do not know any history, I do not misunderstand historical explanations, I am merely in no position to judge them. The aspect of the educated mind that is being focused on here is the tendency to avoid error rather than the tendency to avoid ignorance. The mind that cannot distinguish between the nature of a fundamental religious claim and an empirically demonstrable claim, or between claims in the realm of geometry and claims about the value of art, misconceives. Misconception and error are the marks of the uneducated mind, rather than lack of information or inability to experience certain states of mind.

The classification of knowledge that is of most pertinence to this particular concern is Hirst's (1974) view that there are seven distinct forms of knowledge: mathematics, natural sciences, morality, religion, interpersonal knowledge, philosophy, and literature and the fine arts.[19] An area of knowledge constitutes what Hirst calls a form, if it meets three criteria: it has its own central and distinctive concepts (as notions such as obligation, wrongness and integrity are basic to morality); the range of things that one can meaningfully say while employing the basic terms is limited (one cannot just say *anything* about obligation: one cannot discuss its colour, add it up or measure it); and the utterances it gives rise to have to be approached in a distinctive way if we are to seek to establish whether they are true or false. (One does not seek to ascertain whether it is true that the angles of a triangle add up to 180° in the same way that one proceeds to test whether cigarettes cause cancer). Hirst's view is that an utterance such as 'The opposite angles of a parallelogram are equal' is a distinctive kind of proposition by these criteria (a mathematical one), as would be 'A current of 1 amp is flowing in this circuit' (natural sciences), 'one ought not to tell lies' (morality), 'God is omnipotent' (religion), 'He left her because he believed he owed it to her to allow her to start life anew' (interpersonal), and 'there are seven forms of knowledge' (philosophy).

Literature and the fine arts as a form of knowledge is *not* to be identified either with aesthetic judgements about works of art (which would presumably be philosophical utterances for Hirst) or with the message overtly conveyed by the work of art, such as the story of a novel or the verbal explanation accompanying programme music. It is the work of art itself that is taken by Hirst as the utterance: thus Beethoven's 5th Symphony has to be taken as a statement, capable of truth or falsity. Understanding such a work requires being at home with not so much the technicalities of musical composition, as the concepts basic to artistic expression and the logic that governs such expression. This is the sort of understanding that allows us to dismiss some works as inauthentic, while recognising others as authentic.

The essence of Hirst's claim is that any proposition that one could utter would necessarily be philosophical, scientific, mathematical, religious, moral, interpersonal, artistic, or a complex utterance that could be broken down into further utterances belonging to two or more of the seven forms of knowledge. Each of these types has its own distinctive kind of logic or, more simply, has to be handled in a distinctive way; a claim about somebody's motivation is not merely concerned with different subject-matter than a claim about God's existence; it has to be examined in a logically distinct manner.

There is certainly room for argument about some of the details of Hirst's view. Are utterances involving interpersonal claims really unique in kind, or are they, perhaps, merely a type of empirical claim that is in practice impossible fully to substantiate? Should we accept that works of art make a unique kind of claim (as opposed to giving unique kind of expression to more familiar claims)? Would Hirst's theory not be improved if he modified his third criterion to allow for the possibility that some of his putative forms do not in fact give rise to propositions that are capable of being true or false? On certain views of the nature of morality, for example, most utterances, while clearly having significance, are not thought to be expressing propositions, which is to say utterances capable of being true or false, at all.[20] Instead, a seeming proposition such as 'That is bad' is interpreted as an emotive expression of distaste — 'Ugh' — which cannot be true or false. By recognising a moral form of knowledge, Hirst is already committed to the rejection of any such account of morality. By amending his third criterion to 'a distinctive manner of establishing the coherence of an utterance', he could avoid this problem.

However, for our purposes it is more important to stress the respects in which Hirst is evidently correct. Whatever the outstanding problems in making sense of religious claims, establishing what is involved in the fine arts as a form, and giving a generally acceptable account of the moral domain, it remains true that there are a number of fundamental disciplines that do not merely have their own subject-matter, but that also involve procedures and give rise to claims that have to be dealt with in a unique way. There is a range of claims centred on the concepts of the natural sciences that we assess by empirical means, relying on our senses. Moral claims have to be approached in a quite distinct way: they are not the same kind of claim, and we do not assess the rightness of an act by empirical inquiry. Different again are claims in the realm of mathematics, where the coherence of assertions has to be determined in the light of certain axioms and definitions based upon a limited number of specialist concepts. In so far as there is any logic to religious claims, these too would seem to be *sui generis*, such that estimating the plausibility of the claim that there is papal infallibility would require understanding of the basic concepts of religion. Unlike Hirst, I do not think that claims about motivation and attitudes towards other people have to be examined in some special way; rather, I see them as scientific claims, even though estimating their coherence is, in practice, a great deal more difficult than estimating the coherence of claims about chemicals. I also believe that his notion of literature and the fine arts is misconceived, for even if it were true that a work of art offered a unique kind of utterance (as opposed to what may be readily conceded — that it offers a unique way of uttering an already familiar claim), then, by definition, there could be no way of explaining or expounding on this verbally. On the other hand, it does seem clear to me that straightforward aesthetic utterances do represent another unique kind of proposition, the coherence of which can only be assessed by those who understand the concepts and logic of aesthetic discourse. (Note that this is not the same thing as appreciating art.) Philosophy as a form of knowledge would comprise those claims the coherence of which could only be estimated by concern for conceptual precision and logical relations.

The significance of this for rational curriculum planning is obvious, even though it is true that an accurate depiction of the nature of knowledge will not in itself give us much in the way of detailed curricular prescription. The argument has been that schools should, amongst other things, educate; that to educate involves developing the mind; and that developing the mind involves, at least, promoting understanding in such a way as to minimise error and misconceptions, which will necessarily include the ability to recognise such logical distinctions as may obtain. We are now in a position to specify that among the logical distinctions that obtain are those between the moral, scientific, religious, aesthetic, mathematical and philosophical forms of understanding. It follows, therefore, that by some means or other our curriculum ought to give students understanding of the distinctive nature of these forms, so that they are in a position to appreciate the differences between them.

Hirst himself has made it clear that he does not see the theory as demanding that the forms are taught as separate subjects or in any other particular way. Some commentators feel that the fact that the general prescription has not been converted into any specific curriculum proposals renders it somewhat irrelevant to curriculum concerns. I find this line of reasoning extraordinary. The theory has told us something of what we should be trying to achieve. It provides a clear criterion against which to judge the educational worth of what we do. 'But it doesn't tell us what to do specifically.' That is true. But it does tell us how to *judge* what we do specifically, without which specification is useless and unwarranted.

Furthermore the assumption that we should be providing very specific curriculum guidance has been questioned in Chapter 3. There is no merit in giving detailed specification for its own sake. It may be that we are in no position to be more specific. It may also be that there is good reason not to be more specific, because there are many acceptable ways in which to proceed. It may not actually matter very much whether one teaches the forms as distinct forms, for example, or provides an integrated curriculum whence students acquire a sense of the distinctions for themselves.[21] (That is the view to which the argument of subsequent chapters leads.) It is curious therefore to find Kelly (1977) offering the opinion that 'either epistemological considerations of a purely philosophical kind must dominate curriculum planning . . . [or] they are of no real help in curriculum planning at all.'[22] That is precisely the reverse of the truth. They must not dominate, for there are other considerations to be borne in mind of no less importance, and in any case, as just suggested, the curriculum implications of epistemological truths are not always so specific as to warrant the idea of domination. On the other hand, they are not only of 'real help', they are a necessary part of adequate curriculum planning. How could one plan a curriculum designed to ensure development of the mind without a coherent account to give of the nature of knowledge?

7. OUTLINE OF A CURRICULUM

(See also Chapter 2, s.5.)

We are now in a position to offer an outline of the content of the school curriculum that is rationally justifiable. Rather than hiding behind empty truisms ('The curriculum should be based on children's needs'), meaningless because incomplete catch-phrases ('The curriculum should be relevant'), unacceptable demands ('The curriculum should consist in what individuals want to do'), or, at best, problematic and contentious claims ('The curriculum should consist in inherently worthwhile pursuits'), we have established that the content of the school curriculum must be arrived at by combining due consideration of the nature and purposes of schooling with a proper understanding of the nature of knowledge and our cultural legacy.

I have suggested that the school's main functions are to educate, to socialise, to procure moral and emotional development, and to superintend healthy physical development. In order to move from such a list of functions to more specific curriculum requirements, one needs to have a clear conception of what is involved in being educated, being morally educated, being emotionally mature, physically fit and healthy, and socialised.

Some of these concepts, such as that of moral maturity, are complex and contentious to the point at which even experts dispute aspects of rival conceptions. Others, such as that of physical health, can be more safely and uncontentiously left to be interpreted by experts. This, it seems to me, entails the conclusion that it is not really part of the remit of the curriculum theorist to get engaged in detailed prescription in respect of the latter. Not only, as was argued in the previous chapter, is there no case for a regiment of dunces telling us how to set out detailed accounts of what we intend to teach every second Tuesday till next autumn, but it is also both unnecessary and inappropriate for curriculum theorists to seek to specify the sort of content that should enter the curriculum under the heading 'Physical Activity'. There are no doubt hundreds of different activities and programmes that would subserve the overall aim of developing and maintaining physical fitness and health, just as there are many ways of organising one's chosen programme and, should anybody strangely insist on this, writing it out. It thus seems clear that what should actually take place in physical activity classes does not need to be, and cannot profitably be, specified in advance in general terms. It is a matter to be left to individual teachers who should plan their activities in the light of their understanding of the facts about physical health, fitness and strength. The curriculum theorist's task ends with establishing that physical development has an important place in the school curriculum, whereas developing skills as an ice-skater does not necessarily.

What is required in order to contribute to moral and emotional development is more open, more complex and more contentious, and therefore more the concern of the curriculum theorist, as contrasted with the practising teacher, for it is important that whatever is done in the school should cohere with the conceptual implications of the justification that has been given. Some religious sects, for example, might, in the name of moral education, simply indoctrinate students into the moral values of their code, but such activity would not count as *bona fide* moral education in the sense that it has been argued schools ought to provide moral education. Moral education implies understanding the nature of moral discourse, and is not to be confused with moral training, which implies habituating people to behave in particular ways, nor moral indoctrination, which implies instilling in people an unreflective commitment to a particular code of values. Although, as in the case of physical development, there may be many equally reasonable ways of proceeding, it is necessary that whatever is done in school in the name of moral education should involve making a genuine contribution to increasing understanding of the logic of moral discourse.

Emotional maturity, which is presumably the goal of emotional development, consists not so much in controlling, suppressing or even giving expression to one's emotions, nor yet in developing the capacity to experience them. It consists rather in being able to recognise in oneself and others the emotions that actually are being experienced, and to be aware of when emotions are appropriately experienced. Emotionally mature people do not confuse lust with love or admiration with covetousness and, though they may feel jealous for no good reason, can at least recognise an inappropriate response for what it is. To develop the individual's emotional side, therefore, requires taking such steps as may foster clear conceptions of the various emotions and facilitate the individual's capacity to recognise emotions.

Socialisation is a relatively straightforward notion and obviously requires that we impart to students knowledge of their culture, including awareness of its place and time. They need to know what their society is like and what it expects of them, something about how their culture arose and the cultural differences with which it is to be contrasted. Being educated, as we have seen, involves developing the mind in such a way that it has a grasp of logical distinctions. To this we should add the need for conceptual finesse, by which is meant the possession of a storehouse of concepts that are both clear and specific. The educated mind can shift beyond generalities and vague classifications; it is capable of making the kind of fine distinctions in ordinary discourse that the academically clever mind makes in a specialist discipline.

From these considerations it is easy to draw the conclusion that the school curriculum ought to contain physical activities, science, mathematics, religion, literature and history. We are not committed to the conclusion that nothing else should be on the curriculum — that nobody should study music or engineering, for example. But what has emerged so far is the skeleton of what might reasonably be regarded as a core curriculum, one that all students ought to experience.[23] In excluding certain things from this core curriculum we are not suggesting that they are worthless. What we are saying is that there is a clear case for all children to engage in these activities, whereas there is not a clear case for all students to engage in others, whatever their intrinsic worth as activities or educational value for some individuals. (In passing we should observe that the fact that this curriculum has a familiar ring about it is neither here nor there. Possibly that is because our forefathers were not as foolish as some contemporary curriculum gurus. Be that as it may, the question is whether the reasoning that has led us to this point is sound. If so, so be it, regardless of what prejudices this curriculum may serve or offend. If not, the reasoning must be corrected.)

The inclusion of physical activities is self-explanatory. Science, mathematics and religion earn their place straightforwardly on the gounds that they are forms of knowledge. What, then, of the other forms of knowledge, and where have history and literature emerged from? History and literature have emerged as the obvious means whereby to promote aspects of socialisation, conceptual finesse and, at the same time, cover the remaining forms of knowledge: moral, philosophical and aesthetic. For literature and history can reasonably be seen as the corpus of material that may tell us about ourselves, our past, our present way of life, and our ideas in relation to all issues that have not been hived off as distinct disciplines. Where do we house the world's stock of intelligent thought about morality, about art, about marriage, about war, and so on? In the pages of literature and history. To bring children up in such a way that they can read with ease and pleasure prominent works of history and literature is one and the same thing as to develop their conceptual finesse over a wide general area, and it is also to involve them with a range of ideas and outlooks that, in conjunction with the specialist subjects referred to, ensures a true development of mind.

Whether we can say anything more specific about curriculum, or whether we need to, depends not on an unquestioned assumption that the curriculum should be specific, but on whether we know anything of importance about such things as sequencing of material, child psychology, effective means of teaching and techniques of evaluation. To these questions we shall now turn.

5 Educational Psychology, and the Timing and Organisation of Curriculum

I have argued that the curriculum ought to contain a certain minimum content, which I have specified in outline. Further specification, if in fact it is appropriate for curriculum theorists or planners to offer further specification, must wait upon consideration of the question of what we know about how such material should be organised and presented. In this chapter we shall consider what we can learn from educational psychology and what we know about timing and organisation of content that is useful for curriculum.

It is likely that many readers will assume that psychology, particularly when it is conceived of as an empirical discipline, is one of the more practical and useful branches of educational theory. The prominence given to the subject in teacher preparation, particularly in North America, serves to reinforce this point of view. Without question, the problems to which psychology addresses itself are of educational interest. I shall argue, however, that there is very little of importance for educators that can be gained from the study of such things as learning theory, child development and personality. I should make it clear at the outset that I do not need, and I therefore do not intend, to suggest that the study of psychology is in itself valueless. My argument is that we do not gain any significant knowledge of which practical use can be made in planning curriculum. Research into child psychology and the sequencing and presentation of curriculum material yields a startling number of disguised tautologies, unsubstantiated empirical claims and truisms, few of which in any case can be made use of when considering how to plan one's teaching, since they are at best generalisations that do not necessarily have, and cannot be known to have, application in particular situations.[1]

1. LEARNING THEORY

Maggie Inge (Lawton *et al.*, 1978), while conceding that what one generally gets from learning theory or psychology of learning does not give much immediate guidance to teachers, none the less makes the more moderate claim that 'it is necessary to have some "theory" of how learning takes place and which conditions make for the most efficient learning.'[2] It is important, however, to stress the distinction between learning theory in the form it usually takes, and research into the conditions that make for efficient learning. It would indeed be useful to know about the latter, and in subsequent sections we shall consider what we do know about such things as the effects of anxiety, sequencing of material and motivation on learning. Learning theory, on the other hand, (or some types of learning theory) involves something rather different in kind from understanding of optimum learning conditions, and something which is not self-evidently an asset or a necessity for teachers. Learning theory describes what happens when learning takes place, rather than why or how it takes place. It seeks to offer an explanation of what goes on in the process of learning. Even on the admission of some of those who take it seriously it is 'a confused area' (Fontana, 1981), and it is not at all clear that well-founded or 'intelligent teaching requires understanding of learning processes' (Tomlinson, 1981) in this sense.[3] Intelligent musical composition does not necessarily require understanding of the creative mind; intelligent building does not necessarily require understanding of why bricks have solid substance; and human relationships are not necessarily improved by understanding of *why* we are as we are. It is often enough to know, for these purposes, *that* things are as they are. The same might well be true of teaching.

It is not clear that we know very much about learning anyway. The reason for this is not, as some philosophers claim, conceptual. It is not that there is ambiguity or incoherence in what 'learning' means, as there certainly is in the case of, say, 'creativity', 'intelligence' and 'education'. It would be generally agreed that to learn is to acquire knowledge, not previously possessed, of propositions or skills. So far as the meaning of 'learning' goes it does not matter whether this acquisition of knowledge is accidental, deliberately imposed from without, or sought after. Nor does the length of time one retains the knowledge cause any serious problem, though one would hope that what is learned is retained for some time, and might quibble about the case of somebody who forgot as soon as he had 'learned'. There are no immediate problems in understanding this account of learning. Any conceptual problems that there may be arise indirectly from the fact that it involves reference to knowledge, where there are some problems, but again not overwhelming ones for the purpose of being understood. It is generally accepted that to 'know' means to believe something that is true, with sufficient evidence to support that belief; it follows that to learn something is to acquire evidence, which must be construed to include such things as appreciating reasoning, to support a true belief. There are problems about what may count as evidence and whether the evidence that people have acquired on particular occasions is sufficient, but these are not problems about the meaning of learning.[4]

This definition of learning is admittedly not couched in the sort of terms that learning theorists themselves tend to use. 'Most psychologists would agree that learning is a relatively persistent change in an individual's possible behaviour due to experience' (Fontana, 1981).[5] But the differences are only superficial. It is characteristic of psychologists to use the broad term 'experience', and to emphasise change in behaviour. But in this instance what is meant by behaviour includes reference to verbal behaviour, so that the ability to recite some dates would count as a change in behaviour no less than the ability to tie one's shoelaces. Experience, likewise, is not narrowly conceived to cover only cases of learning through first-hand experimentation or discovery, but to cover also cases such as having information provided, or points explained. Reference to experience is designed to contrast with changes in behaviour that come about automatically through maturation and physical development. Consequently this formulation, though its phrasing might prove slightly misleading, does not essentially involve a different conception of learning.

We therefore return to the question of whether anything that is either useful or necessary for the practising teacher or the curriculum planner to know can be said about the process or the processes whereby people come to learn.

When spelt out in this way the first thing that strikes one is surely that the very phrase 'process of learning' may be suspect. Is there any such thing as a process of learning? Presumably we are not here concerned with the physiological level, for although there must be a tale to be told about the neurophysiological occurrences that take place when people perceive or come to understand things, this would parallel knowledge of physiological changes that take place when somebody is sick, or knowledge of the theoretical physics that explains what happens when an automobile engine functions efficiently. In either case it is neither necessary nor sufficient to have such knowledge in order to remain healthy or to maintain one's automobile in running order. Even a doctor or mechanic may successfully operate at the level of knowing what to do, while being ignorant of precisely what is happening. Indeed that is how, very often, we have to operate. To this day the medical profession is unable to give a clear account of how or why Aspirin functions as it does, and many garages throughout the world are staffed by excellent mechanics who do not have a grasp of physics. There certainly seems no case for saying either that teachers need knowledge of the physiological transformations involved in learning or that, with it, they would necessarily be any better equipped for facilitating learning in their students.

But is there a process of learning, in any meaningful sense, at any other level? Certainly there is not a process as there is a process of mixing cement. For while it is true that there is a proper way in which to mix cement, such that radical departure from it will result in a failure to produce cement, there is not one way to proceed in order to learn. People may come to learn different things in a variety of different ways, and different people may learn the same things in different ways. Anything that is common to all instances of coming to learn something, such as perhaps that experience of something must always precede recognition of it, and that recognition must always precede analysis of what is perceived, seems to arise directly from the meaning of learning and anyway seems to be trivial in its practical importance. Naturally one cannot analyse or make sense of a proposition or an occurrence prior to recognising or focusing upon it in some way or other, for prior to recognition there is nothing there to analyse. Equally, one cannot recognise or focus upon something unless it is first presented to one's experience, since recognition logically presupposes experience in this broad sense.

This view is borne out by the fact that the theories of learning that have been produced have either been extremely implausible or a mere business of labelling with new terms steps that are not thereby any better understood. An example of the latter is provided by one part of Gagné's work on learning theory, which, despite being widely taught in colleges of education, is little more than a somewhat obscure account of what might be going on when people are learning, at a quasi-physiological and partly psychological level. Gagné depicts learning as an information-processing business, on the model of the workings of a computer (Gagné, 1974). The central nervous system is posited to contain receptors, a short-term memory, a long-term memory, and a response generator. These of course are not actual identifiable parts of the nervous system, as the heart, the cerebellum and the liver are identifiable parts of the body. They are names given to fictional entities that represent certain things people do. People remember some things for a short time only, so a short-term memory bank is conceived to exist; people respond to external stimuli, so a response generator is posited. There is no reason to suppose, and Gagné is not committed to claiming, that there actually is an organ that generates all responses. He merely offers a rather mechanistic way of talking about some fairly obvious features of human behaviour. His procedure is comparable to talking about the weather in terms of the behaviour of the Greek gods: it thunders, so we say that Zeus is angry. A person forgets something, so we say his long-term memory is on the blink.

Gagné goes on to say that what happens when people learn is that information from the environment is coded by their receptors, and then that initial perception is transferred to the short-term memory. Things that make some impression, and are not more or less immediately to be forgotten, are then said to be transferred to the long-term memory. The response generator activates behaviour of some kind, aided by what are called the 'executive control' and 'expectancies', which refer respectively to such things as cognitive strategies and motivation.

To consider whether this account is true or nonsense is hardly to the point. It is a metaphorical way of talking about phenomena we are all perfectly well aware of. The important questions are whether it is a useful way of talking about them, and whether such talk has any practical interest for educators. As to the first point, I would suggest that it is not a useful way to talk, since it misleadingly oversimplifies and suggests a mechanistic chain of cause and effect that may be wildly misleading. It implies that we have some apparatus within us that autonomously processes stimuli from the environment, as the kidneys process liquid. As to the second point, it is difficult to see anything that follows from this account that is of relevance to teaching, curriculum planning, or indeed the business of learning itself.

It is true that Gagné has done a great deal more than posit this one learning model.[6] He has offered a classification of eight types of learning; he has filled out the contours of the basic model by suggesting eight elements in a typical act of learning; he has attempted to summarise external conditions that may affect the process of learning; and he has sought to draw on all of these to propose a theory of instruction that, by outlining important steps in a learning sequence, tells teachers something about how they should proceed. Unfortunately, in all of this work we do not appear to advance beyond statements of the obvious and unwarranted or artificial mechanistic descriptions and prescriptions that, when they are not logical necessities apparent to anyone who thinks about the terms involved, are backed by no reasonable empirical evidence.

The eight types of learning classified by Gagné (1970) are: signal learning, stimulus response learning, chaining, verbal association, multiple discrimination, concept learning, rule learning and problem-solving. Although the broad nature of the various categories can be grasped readily enough, Gagné does not offer a very clear account of what he means by some of them. He tends to adopt the technique of explaining by means of example, which was criticised in Chapter 1. But the distinctions are roughly as follows: signal learning refers to cases where the child makes a conditioned response of a non-specific type to a stimulus. Stimulus response refers to cases where a specific response is elicited by a stimulus. Chaining refers to the ability to join two or more stimulus response connections together. Verbal association involves chaining in respect of verbal response connections. Multiple discrimination is the name given to the business of identifying different stimuli that resemble each other. Concept learning refers to the ability to respond appropriately to a class of stimuli — for example, to treat all dogs as dogs. Rule learning refers to the type of learning involved in recognising that if A, then B. Problem-solving describes learning to combine the sort of principles learned in rule learning to form higher order rules.

It is readily apparent that here again we are merely being presented with names for familiar phenomena. We are all aware that sometimes children (and adults) respond in a quasi-automatic way to stimuli (stimulus response learning), that sometimes they come to acquire concepts, which is to say learn to recognise particular instances of dogs as being dogs or grasp what is common to all dogs (concept learning), and that sometimes they may come to understand logical rules (rule learning), or combine rules and draw conclusions (problem-solving). We are not being given any insights into these various types of learning by this classification; we are not learning anything about them. And it is quite possible that some people will infer from the manner of classification that these eight types represent discrete forms of learning. If so, it is not clear that the inference is warranted, for it is not at all clear that verbal association and multiple discrimination, for example, might not be part and parcel of problem solving.

Gagné himself believes that these types of learning are not merely distinct, but that they are also hierarchical. He is explicitly committed to the view both that the individual's learning must proceed through these stages in the order in which they have been presented, and that learning of particular subject-matter must proceed through these stages. But what truth there is in these views seems to be a simple matter of logic. Of course problem-solving, as defined, presupposes rule learning, since it is defined in terms of combining rules, and, of course they both presuppose concept learning, since one could hardly understand a rule if one couldn't understand the concepts involved in the rule. But that is not the same thing as saying that these are separate steps through which one passes one at a time: a person who has learned to solve problems may still have many concepts to learn, and he may still sometimes operate on the level of stimulus response. A person learning something new may be involved in verbal association, chaining, mutiple discrimination and rule learning at one and the same time.

More importantly, it therefore does not follow that particular subject-matter has to be presented in a way that matches the eight types of learning in hierarchical order. Certainly, Gagné is correct to say that if the child is to 'learn rule IIc, "identify and draw the intersection of lines or parts of lines taken two at a time, as more than one point," he must know the rules that govern the construction of lines . . . and intersections of sets of points . . . and also the rules pertaining to various parts of lines.' But that is because, as Gagné says, 'the higher-order rule incorporates these other rules.'[7] What he does not appear to realise, as Phillips and Kelly (1975) have pointed out, is that to say that is to say that this is a logical and not an empirical point. There is no such logical necessity involved in a general prescription to the effect that when introducing new subject-matter we should start by concentrating on signal learning and proceed through the other seven stages in order, or in Gagné's specific proposals for organising particular subjects such as the teaching of reading. And he does not produce any adequate empirical evidence for the advantages of adopting his approach. He has given us no good reason, therefore, to accept his contention that the teaching of reading should proceed by getting the child to master the art of distinguishing similar words, *then* to master nouns, verbs, prepositions and connectives, *then* to master the intricacies of word order, and *finally* to master the organisation of paragraphs and larger units. Quite apart from the fact that one might be teaching the child all these things at the same time, or switching between them as new concepts and rules arise, there is no obvious reason why one should not concentrate on these elements in a different order.

The eight elements in a typical act of learning listed by Gagné are: motivation, apprehending or focusing, acquisition, retention, recall, generalisation or applying knowledge to new situations, performance or making use of knowledge, and feedback or obtaining knowledge of results. The external conditions or principles of procedure for enhancing learning that he lists include such things as the need for repeated practice when developing motor skills; the need to activate student attention by variation in the manner of presenting verbal information; the need to use a variety of contexts to promote transfer when developing intellectual skills; the need to pose novel problems when developing cognitive strategies; and the need to provide feedback in order to promote a positive attitude to learning.

It is rather difficult, when faced with this kind of theorising, to understand what Gagné thinks he is doing. Are the eight elements supposed to constitute a description of the events in a case of learning? If so, it seems a poor description, since motivation might be a cause of learning but is not part of learning — and one may learn something without putting it to use and without receiving any feedback. It seems more reasonable, therefore, to see both the list of elements within an act of learning and the list of external conditions as a prescription for enhancing learning. As such it is by no means to be dismissed out of hand, but it must be recognised that it is not saying very much that any thoughtful teacher wouldn't think of (motivate, give practice, put the knowledge to use, vary one's approach, provide feedback), that some of the points are true by definition (given what has been said in Chapters 3 and 4 about the transfer of training, it is obviously the case that if one wishes to develop critical thought generally one needs to call for it in a variety of contexts), that no evidence is being produced to support the claims that are not a matter of logic and, above all, that no guidance is given in respect of what the teacher should actually do. Advice of the order 'be varied' or 'pose novel problems' is not exactly useful.

And so we come to Gagne's specific proposals embodied in his theory of instruction. He claims that the teacher should follow five steps. First, he should inform the students of what is expected of them, and do so by presenting a list of his own objectives. Secondly, he should question students in such a way as to have them recall earlier aspects of learning which are necessary to the new task. Thirdly, he should present cues to the students that help them put together the current learning as a chain of concepts in the correct order. Fourthly, he should question the students in ways that allow them to display application of the new learning. And finally he should elicit from them statements of the rules learned.

It is not my intention to suggest that any of these are bad things to do. But what I hope is clear by now is (i) that these prescriptions are in no obvious way related to the initial theory of learning, which is therefore not shown to have any implications for teaching; (ii) that some of them appear to be self-evident (who could fail to see that good teaching requires taking steps to help students make sense of what they are learning, which appears to be the meaning of the third step?); (iii) that no adequate reasoning has been produced to suggest that any of these steps ought necessarily to be taken (why, for example, should a teacher necessarily spell out his objectives to students?); (iv) that no case has been made for the necessity or even the desirability of always following all these steps; and (v) that, given the generality of the prescriptions, they offer no practical guidance to teachers. (It is made quite clear, for instance, that what are here referred to as 'questions' might take many forms, including such things as requiring project work or providing straightforward instruction.) It is not that what Gagné has to say about the steps in instruction is necessarily false or objectionable, so much as that at worst it is empty rhetoric and at best there is no obvious reason for us to be governed by it. It is difficult to avoid Sockett's (1976) conclusion that Gagné's account of the learning process, along with various other psychological accounts of the learning process, such 'as SR, the forming of gestalts, assimilation and accommodation . . . are largely metaphorical ways of describing this mysterious (and not worth searching for) process.'[8]

There are certainly learning theories that do have bite, in the sense of clear and specific implications for how we should teach, but they only seem capable of providing the bite at the cost of considerable implausibility. An example is provided by B.F. Skinner (1969), who takes the view that conditioning, in the sense of connecting a response to a particular stimulus, is the basic unit of learning. Starting from that premise he comes to the view that just as rats can be brought to press levers by reinforcing such behaviour with a food pellet so, in principle, proceeding one step at a time, human beings can be brought to learn items (whether of behaviour or propositional knowledge) by a process of reinforcement.

The basic problem here is that, regardless of how true it is that human beings can be conditioned, this simply ignores both the fact that humans have the capacity to do new things because they understand the reasons for doing them, and the evaluative assumption that education is concerned with our specifically human side, which is to say with providing something other than mere conditioning. Even if it were possible to get people to learn the causes of the Peloponnesian War or Euclidean geometry by means of operant conditioning (which despite what has been achieved by those of a Skinnerean persuasion seems extremely unlikely), and even if one chose to call conditioned acquisition of a coherent view 'learning' (which, because learning is conceptually tied to *appreciating* evidence, we should resist), it could still be said that this is not the kind of learning that we want to encourage in schools.

It may well be that all learning requires, or at any rate benefits from, reinforcement. Provided that 'behaviour' is understood as a very broad term that includes verbal, imaginative and cognitive behaviour, Skinner's view that all learning takes the form stimulus-behaviour-reinforcement could be said to be reasonable. But then it tells us nothing about the wide variety of stimuli to which we may be subject, ranging from merely being in certain situations to being deliberately acted upon by others; and it tells us nothing about the different kinds of reinforcement that might be appropriate for different kinds of behaviour. The truth is that learning not to wet the bed, learning the date of the Battle of Waterloo, learning the concept of time, learning a foreign language, and learning the causes of the Peloponnesian War are rather different in kind, and any account of learning designed to cover them all is necessarily going to be general to the point of emptiness. What we need to know is what kind of stimuli and what kind of reinforcements are most appropriate to enhance learning in each case. The danger, illustrated time and again in the work of those committed to operant conditioning, is that 'stimulus' and 'reinforcement' will in practice be interpreted very narrowly to exclude such factors as satisfaction in understanding, and that the part that may be played by the mind of the learner in perceiving and making sense of stimuli and in providing its own reinforcement will be ignored. When that is the case the theory ceases to be reasonable.

Gagné and Skinner may both be classified as adherents of a behaviourist theory of learning. By contrast Bruner (1966) adopts a cognitivist theory of learning. He emphasises the importance of activity of mind in learning and correctly stresses that a great deal of human behaviour is not simply reflex. Learning in many cases involves acquiring information, sorting it out or making sense of it, and testing it in various ways. One of the characteristics of human beings is the ability to ignore stimuli altogether. Bruner's view is that there are three systems or ways of making sense of incoming information. The enactive mode refers to learning by doing and is, typically, the type of learning involved in acquiring motor skills. The iconic mode involves the use of imagery, but not language, and refers to the type of learning involved in the ability to recognise instances of something without being able to give an account of the concept, or to picture things that one could not describe. The symbolic mode refers to learning through language.

Bruner's view seems rather more sensible than either Gagné's or Skinner's, but that may well be partly because it is very much less specific. Bruner himself is well aware of the fact that an individual may employ the iconic, the enactive or the symbolic mode of learning at any time (and, presumably, in conjunction with one another). This is not therefore a hierarchical model of learning such as Gagné offered. All that we are actually being told is that learning is not generally, if at all, just a matter of reflexive behaviour being reinforced by outside consequences. Rather, the agent's mind plays an important role, and there are some things that will be learned through constant repetition, some things that will be understood in pictorial terms, and some things of which the agent may learn to give some kind of account. This kind of theory of learning, therefore, although it is not obviously false, still does not tell us anything of practical significance for encouraging learning. The game is still one of providing labels for fairly self-evident phenomena. We are not being provided with any kind of reason for doing anything in particular when we wish to facilitate learning of various particular things.

The above may tempt us to adopt the view that thinking in terms of learning processes is preferable to thinking in terms of a learning process. That, I think, is true, provided that we don't repeat the mistakes inherent in the above accounts, and assume that it is merely a case of recognising a relatively small number of processes which we can set in motion at appropriate moments. For that is where the mistake lies. There are not, as far as we know, a number of ways of learning that people are capable of adopting and which may be tapped by the teacher, as there are a number of ways of pruning roses, arranging the furniture, or building a house, between which we may choose, or about the merits of which we may argue. Rather, people come to learn different things in different ways, partly as a result of difference in content, partly as a result of difference in context, and partly as a result of being different people, preferring or finding it easier to acquire understanding in different kinds of situation. If we wish to learn more about how children may come to learn, we need to acquire greater understanding of various particularities in the nature of what it is that is to be learnt, and of what individuals most readily respond to out of a more or less limitless number of things we might do and situations we might engineer.

It is sufficient to assert the conclusion that learning theory, as it has been institutionalised, gives a spurious scientific respectability to what is at bottom an awesome mystery, and what, in more practical terms, requires far greater understanding of individual differences. As Peters (1974) says 'the fact is that very little of learning theory is of much interest or relevance to the educator.'[9]

2. DEVELOPMENTAL THEORY

Are developmental theories likely to prove any more helpful to the educator? In 1959 David P. Ausubel took the view that the study of growth and development could offer 'only a limited number of very crude generalisations and highly tentative suggestions'.[10] In my view that was a very fair summary of the situation, though it is important to distinguish here between insights and theories. Many of the perceptions of individual theorists are plausible and should be made familiar to practising teachers if they are not already familiar; reasonable generalisations, although of limited practical value, are important in so far as they oust false generalisations, and insights such as that young children do not normally operate at an abstract level, though they rapidly become commonplaces, do need to be recognised. What is to be avoided is either the assumption that these generalisations have been empirically validated, or the adoption of an exclusive monolithic theory of development that is treated as the pattern for planning all curricula or organising all teaching. Theories of development, as we shall see, even if they are regarded as beyond criticism in themselves, do not yield practical guidance for curriculum any more than learning theory does.

What, for instance, does Sigmund Freud have to offer educationalists, let alone curriculum planners, such that the study of Freud should be regarded in some institutions as crucial for the education of teachers?[11] Freud made two decisive contributions to psychology: first, the method of free association (which might either be an instrument of research or an instrument of therapy in the right hands). He then evolved a theoretical position as a result of his experience and his conclusions using the technique of free association. The most famous elements in this theory are his terms the 'id', 'ego' and 'super-ego' to represent, roughly, appetite or instinctive needs, the executive will or spirited part of man, and the moral element.[12]

But the basis of Freud's theoretical position includes belief in causation for mental events. This is not to say he believed that mental events, such as love, fear, determination or anxiety, were determined in the sense of being unavoidable, but he did believe that they were explicable in terms of prior events, material or mental, rather than random moods, fancies or desires. He also believed that the causes of mental events were very often unconscious and, more specifically, the product of very early relationships. We should also add reference to his notion of the libido. Freud believed that sexual drive was far wider in scope than had previously been generally supposed; for example, he accepted homosexual activity, voyeurism and other taboo practices as straightforward manifestations of the sexual drive, and not as perversions of it. He also noted that many people can actively embrace more than one manifestation. His theory finally goes on to suggest that much of our behaviour is a transformation of early sexual drives into non-sexual activity.

Clearly one problem with making use of Freudian theory is that it is not necessarily correct. This is not because it is theory. As we saw in Chapter 1, theory is not inherently more specious, uncertain or false than practice, and the polarity between theory and practice is greatly misconceived. But Freudian theory is at best to be treated tentatively because it relates to an area in which it is very difficult to gain certain and total theoretical knowledge. Even many who classify themselves as neo-Freudian will often stress a lack of plausibility about some parts of the theory. Explaining all behaviour in terms of transformation of sexual instincts, for example, is not widely held to be very convincing. As J.A.C. Brown (1964) observes: 'experience suggests that for every stamp-collector who is satisfying his libidinous needs at the anal level, there are dozens who collect because it is profitable to do so, because their friends collect too, or simply because they were given a stamp album.'[13] This and other similar reservations about aspects of Freudian theory shade into what for our purposes is the more important point. Given that it is only a tentative theory, given that few, if any, embrace it wholeheartedly, and given that most people would see it as at best a possible explanation of some parts of some people's behaviour and personality, how helpful does it become in practice in our daily dealings with people? In particular, how useful is this theory of development to educationalists? How legitimate is it, given that no student can study everything, to devote part of the intending teacher's time to studying one such theory?

It is arguable that people concerned with the upbringing of very young children should be aware of the general claim about the importance of early relationships and practices, but only on condition that they do not imbibe it uncritically as a total explanation and a proven truth. One might also accept that teachers should be aware that some few individuals might benefit from psychoanalysis, provided we don't make too much of the point. As Morris (1958) remarks, although 'teaching is in some respects necessarily a therapeutic relationship . . . the therapy required is largely that of spontaneous intuitive understanding . . . not an extensive academic knowledge of the more intricate parts of dynamic psychology.'[14] But the practical value of awareness of these broad claims is necessarily very limited, since, even if the claims were true without qualification, we should still need to recognise in individual cases what significance what early experiences had had, and what we should therefore do about it, if we wished to take practical advantage of our theoretical insights. The famous Oedipus complex element in Freudian theory, if well-founded, warns us to appreciate that at about the age of four or five the individual comes to terms with his or her Oedipal stirrings. But the theory does not tell us how to recognise what is going on, how to interpret it, or what to do about it. Beyond the value of being aware of such very general points, it is difficult to see what relevance Freudian theory could have to practising teachers or curriculum planners, despite the fact that lectures on Freud play a part in many educational psychology courses.

Morrish (1967), a restrained and cautious commentator, suggests that a study of Freud leads us to seeing the need for teachers to have 'a fully realised personality' and to make 'good relationships', while more generally it leads to the view 'that really effective learning takes place only when a child's energies and drives are properly and fully employed.'[15] But the last remark is either a truism or untrue, depending upon interpretation, is not exclusively dependent on Freudian theory, and is not of much practical use. It is simply not true that people *cannot* effectively learn when frustrated or depressed, for example. So this knowledge does not lead directly to a general prescription along the lines that children should never be allowed to experience frustration or depression. If, on the other hand, it is claimed that necessarily learning would be more real if cheerfully engaged in, that becomes a definition of learning rather than an empirical observation. For granted that a person could learn something while depressed, the only way in which it can necessarily be true that it will not be real learning is if one arbitrarily defines true learning as 'learning cheerfully acquired'. But the main point remains that while no one would dispute the importance of recognising that learning may be inhibited by psychological problems which are sometimes the product of early experience, the questions of importance are what are the problems of particular children, what caused them (to which Freud offers one possible kind of answer, but still not a specific one) and how to deal with them in practice. Freudian theory does not offer an answer to such questions because it is not supposed to. Of course, if one were an uncritical committed and simple-minded Freudian, there would be some kind of answers, and the immediate conclusion would be that teachers should become Freudian analysts. But that is quite unacceptable as a general prescription, given the extremely tentative and contentious nature of the theory.

Superficially more plausible than the idea that pure psychological theory is of especial value to those concerned with teaching is the idea that developmental theories, such as those of Piaget or Isaacs, and offshoots of these such as Kohlberg's theory of moral development, are of great importance for educational practice.

Susan Isaacs (1930) categorises stages of development into infancy (0-1 years), early childhood (1-5), later childhood (5-12), early adolescence (13-16) and later adolescence (16 +). The differentiation between the stages is arrived at by reference to various alleged general truths of the order that the period of later childhood is marked by changes in emotions, a turning away from parents and towards other children, a move away from fantasy to the real world, an increase in linguistic skills and sociability, and an increase in the tendency to look for purposes. Devising such a theoretical structure is therefore a matter of assessing, and seeking to verify empirically, what seem to be particularly noteworthy age-spans in respect of the clear emergence of various itemised aspects of personality. The plausibility of any such theory has to be judged while bearing in mind that it consists of generalisations, and that their verification is not a simple matter of observation, since what counts as, say, an increasing interest in the real as opposed to fantasy is both difficult to conceptualise and, once conceptualised, difficult to discern. It is a matter of judgement as much as looking.

The value of any such theoretical account is less a question of truth than one of usefulness. For, provided that one's observations about the general tendency for children to develop certain characteristics at certain broad ages are not manifestly false, what matters, from the point of view of those debating how important the theory is, is whether the changes focused upon are of practical significance for some purpose or other. In addition, it is important to note that if anybody, such as a teacher, is to make use of the theory, it is not sufficient that he should merely learn the stages and what they involve by rote, as unfortunately too often happens in teacher education. He needs to know precisely what the originator of the theory means by all the itemised features of a stage, and he needs to be aware of the tentative nature of each generalisation, as well as that it is a generalisation. In this case Isaacs' divisions do not appear fanciful or absurd, and there is no reason to doubt the authenticity of the empirical studies backing up her theoretical account beyond reminding ourselves of the very grave general limitations inherent in any such research (see Chapters 2 and 6). The question is of what use this particular developmental framework is to us as educators.

Because the theoretical structure only claims to give us generalisations, we cannot apply the theory in any direct way when planning our curriculum or our teaching. We obviously cannot say: 'This is a class of ten-year-olds, so they must all be moving away from their parents and towards their peers.' (Nor can we say that they *should* be doing this, for the theory only purports to describe what normally happens; it would be quite illegitimate to deduce that this is the way things ought to be.) We have to look at each individual child in the class and make a judgement as to whether he does conform to the norm set up by the framework. This means that for practical purposes the art of recognising this and other elements of the items listed in the stage in question is more important than knowing the details of the stage. Learning the elements listed by Isaacs for the stage of late childhood may serve as a useful check-list of things to look out for, but it does not in itself help one to recognise them and, if it is treated as comprehensive, it will deflect one's attention from other features of particular children's stages of development. By contrast, the art of recognising what particular children are experiencing and what they are like is both necessary to taking any appropriate action, and sufficient, so far as anything that knowledge of any theoretical structure could add: if you recognise that John is growing away from his parents, increasingly interested in the real world, and so forth, you know what you need to know as a prerequisite for suitable action, and nothing would be gained by knowing in addition that John's state represents what Isaacs had chosen to term late childhood.

Secondly, it does not appear that the stages named by Isaacs introduce any new concepts, which is to say new ideas or, more colloquially still, things that nobody had previously thought of. The notion that a person might be more or less drawn to fantasy, for instance, is not one that was created by Isaacs. She has merely chosen to emphasise certain items (and sometimes introduced new names or descriptive phrases for them) with which many parents and teachers are already quite familiar, though perhaps under different names.

Thirdly, it is not at all obvious that the majority of the features of the various stages are of any great importance for educators. One should, no doubt, be aware that children do grow away from their parents, that they begin to develop an interest in the real world later than they do in fantasy, and that they gradually develop linguistic skills at the pre-puberty stage, because such knowledge may help to guide one's understanding, expectations and practice. But clearly one should not make too much of this. It is not going to make a very significant contribution to curriculum planning or teaching strategy, since it provides only rough guidelines to general points along the lines of 'one can usually afford to be more abstract with older children', or 'one can often gain a more positive response to facts about the world as children grow older.' But these general guiding principles are not exclusive to or dependent on particular theories of development; they are part and parcel of a general awareness that there is development in children.

The matter would be very different if, besides providing precisely articulated accounts of the various stages and pinpointing some rather more specific ones, we could tie them firmly to various ages. There are one or two people, such as Gesell (1928), who have tried to do this. But in no case has there been any adequate empirical backing for the claims, and indeed it seems clear to most of us, including developmental theorists, that it just isn't true, for example, that the child *necessarily* walks holding on to furniture at nine months of age, stands alone well at eleven months and walks well at twelve months (Frankenburg and Dodds, 1967). The best that we are able to do is put up a case for saying that the order of certain stages of development is invariable, as Kohlberg has argued for certain unchanging sequences in moral development, and that is not good enough for helping us in any significant way with curriculum planning or teaching.

Kohlberg's (1969) view is that any individual in any culture necessarily develops some way along a line of moral development through six stages which must be passed through in this order: a stage of simple unreflective obedience, a stage of naive egoism, a good boy/girl orientation stage, a stage of deference to authority, a contractual stage in which moral behaviour is guided by a sense of honouring agreements, and a stage in which the individual is guided by his conscience. Kohlberg associates the first two 'pre-conventional' stages with the years 2-7, the next two 'conventional' stages with the years 2-11, and the final 'post-conventional' stages with 12 and beyond. But as the overlap between the ages given for the pre-conventional and the conventional stages mildly indicates, he is not committed to a firm view about when these stages will occur, and in fact explicitly concedes that anybody might be at any stage.

Kohlberg claims that nobody could be at stage five without having previously passed through stages one, two, three and four, in that order. If somebody is at stage two, he will necessarily proceed to stage three, if he proceeds at all. This is not surprising, since the later stages are presumed logically to presuppose at least some of the earlier ones. How could anyone display deference to authority who did not already have a developed sense of obedience? How could an individual act autonomously in response to his own conscience if he had not previously acquired a conception of such things as the distinction between naive egoism, good-boy orientation and deference to authority? The main empirical claim is that progression from stage to stage is not brought about directly by the teaching of adults.

What precisely Kohlberg means by these claims, and whether he can convincingly maintain that he has demonstrated them, may be open to question, though I do not intend to challenge them here.[16] Our concern is with the practical value of such schemata for curriculum. What does the planner or teacher gain from this rather formalised theoretical account of moral development that is not encompassed by the commonsense observation that children slowly develop from being non-moral creatures, by means of a realisation of the value of cooperation, through to an abstract sense of justice? And how does knowledge of either help him to judge the state of the individual before him or lead him to the best way to teach that individual? Kohlberg's most significant claim would appear to be that the way to advance an individual from one stage to the next is to communicate with him in terms of the stage beyond his present one. But this again seems a matter of common sense; in order to advance learning or development in any sphere, it is clearly necessary to go beyond the individual's present state, and it is clearly foolish to communicate in terms far in advance of that state. We would gain more from Kohlberg if we had a clearer and more specific account of what is involved in the various stages, so that we had more guidance as to how we should actually proceed.

Just as relatively single-minded theories of learning are potentially more useful than general theories, but correspondingly more contentious, so relatively specific schemes of development, such as Piaget's, might conceivably prove more useful than a relatively plausible but open and general one such as Isaacs', but are also likely to be more debateable in their content.

Piaget's (1924) view is that how we handle concepts varies as we develop.[17] He has posited the following stages of development: the sensori-motor stage, which involves reflexive, non-thinking behaviour, generally associated with the years between birth and 2; the pre-operational stage, associated with the years 2-7, which may be broken down into the pre-conceptual stage (2-4), which involves recognition of particular signs and symbols, and the intuitive stage (4-7), which is characterised by thought centred on the self, thought centred on an isolated aspect of a situation, and irreversibility, by which is meant the lack of ability to work on an operation backwards. For example, the child can add 2 and 4 together to make 6, but not appreciate that 6 minus 4 equals 2. The next stage is that of concrete operations, which involves the ability to group and serialise objects, and is associated with the years 7-11. The final stage is that of formal operations, involving the ability to hypothesise and relate points to one another and associated with the age 12 + .

There are a number of serious questions to be asked about, and grave problems in, this work. In the first place, has Piaget correctly understood and described what he observes? Many commentators think that he has often not done so. Isaacs, for example, challenges his view that what children are actually doing at the pre-operational stage is engaging in 'collective monologuism', and therefore rejects the characterisation of this stage as egocentric.[18] Hamlyn (1967, 1978) raises the more general point that some of his apparent findings may be due not to the developmental stage a child has reached, but to a misunderstanding between children and researchers. Thus the famous conservation experiment, designed to show that children at a certain stage cannot appreciate that volume is distinct from depth, could conceivably arise out of a conceptual difference between child and adult relating to the instructions given, rather than out of an inability to perceive or conceptualise volume. The children, when asked such questions as 'Is this the same amount of liquid?', may understand something different by that phrase than we do. It would not then be that they fail to appreciate that it is the same amount of liquid, as we would phrase it, but that they fail to understand what we mean by that phrase.[18a] If it be said that that is an implausible interpretation of what happens in the research, then it follows that our reasons for accepting Piaget's view that children do not have the concept of volume are not purely experimental, but are partly judgemental: we think it likely given what we observe and how we interpret it, that children cannot see that volume is distinct from depth. We may be correct, but we have not unequivocally demonstrated it.

Secondly, there is the question of how much of Piaget's theory is empirical and how much a matter of logic. (Piaget himself is equivocal on this point, merely acknowledging that his work is not simply empirical.) Is it, for instance, an empirical point that children cannot at first see the reverse implications of particular processes of thought they can engage in, or a matter of inevitability? If a child has not been introduced to the idea of subtraction, why should we expect him to see that since $2 + 4 = 6$, then $6 - 4$ must equal 2?

Thirdly, the previous example brings to the fore the question of the extent to which development through these stages is a matter of maturation and the extent to which it may be affected by teaching. Povey and Hill (1975) claim that children supposedly at the pre-conceptual stage can in fact handle concepts such as dog and food, in as much as they can correctly identify instances of them, provided that pictorial rather than verbal material is used. And Bryant and Trabasso (1971) claim that children at the same stage can be taught to appreciate reasoning of the form 'if A is bigger than B and B is bigger than C, then A is bigger than C', provided it is done carefully and firmly. If such claims are true, and they seem to be in accord with the experience of many people who deal with young children of their own, they suggest that some of the detailed elements in the various stages do not necessarily belong there as a matter of empirical fact, as well as that they are not a simple matter of maturation.

They also raise a fourth point. Given that the ages given are only contingently linked to the stages, and given that by taking certain steps we can bring children who might be expected to be at the pre-conceptual stage to operate in ways associated with the concrete and formal operational stages, how does one determine the stage which particular children have reached? Clearly it would be inadequate to reply 'by setting the child the sort of tasks that Piaget used in his research.' For the implication of the points raised by Isaacs, Hamlyn, Povey and Hill and Bryant and Trabasso, different as those points are, is that the Piagetian approach is not necessarily reading the situation correctly.

Such criticism at the theoretical level is obviously of great importance in itself, but again it should be recalled that from the point of view of curriculum the crucial question is not about how to interpret data and whether particular arguments are sound, but what their use may be. Developmental psychologists are, after all, concerned essentially with the *order* in which mental growth proceeds, not the actual ages at which things happen. In fact, the age ranges given as typical for particular stages of development in Piaget's work represent approximately 75 per cent of children tested. In other words, one in four children aged between 11 and 16 might be expected *not* to be at the stage of formal operations. This means once again that the teacher prepared with knowledge of Piaget's theoretical framework is not very well armed by that alone to deal with the individual children in his care. What he needs to know is which of his children can cope with abstractions, which of his children have developed what linguistic capacity, and so forth; and, of course, if one can recognise the particular, the generalities cease to be of importance. It must also be repeated that Piaget's primary interest is in the development of mind as it takes place without special intervention from people such as teachers. Unless this is clearly understood, studying Piaget can actually be very misleading. If it is understood, the value of the Piagetian framework to the teacher becomes less. Schooling is an activity based on the idea that by taking active steps and taking account of social factors that may alter expectations and possibilities envisaged within a psychological developmental framework, we can significantly hasten development.

Even if Piaget's claims were judged to be reasonable, they surely have far less practical pay-off for educators than the time usually devoted to them in courses for the preparation of teachers would suggest. It is true, as Stenhouse (1975) says, that developmental psychology in general helps us 'to set limits to readiness',[19] in the sense that it provides tentative hints as to what not to expect from children of various ages; but the limits set are for the most part fairly obvious (e.g. 'Don't expect elementary school children, as a rule, to be able to discuss democracy in abstract terms'), and, when faced with individuals, we still have to establish whether the generalisation applies.

It may perhaps be said that if the generalisations seem obvious they have become so thanks to developmental psychology. It seems possible to doubt that. Certainly several hundred years ago Plato had grasped the point that young children cannot usually handle abstractions, and it is difficult to think of any other generalisations from the corpus of developmental theory over the past fifty years that involve literally putting new ideas into our heads. But in any case the prime issue is not whether Piaget did or did not discover new truths, nor whether his work has, as a matter of fact, led to wider currency for old truths. The issue is whether studying Piaget is a valuable activity for those who wish to teach or to plan curricula. Stenhouse may be correct to suggest that the value of developmental theory lies in a provision of norms for diagnostic and individual purposes, that is to say as a pointer to the sorts of consideration one might look for in order to explain the problems of particular individuals; but in that case what curriculum planners need is an awareness of general points, such as that children develop increasing powers of abstraction, that young children tend to be egocentric, and so forth, rather than a particular developmental framework, and what teachers need is experience at judging the problems of individuals. Given these observations (about the generality of such theories, their tentative nature, the need to make individual judgements, and the effects that social factors and the act of teaching itself may have on the generalisations) it cannot be right to plan a curriculum or teach a class by reference to a developmental theory, even if such theories had it in them to prescribe what we should do given a particular developmental stage (which they do not). The fact that John Stuart Mill could speak Greek and handle abstract concepts at the age of 4 better than some

44-year-olds does not 'disprove' Piaget; what it does is illustrate the practical limitations of such theory.[20]

Kieran Egan (1979) has recently argued strongly against the coherence and value of psychological developmental theories, and asserted instead the need for a truly educational development theory, such as, he contends, Plato and Whitehead tried to offer.[21] A minimal aspect of such a theory would be that it looked at development in the context of the school, precisely as Piaget did not. He himself offers the outline of such a theory, involving a mythic stage, associated with the years 4-7, characterised by the child's attempt to make sense of the outer world in terms of his own inner world and centred on the emotions; a romantic stage, associated with the years 8-14, in which the child sees the outside world as separate from himself and tends to identify with hero figures; a philosophic stage, between the years 14-19, characterised by enthusiasm and wholehearted commitment to causes and ideas; and finally, an ironic stage, which assimilates the previous stages but overlays them with an appreciation of the significance of mind.

While his emphasis on the question of what we can achieve, rather than what would happen if we didn't try to achieve anything, is welcome, and while his educational development theory should in many respects prove more appealing to those interested in *education* than psychological developmental theories, his approach seems vulnerable to many of the criticisms we (and he) have directed at the latter. The status of his stages seems frankly prescriptive, with perhaps a small admixture of empirical support. But he offers no evidence that children are as he depicts them, and no strong case for saying that they ought to be so treated. Above all it is very difficult to see what specifically follows in terms of practical guidance for educators. Egan is working on the latter issue, but he does not yet appear to have produced any argument to support the adoption of his particular curriculum proposals, even supposing we were to accept his stages as a framework to be adopted.

Maggie Inge (Lawton *et al*, 1978) writes: 'Piaget may tell us that the concept of conservation is not reached until the stage of concrete operations; a theory of instruction should set out the best ways of promoting understanding of conservation. This involves not only psychological theory, but a sophisticated understanding of what is to be learned, of the structures of knowledge.'[23] Although she is correct about the need for the latter, we must conclude that a theory of instruction has no need at all of psychological theory, at least of this kind. A theory of instruction, if such is possible, should tell us simply how to teach conservation to those who apparently do not understand it. The question that begins to emerge is whether there can or should be such a thing as a theory of instruction.

3. ORGANISATION OF CONTENT

Even though it may be necessary to exercise great caution about the claims of learning theory and developmental theory, few would imagine that it makes no difference how one presents material or content to students. There may not be many verified and useful principles of sequencing, learning or organisation, but there are some established — if sometimes obvious to experienced teachers — points, and a few more reasonably well-attested and intuitively plausible suggestions. It is, for example, plain that ideally material should be presented at a level suitable to individual children's competence at abstraction, that it should be presented to students when they have already learned anything that is presupposed by it, and that it should be presented when they are, or in such a way as to make them, well-motivated. Usually it is foolish to expect a class of 9-year-olds to grapple with abstract concepts, such as justice, love or democracy; any attempt to introduce such ideas to such an age-group would in all probability need to proceed by using concrete examples. That kind of consideration should of course govern curriculum planning and teaching, but such considerations cannot be elaborated to the status of principles or taken as definitive rules to structure the procedure, for all the reasons advanced. They can only be points to be borne in mind.

As to the structure of subject-matter, here too, in the zeal for certainty, a lot is assumed that is highly questionable. It is sometimes said that it is imperative to observe the logical order of the subject matter or, more frequently, that logical prerequisites must be set out in any curriculum and seen to be met by any students who would undertake the course. But it is not at all clear from those who use such phrases just what they suppose a logical order or logical prerequisites are (nor why students must be seen to have met them. Why not adapt one's approach to include making good deficiencies, if and where detected?). Of course, sometimes there are things that are presupposed by a curriculum. A course in algebra presupposes basic numeracy. Understanding certain historical events presupposes understanding others. A course in human biology may presuppose knowledge of plant life. In what sense even these considerations are 'logically necessary prerequisites', however, remains unclear. They are logically necessary conditions of undertaking the studies in question as conceived, but that is a mere tautology: the courses are defined in such a way as to demand prior knowledge of a certain sort, which therefore becomes by definition logically necessary. But the courses didn't have to be designed that way. It is not an unavoidable truth that he who would understand algebra must previously have become numerate. They are at best logically necessary conditions of understanding the study in question in that they are a necessary part of the study in question, but they do not necessarily have to be mastered beforehand: they might be introduced as part of the course in question.

A far happier way of phrasing it would be to say that any proposed curriculum should be prepared with a full awareness of what is involved in coming to grips with it, in the light of which sensible *ad hoc* decisions can be made as to whether particular individuals are in a position to cope with it. Beyond that it is not at all clear that subjects have a logical order in the sense of discrete stages, elements or facets that necessarily must be encountered and mastered in invariable sequence. There is nothing specifically logical, for instance, about such assumptions as that the study of one's own land should precede that of other lands in geography; that the study of history should proceed in temporal order (it is anyway part of the stuff of history to argue about what knowledge is required to understand particular events); that grammar should be mastered first; or that one should learn to decline nouns before conjugating verbs when learning Latin. These are, at best, more or less sensible proposals to be borne in mind and thought about. Different individuals may quite reasonably hold different views about them. More precise schemes of sequencing, such as may be encountered in particular reading schemes, programmes of physical development or mathematics, cannot legitimately claim to be 'logical' in other than the weak sense of 'reasonable', so long as there is as much *bona fide* contention about them as is evidenced by competing schemes and programmes. It is conceivable that there is an ideal way in which to structure reading programmes, but it is unreasonable to claim that we know what it is in the present state of knowledge, and it is equally plausible to suggest that there is no one logically preferable way, but several equally sensible ways of ordering the same material.[23]

That does indeed imply that those who are going to teach reading should give thought to the sequencing of their material, but it also implies that the way to set about that is not to imbibe one philosophy of teaching reading, or even two or three, but to attempt to understand what is involved in reading, so that one can create one's own programme and adapt to one's own students and circumstances as they change. Planning a humanities curriculum or a music curriculum needs to be governed not by an *a priori*, and necessarily questionable, theory of what has to precede what, but by a proper appreciation of what one wishes to get across during the course and what individual students may be capable of. In the event there will be prerequisites presumed, but these will seldom, if ever, be logical prerequisites, and they cannot be determined by outside planners. Rather they will be determined as prerequisites by the teacher for reasons of convenience and control.

If I am planning my university course on curriculum itself, I do not set out on a vain search for those things which, in the abstract, people must necessarily have studied in order to understand any such course. I come to a clear understanding of what ideally I would like the course to involve, I then make clear the things that, given my knowledge of likely applicants for the course, I insist on presuming they already know. But another instructor, or I myself in a different term or with a different group of students, might well alter those presumptions. There is nothing necessary about them, and they cannot reasonably be laid down from without by centralised curriculum planners. Not even the ability to read is a 'logically necessary' *pre*requisite; it is at most a logically necessary part of completing the course as I have planned it. The important thing remains to understand what is involved in what one is teaching rather than to formulate *a priori* lists of requirements. Understanding gives one flexibility; lists constrain. It is a matter of being aware of what one *intends* to take for granted with particular groups or individuals, not of working out what is necessarily the proper order of events.

It is not that one wants an illogically ordered curriculum. But the dictum that the curriculum should be organised logically is formal and empty, in the way that the more general claim that curriculum should meet the needs of students has been shown to be. Subject-matter does not contain a logical order as the human body contains a skeleton. The logical order, if the phrase is apposite at all, in which to present a subject depends partly on the state of the students, and partly on one's resources and intentions; and even then there may be more than one logical way to proceed. It may be said that, none the less, certain aspects of a subject do have a logical priority over others in that they are more fundamental or general, but even if that is sometimes true in some sense, it does not follow that one has to acquire understanding of the more fundamental elements first. Indeed, as we have seen, there is some reason to suppose that children cannot understand more fundamental general principles until well after they have come to recognise concrete instances of those general principles. If 'logical' is taken more loosely to mean 'rational', then it is true that the curriculum should be organised logically, but that observation will not take one far on its own. One needs to develop a rational organisation of one's material out of an understanding of that material, the students in question and one's purposes.

The notion of sequencing one's material in terms of relative difficulty is not unproblematic either. Is it not rather a question of difficulty for certain people at certain times or stages of intellectual development, which may vary considerably and which needs therefore to be assessed by individual teachers rather than by curriculum planners? Obviously some things may be more complex than others, some more abstract, and so forth, but since some people are more at home with complexity than simplicity, or with abstractions than concrete particulars, it is mistaken to equate such specific features with a general notion such as difficulty. At best one might say that in general people find more complex material more difficult. (There is a danger of turning this into a tautology, by making 'complex' just another word for 'difficult'. It is important, therefore, to have a clear idea of what one means by complexity, if one wants to appeal to the broad empirical claim that for most people complex issues are relatively hard to come to grips with.) This, generally, is what the schooling system does tend to assume: by and large, our teaching becomes increasingly general, abstract and complex. And we have some warrant for proceeding in this way. But we do not have enough clear and determinate rules in respect of that general approach to provide specific guidance for particular age-groups or individuals in particular subjects. Our notion of a suitable 'O' level or Grade 9 examination in physics is very much more based on judgement and experience than on a science of development and a logical map of the order of the subject-matter. There is no sufficient independent evidence to show that certain particular aspects of physics are necessarily more suited to 14-year-olds than others. Still less is there a means of determining the relative easiness of science and history, or any other subjects, in the abstract. The ease of studying one subject or another will vary with individual cases, as a result of such factors as student interest, student talents, student knowledge, teaching methods, teacher commitment, teacher personality, and other extraneous factors such as the ethos of the school and degree of home support.

Readiness on the part of pupils has sometimes been put forward as a desirable criterion for the timing of the material, but here we have another instance of a formally desirable, but in practice inadequate, guide. One should not introduce children to material before they are ready for it, by definition, since not being ready for it means being in some way (intellectually, emotionally, or whatever) unsuited to it. But readiness only provides a *terminus ante quem non* — it tells us when we must not do it before; it does not follow that we should do things as soon as somebody is ready. In any case, we now face the serious problem of knowing whether somebody is ready for something. This is not the same thing as when they think or say that they are ready, nor as when they appear to be ready. But in order to know that somebody is ready to study or understand something, one needs to know various things that make appeal to the principles of readiness redundant. In order to know that Jim is ready to study quadratic equations, I need to know that he has already mastered certain things, that he has the interest and ability to undertake the study, that he can benefit from my way of teaching, and so on; it would be more straightforward, then, to say that these are the sorts of thing that teachers need to make judgements about when embarking upon particular courses, rather than to suggest that there is some quality, 'readiness', that one may become trained to detect. Certainly, states of readiness in respect of particular subjects are not universal enough, nor closely enough related to age, to allow us to prepare any general scheme of readiness.[24]

At this point further reference should be made to needs and interests, but now as possible determinants of timing, rather than as determinants of content. (We have already seen that neither are directly pertinent to content selection.) Those occasions on which interest is aroused (although it should be borne in mind that interest may be aroused by the teacher in the course of teaching), or when a need is correctly perceived, are good times to introduce appropriate material. They are not, however, necessary or sufficient conditions of introducing material. It may be a good idea to override a present interest or current need, or there may simply be good reasons for doing something else, and sometimes it may be reasonable to refuse to await the occasion of either one. But the main problem here is the same one that we encountered with easiness, readiness and logical structure: these are all good ideas formally, but determining what is interesting, what is needed, what is appropriate, easy and logical, is itself a complicated business, and it has to be engaged in in particular situations, which will take us so far beyond these terms as to indicate that they are immaterial as practical guidelines for sequencing material. Say that curriculum material should be accessible to students, and you have said nothing of moment. The thinking begins there, rather than ends there.

A further point that should be raised about the organisation of curriculum is integration.[25] A lot of unnecessary argument has centred on the merits and demerits of integration, which can be set aside if we bear in mind that integration may take a number of forms. Some writers would like to confine the word to a particular kind of interrelationship between subject matter, others take it more loosely to cover a wide variety of ways of combining subjects. Some, for instance, would regard linking courses in literature, history and music by covering the same time span in relation to each as a form of integration. Others would not accept as a truly integrated curriculum anything that did not break down the very notion of distinct subjects, and approach the study of particular issues from a multidisciplinary point of view. There are a great many other variant definitions of integration that might be appealed to. Provided we do not misunderstand each other by using the word in different senses, it does not greatly matter how we decide to use the particular word.

Regardless of the word 'integration,' it is clear that one might in principle organise one's material in more or less discrete blocks according to a variety of different criteria such as methodology, subject-matter, period, topics and interest. That is to say, whether one sees oneself as teaching subjects, disciplines, activities, topics, forms of knowledge, experiences or some combination of these, one may keep the study of the various distinguishable elements separate or link them to a greater or lesser extent in a number of different ways. The main argument for closer integration between elements (in very practical terms, between the individual contributions of teachers) has tended to be the claim that it would give the children a sharper understanding of the relationship between, and the relevance to one another, of the various things that they study. Opposition to the idea has usually centred on the claim that it is impractical, or that it is important for students to appreciate such distinctions as there are between subjects, especially between disciplines.

If one believes, as it must be admitted the quasi-scientific tone of much curriculum writing tends to lead people to believe, that this is a problem that must in principle have a correct answer (to integrate or not to integrate), then one is doomed to many fruitless hours, pitting a number of equally fair points and arguments against one another. But there is no correct answer here. The fact is that there are good reasons for relating what we teach more closely, such as increasing awareness of the interplay between historical and artistic events, or between moral considerations and scientific advance, or simply enhancing appreciation of the various elements: music has an added dimension if it is understood historically as well as musically. But it would be beyond credibility to say that any such arguments are evidently overwhelming. Conversely, reasons can be given for preserving something like the distinctions we have between subjects: teachers are better equipped to teach, and therefore may be expected to teach better, by way of specialisms; some of the distinctions between subjects represent a logical difference, being not a matter of differing content, but a matter of different kinds of procedure. But these reasons are not decisive either. (See also Chapter 4,s.6.)

When one is faced with a number of good reasons for doing different things, it is surely plain that the issues should be settled on an individual basis through judgement exercised by those directly concerned. It is not for curriculum planners to determine whether the total curriculum should be integrated or not. For curriculum planners should operate at the level of general argument, and we have just said that there are no decisive general arguments. It is for particular schools to determine what, on balance, is the degree and type of integration most suited to their resources. Incidentally, although Kelly (1977) has said that 'no logical problems are created when we wish to integrate subjects, but only when the integration of separate disciplines is involved', it should be noted that there is no necessary difficulty in the latter case either.[26] The fact that science and morality are agreed to be logically distinct areas or forms of knowledge, and not simply concerned with different subject-matter, does not prevent us from integrating them in a number of ways, if we want to. All that is required of any proposed integration, which is to say systematic interconnection of some sort between subjects, is that the links should have some defensible purpose, that they should be practicable, that they should not prove confusing to the student, nor destroy or obscure other equally important concerns. For example, if morality and science were to be integrated it would be important to do it in such a way as to avoid blurring the logical distinctions in students' minds.

4. MOTIVATION

In this section I shall take up the question of what we know about the sorts of factor that may affect learning in particular cases. (The act of teaching itself will be considered separately in the next chapter.) I shall refer to certain aspects of personality and classroom approach that may affect learning as well as more direct motivational factors.

It seems to be widely agreed that reward and encouragement are to be preferred to punishment and chastisement as ways of motivating children.[27] This is not so much because of any clear evidence that the former are more effective means of reinforcing behaviour, as because the latter have certain clear disadvantages. The use of punishment may promote anxiety in the child, it may tempt the child to do various undesirable things such as lie and cheat in order to avoid punishment, it may impair the child's relationship with the teacher, and it may suggest to the child that it is reasonable for the strong to impose on the weak. These can hardly be said to be decisive points against the use of punishment, since the actual effect will clearly depend upon such further factors as the situation, the nature of the punishment and the individual's nature, and since rewards may also be mishandled to detrimental effect. But they might reasonably incline one to be cautious about the use of punishment and chastisement in general. It might in addition be argued that there are moral objections to the use of punishment, at any rate when there are alternatives available.[28]

Research into age, sex and social background has produced a number of claims, such as that girls tend to be more verbal than boys and to have fewer general backwardness problems, while boys tend to be more numerate when they come to school (Davie *et al.*, 1972). Girls tend to have less self-esteem than boys, and high self-esteem is said to be linked to achievement (Coopersmith, 1968). Many studies relate particular achievements to particular age levels, as we have seen in discussing child development. A high correlation between achievement and socioeconomic status has been frequently reported (e.g. Coleman *et al.*, 1966; Davie *et al.*, 1972).

These findings, however, and other similar ones involving claims about correlations between various factors, have to be treated extremely cautiously. First, there are problems about the concepts employed in the research: what, for example, is self-esteem and has the research in question found an adequate way of recognising and assessing it? Secondly, there is the question of whether the correlations claimed are actually correlations between the items referred to: is it really socioeconomic status that correlates with achievement, or some particular aspect associated with that status, such as parental encouragement? Thirdly, there is the question of whether the measures of achievement are adequate: how does one assess 'general backwardness', for example? Fourthly, there is the problem, intensified by the previous difficulties, of establishing controls on various other potentially relevant factors to ensure that something else is not the real reason for what we observe. It has been pointed out, for instance, that most children are initially taught by women.[29] Perhaps that explains in some way some of the differences reported between girls and boys. If that were the only possibility we could of course research into it. The trouble is that there are hundreds of possibilities. All of this leads up to the main problem, which is that we cannot reasonably infer cause and effect from reported correlations. It would be quite unreasonable, for example, to conclude that girls have low self-esteem because they are girls. Finally, since none of these claims purports to be more than a generalisation, and since the individual children a teacher faces may be the exceptions to the rule, one cannot draw any specific conclusions for practice. (These points will be discussed in detail in the context of research into teacher effectiveness).

The notion of interest should be introduced yet again in this context, for although interest must not be allowed to determine content, and although it cannot directly serve as a principle for sequencing material, it is clearly advantageous to motivate by taking advantage of students' present interests or by seeking to cultivate new interest. In much the same way, although attention to perceived needs should not necessarily determine the content of what is taught, a sense of having their needs met is likely to motivate students.

That success breeds success, and failure breeds failure seems well attested (Bloom, 1976), as well as commonsensical.[30] There is a certain amount of evidence that children respond to and learn well in situations that involve some degree of team competition. At any rate, it has been claimed (Michaelis, 1977) that individual competition produces higher standards of achievement than the use of individual rewards, group rewards, or group competition. But since it has been suggested, as against this, that cooperative structures are more effective in producing group productivity (Johnson and Johnson, 1974), that most children prefer cooperative settings (Madsen, 1971), and that one should encourage cooperation on moral and social grounds, it is reasonable to argue that group competition is, by and large, a desirable practice to bring into schools. The separate claims mentioned would seem to gain a degree of support from the suggestions (Julian and Perry, 1967; Devries and Edwards, 1973) that team competition produces more insight into problems, less anxiety for individuals, higher self-esteem and more peer cooperation, though it is worth pointing out that the effects of team competition or anything else might well change if they were adopted to a greater or lesser degree. That is because human beings, unlike inanimate matter, change as a result of the changes we introduce. The conclusions of any research into human behaviour therefore have to be handled carefully, even when we do not doubt them. What we correctly observe to be the effect of a particular practice in the current situation might well materially alter if this practice became more widespread, particularly if it were to be more or less exclusively adopted.

There is also research that suggests that the quality of students' performance increases when they are given specific goals. It is important not to confuse this point with any claim about the value of precisely formulated learning objectives, still less specifically behavioural ones, on the part of teachers (see below,s.5.) The claim here (Bryan and Locke, 1967) is that if people have a clear idea of what they are trying to do they are more likely to do it successfully. This is not the same thing as saying that a teacher should have pre-specified objectives for every class, or even every course, since it is possible to give students a clear idea of what one wishes them to achieve, without specifying what one wishes them to gain from it. A teacher of English might have no formulated account to give of what he hopes students may gain from studying a poem, but none the less provides the students with clear tasks to perform in respect of studying the poem. The argument for clarity of procedure is supported by a number of studies that suggest, not altogether surprisingly, that people feel more satisfied the more they can feel they have reached particular goals (Locke *et al.*, 1970; Hamner, 1974). (It does not seem to me that the research in question shows that people need to know what the goals are beforehand in order to feel satisfied, as is sometimes supposed. Rather it suggests that people feel satisfied when they see a job well done, which can happen *post eventum*).

What some may regard as one of the most plausible, not to say obvious, suggestions, namely that the personality of the learner may have some effect on the conditions in which he will learn best, is also attested by some research (see Chapter 2,s.3). Broadly speaking (according to Johnson, 1974), introverts tend to prefer learning from books, while extroverts prefer learning from an instructor. This does not perhaps seem very surprising, when one considers the introverted nature of the act of reading as compared with even a relatively informal teaching situation. And a more practical reservation would be that most people are a mixture of introversion and extroversion.

There is material relating to so-called 'field-dependent' learners (Witkin *et al.*, 1977), by which are meant people who tend to judge things in relation to their context or field rather than on their independent merits (although it is not altogether clear to me what that means), which suggests that such people are more susceptible to the influences of their surroundings and more inclined to see things in personal terms. But this particular research begins to raise again some of the problems with which we are now becoming familiar. Leaving aside the question of its reliability, it is difficult to see what practical guidance we can derive from it. Even assuming we know some such general truths about different personalities, in practice and in detail, as Pratt (1980) remarks, 'it is far from clear how instruction should be adapted to match the personality characteristics of learners.'[31] It is also hard to see how teachers are supposed to recognise the various personality types referred to in research, except by way of the very tendencies that are said to be concomitant to them, and which, when they are recognised, make it self-evident what needs to be done. There seems no need for teachers to study or learn Stern *et al.'s* (1956) conception of stereopaths and non-stereopaths, in order to watch out for the anxiety that the former tend to exhibit. What one needs to do is to watch out for the anxiety of students and take what steps one can to alleviate it to the point that one judges alleviation desirable. The case would be different if, generally, actual individuals conformed neatly to one of these various stereotypes defined in terms of clusters of features. Then in recognising trait A in an individual, one could presume the remaining traits that invariably accompany A. But that is not the case. We do not, for the most part, conform to isolated stereotypes.

One area of research that cannot be passed by in silence, since it is both big business and yet based on a fatal flaw in argument, is that concerned with individual instruction. North American education in particular seems very often now to accept the dictum that individualised programmes of instruction are shown to be desirable. That is not in fact the case. (I have no wish to suggest that they are necessarily undesirable or to be deplored; merely that it has not been *established*, claims to the contrary notwithstanding, that group or class instruction is necessarily inferior.)

The logical flaw in argument in favour of individual instruction consists in moving from the truism that individuals differ, and therefore may ideally need different things from their teacher, to the conclusion, which does not necessarily follow, that they need to pursue individually designed programmes. It does not follow, because there is no necessary reason why, within a group setting, even with the teacher unashamedly offering instruction to all at the same time, individual programmes should not emerge. In fact, if we are looking for something that might reasonably be called certain, it is that, precisely because the individuals are different, what they variously make of the teacher's instruction will be individualised. The important question, of course, is whether what emerges for each individual is satisfactory, or the best they might reasonably be expected to get. But there is no evidence at all that I know of that establishes necessarily that of a given group of twenty students, each or even most would gain most from pre-designed highly individualised programmes. As Anne Yeomans (1983) has convincingly argued, the research in this field has tended to suggest the opposite by dint of a process of cross-misquotation and misunderstanding. And as against any such proposal, it should be argued strongly not only that such individualised programmes make demands on teachers that they may well be ill-equipped to meet, and that therefore their achievement will be less than it might have been had they adopted a more congenial approach, but also that such programmes cut out the benefits to be gained from peer group interaction. This is a good example of a case where researchers may be in danger of seriously harming education. An inadequate conception on the part of researchers and critics alike of what it is, if anything, that they are establishing when they observe and report on individualised learning, leads to a widespread call for a change in practice, that while it may certainly have its merits, is not in any way shown to have been desirable. I choose my words carefully: *shown* to be *desirable*.

Mastery learning is a variant, or some might say a sub-species, of individualised instruction. It refers to the practice of bringing children to high standards of achievement in respect of particular tasks, rather than setting them to compete with one another so that some are bound in relative terms not to master the subject-matter. If this approach to teaching is accepted, it is clear that what would be needed for each individual is a course of instruction that provides 'the appropriate prior and current conditions of learning' (Bloom, 1976).[32] The problem with this idea, apart from the fact that it is not clear that full mastery of particular subject-matter is all that education should be concerned with, or even whether it should necessarily be concerned with it at all, is that it is practically impossible to teach everything in the programmed sort of way that this presupposes.

One could easily enough devise a mastery learning programme for something largely consisting in uncontentious facts, such as physics or social studies conceived of as the imbibing of information. But could one satisfactorily devise such a programme for studying literature? And if it be replied that one could, provided that one is not too fussy about what counts as mastering various aspects of literary study (nay indeed, it has been done), then surely we are entitled to question whether we want literature to be approached in this sort of way. Certainly, what I understand by developing literary appreciation could not possibly be converted into a course of mastery learning.

Furthermore, mastery learning does not do away with the need for the teacher to make judgements of value about student peformance; there is still a need to determine what standards of achievement are desirable, both in the abstract and for given individuals. Here, as so often, one is tempted to conclude that the point that lies behind the idea of mastery learning — that with many students we could achieve higher standards, if they did not perpetually have to see themselves as inferior to others at specific tasks — is more important than the single-minded solution zealousy based upon it. There is no reason to suppose that a widespread commitment to mastery learning programmes will make us more successful at educating our pupils. The research must not be taken to show that.

Rather more specific, helpful and well-attested is the claim that peer group tutoring, using quicker learners to help slower ones, can be beneficial to both parties involved, as well as helping to solve a practical problem of organisation (McGee *et al.,* 1977).

Another claim to be considered is a broad one concerning the value of discovery learning.[33] Is this to be favoured to more formal types of instruction as a mode of teaching, or is there less to be said for it than its proponents have claimed? Or is this another case where the main thing to be avoided is an all-or-nothing polarisation between supporters and opponents? The notion of discovery learning is often linked to that of learning how to learn, and the main claims made in respect of them are that discovery learning aids learning how to learn and involves better learning. Better learning must presumably mean more thorough understanding, more retention of understanding, or both. Behind such claims, however, lies a certain amount of obscurity.

What is 'learning how to learn'? As with critical thinking, we must avoid talking as if there were some mono-skill, like using a spade, which has to be acquired or developed, and may then be put to use in a variety of circumstances. Robert Dearden (1976) has pointed out the need to distinguish between five facets of learning: (i) developing an inquiring disposition; (ii) developing information finding skills, such as the use of bibliographies, a library index or a computer; (iii) acquiring understanding of fundamental principles of certain well-developed disciplines such as maths and history; (iv) acquiring understanding of basic substantive principles of logical reasoning; and (v) what he terms 'self-management skills'. Even if one chose to argue with the details of this breakdown, he is obviously correct in stressing that to learn how to learn involves some such different elements, which on the face of it need to be acquired in different ways, and some of which are by definition context-bound. Learning by discovery itself may take many forms, ranging from being left to respond in some way to an environment or situation, through to more guided structures none the less designed to enable the student to see vital points for himself, rather than to be informed about them. The question therefore becomes what kinds of learning by discovery or, possibly, learning what kinds of thing by discovery are important for developing what facets of learning how to learn, or for ensuring better understanding.

The answer is that we do not know, but we do not have any particular convincing evidence to support the suggestion that retention of learning will be better if what is learned is through discovery. What is clearly crucial, though not perhaps sufficient, to retention of learning is proper understanding. If the biology I learn is understood, and not just a catalogue of (to me) semi-meaningless names, formulae and processes, then it has a good chance of remaining with me. If I do indeed *learn* something by discovering it for myself, then I do have such understanding. That is a matter of definition; one would have to be sure that I have really learnt by discovery rather than that I was merely put in a position to learn by discovery. In addition, it is necessary that what I learn should be what I am presumed to have learnt. A child wandering around in a garden is in a position to discover things for himself, but it is another question whether he is intellectually and psychologically equipped to learn, and whether he will in fact learn much adequate biology. Conversely, nobody could seriously dispute that it is possible to be instructed in biology in such a manner that one truly understands it, learns it and hence in all likelihood retains it. We have no reason to suppose that children will be more likely to acquire adequate or deeper understanding of the principles of biology (or anything else) simply because they were not formally instructed in them.

What one may presume will be developed by leaving children to find things out for themselves, rather than teaching them about them, are the enquiring disposition, certain information-finding skills and self-management skills. But even in these respects no evidence establishes that discovery techniques must be preferable as a means to development. Most people who do have inquiring dispositions and good information-finding and management skills probably acquired them through instruction (simply because, at this date, most such people, as well as many other incompetent people, were taught by instruction).

The equivocation surrounding discovery learning, as a result of the fact that it may take many forms, also requires consideration. Extreme variants, such as leaving the child to evolve biological understanding for himself out of quite unstructured and unguided wanderings through the garden, are implausible. By what chance should an individual, unprepared and unguided, devise for himself the classifications, insights and theoretical explanations developed by centuries of determined thought and rigorous experimentation on the part of many, sometimes extremely gifted, individuals? If, on the other hand, one adopts a far more structured conception, such as that exhibited by Socrates when he enabled an untutored slave boy to see for himself some basic geometric truths, the emphasis on the phrase 'discovery learning' may become rather misleading. For the Socratic practice of asking leading questions and suggesting that the slave boy might draw certain lines on his diagram, could equally well be characterised as a subtle form of instruction.[34]

The conclusion must be that although there is undoubtedly an important place for discovery learning, in the sense of varying degrees of unstructured problem solving, in the curriculum, there is no case, for the purpose of developing an attitude of inquiry, for basing a whole theory of instruction on it, and no general principles that firmly determine its place. It is for the individual teacher to remember to vary the pattern of his teaching, sometimes unashamedly informing, explaining or outlining, sometimes not, so that the students get some opportunity to find out different kinds of thing for themselves from different kinds of source, as a supplement to various different kinds and shades of instruction.

Beyond the tentative specificities that I have outlined it would seem that at present we cannot legitimately go. A theory of instruction would therefore seem possible only if it takes a very general form. Bruner's (1966) suggestion that an adequate theory of instruction should specify the predispositions necessary, the structure and sequence of the content, and the appropriate reinforcements, is not wholly objectionable, since it is so very general. Even so, one may question whether any such *general* theory of instruction is possible, and whether, in particular cases, the teacher needs to specify all these things in advance. If it is regarded as acceptable, it is difficult to see what is gained by acknowledging it, since it tells us nothing about how to determine predispositions, structures and reinforcements. More specific theories of instruction (such as Gagné's, referred to above) have the demerit of being arbitrary, contentious and inhibiting to the imaginative interaction of teacher and pupil.

The upshot of the debate must therefore be that, while the organisation of material or content must obviously take account of the stage of development reached by pupils, of factors that affect learning, and what we know about the merits of various teaching techniques and modes of curriculum organisation, considerable caution must be exercised. Learning theory has not told us how to facilitate learning, and developmental theories are of far less practical use than their institutional prominence suggests. Something that would be more useful would be evidence relating stages more or less firmly to ages. The information that stage A follows stage B, at the level of generality in which such information is couched, is, besides being fairly obvious to those with experience of children and an ability to see logical implications, of limited value to practice. It would be more valuable if we could add that within specific cultures stage A is reached by a certain age. However, the evidence we have from, for example, Kohlberg's research suggests that we cannot do this.

On balance, Hamlyn's (1967) conclusion seems correct: 'it is . . . possible in principle to produce generalisations in this field, statements which may apply to people in general, although it may be doubted whether these will in fact amount to more than platitudes — that people learn better in general when encouraged or rewarded, when they are given opportunities for practice, when they are given material in digestible amounts and so on.'[35] But always, even then, the nature of teaching is such that we have to convert such platitudes into particular judgements. Children in general may need this, or be at that stage, at a certain age, but this particular child may be the exception that proves the rule. The teacher can never use theoretical frameworks as a substitute for individual judgement, and with the latter he has no need of the former except as an *aide-mémoire*. Their only function is to give a very rough guide to the kinds of thing that the teacher might care to consider. If it is really felt to be the case that the earnest study of the available research is necessary to stimulate the imagination, so be it. But one thing is certain: there do not appear to be sufficient data for a theory of instruction in any specific, coherent and worthwhile sense.

5. BEHAVIOURAL OBJECTIVES

I am moving towards an open and flexible account of what form instruction should take, and how to set about determining it. Now is therefore the time to give more detailed attention to the rigid school of thought which says that what a curriculum theorist needs to work out, what a curriculum designer needs to set out in detail, and what a teacher needs to work with, are clearly defined objectives, so that we can see what methods are effective, evaluate the success of our curriculum and, subsequently, as a consequence, proceed more effectively.

It has been claimed (Duchastel and Merrill, 1973) that 'objectives sometimes help and are almost never harmful' when it comes to motivating pupils, and that 'therefore if the provision of objectives is relatively inexpensive, one might as well make them available to students.'[36] The reasoning here is weak, since motivation is not our sole concern. However, let that be. I do not dissent from the view that we should have objectives, and it is worth pointing out that many who formally deny this would seem none the less to have them. An objective is a purpose. Curriculum planners should have purposes, which is to say aims or objectives, otherwise they are sailing rudderless. Designers, if there are to be such creatures, must conform to some set of aims, otherwise there is no star by which to set their course. Teachers could conceivably operate as instructors without them, but if they are to have some sense of how they are doing, they too need them. The only questions are how specific the aims need to be in each case, and to what extent they need to be consciously articulated. Does a teacher have to have a determinate set of aims or objectives for a particular lesson, for example? How specific does a curriculum proposal have to be about its objectives? But the major issue is to separate the belief in objectives from the belief in behavioural objectives. It is just an unfortunate fact that the dominance of the latter in curriculum material for a period has tarnished the reputation of the former. (Curriculum writing tends to distinguish aims from objectives, by seeing the former as long-term and the latter as short-term. This verbal distinction does not seem to me important, and I shall ignore it.)

The long-standing grip of behaviourism on psychological study, and indirectly on education, particularly in North America, is hard to understand. The obvious inadequacies of behaviourism have time and again been exposed, but still the grip strangles. So on this occasion let me set the issue out very simply. It is quite true that for much human activity behaviour is the only criterion that we have whereby to judge what is going on. Am I walking? Watch me. Am I jealous? What can you do, but watch my behaviour? But it does not follow, and it is not true, that all matters can be fully or adequately characterised in terms of behaviour. Am I in love? Am I thinking? What are you going to look out for in these cases, and can you seriously maintain that whatever signs you choose to rely upon are sufficient to settle the matter? Granted that some behaviour is typical of people in love, and that some behaviours usually suggest that people are thinking, there are no observable signs that are either necessary or sufficient for establishing that I am engaged in either activity.

Futhermore, sometimes behavioural signs constitute the activity in question, whereas sometimes they are merely symptoms or concomitant features of it. Compare the business of walking, where the observable fact of my perambulation is the activity, with being jealous or being hungry, where the observable facts of my throwing tantrums and saying bitter things, or taking something to eat, are signs that suggest that I am, but are not elements in my being jealous or hungry. Since being jealous or being hungry cannot be defined in these terms, they are not wholly reliable indicators that I am in either state. Being jealous is not simply a matter of doing certain things, indeed there are no things that one must necessarily do, if jealous. Being jealous is a matter of seeing certain situations in a particular kind of way, and even though you may sometimes have pretty good reason to suspect that I am jealous, you cannot know how I see my situation just by observing my behaviour. (See Chapter 2,s.5.) Whether I am hungry is not a matter of my doing certain things, such as eating greedily, or the inevitable consequence of certain observable situations, such as going without food for a day. It is a matter of how I feel about it, and that you cannot directly observe. In these two examples, there are merely behavioural hints that suggest whether I am or am not jealous or hungry. In many cases, such as when a person is in love, is happy, is interested, or is appreciative, it would be very foolish indeed to rely heavily on observation of behaviour.

With those points in mind, we need next to distinguish behaviourism as an ideology from behaviourism as a methodology. That is to say, we must differentiate between those who see behavioural tests as, by definition, tests of the real and intelligible, and those who merely make use of them on the grounds that they can be used in a systematic way. The ideological behaviourist is one who does not recognise the existence of things that cannot be observed in behavioural terms. For him love is a matter of various behaviours; it is *defined* in terms of those behaviours, and any alleged essence that goes beyond what is involved in certain behaviours is so much moonshine. The methodological behaviourist, on the other hand, while recognising that 'there must be more to love than this', points out that since he cannot get to grips with it, he is going to concentrate on looking at love in behavioural terms.

To anybody who accepts the distinction, behaviourism as an ideology must seem absurd for, as indicated, it involves denying the reality of experiences such as love, hunger and aesthetic awareness (which most of us know from first-hand experience to be real enough), except in so far as they can be defined in observable terms. But our experience is such as to indicate that their reality is quite removed from those terms. That is altogether different from saying that the only kind of love I can directly experiment with or make observations about would be love defined in behavioural terms. As a methodology behaviourism is obviously acceptable in some contexts, reasonable in some, if used cautiously, and absurd in others. A behavioural approach to vandalism seems sensible, since depicting vandalism in behavioural terms is not a manifest distortion. Not every act of defacing walls, smashing windows or destroying public telephones is an act of vandalism, but it is reasonable to regard vandalism as consisting in such acts. A similar approach with anger might be reasonable as a methodology for particular research, provided one remembers that it is possible to be angry without showing any outward sign of it, or to appear to be angry so far as one's behaviour goes, but not in fact to be so, and that therefore any conclusions from our research must be suitably tentative. But a behavioural approach to love would be highly misleading, as is a behavioural approach to happiness or to teaching, given that the objects of teaching include such things as awakening appreciation, understanding and judgement. There is nothing of an observable behavioural sort that I must necessarily do, if I am truly appreciating poetry, understanding people or physics, or exercising sound judgement in relation to politics. It is simply mistaken to assume either that behavioural symptoms such as spitting and yelling are necessary or sufficient to indicate anger, or that everything must manifest itself either directly or indirectly in observable ways.

The desire to itemise behavioural objectives is, up to a point, understandable. All are agreed that ideally educators need to know where they are going. All are agreed that in order to judge that, one needs a clear account of what counts as arrival. And who could deny that, if we had readily observable signs of arrival, our task would be in various ways easier? What we can and should deny strenuously is that it is always possible to do this laudable thing, this converting of our aims into specified behavioural objectives, without glaring distortions. Sometimes, as a result of confusing symptoms with essence (e.g. yelling with anger), we pat ourselves on the back for eliciting behaviour which may not indicate that the desired educational aim has been achieved. (The children spit. Good, we have made them angry as intended. Not necessarily. They may be joking, having trouble with their teeth, playing, misunderstanding, fooling us.)

Secondly, we sometimes forget that a clear statement of objectives does not necessarily remove ambiguity. Many standard behavioural objectives, widely revered as being at any rate clear are in fact at best ambiguous and at worst incomprehensible. (I cite as an illustration one of Bloom's (1956) objectives: 'Alertness toward human values and judgements on life as they are recorded in literature.' What is meant by 'alertness' here, and what observable behaviours necessarily reliably indicate its existence?) Thirdly, behavioural accounts of some things distort them. Love as measured by behaviourists may not be a poor thing, but it certainly is a different thing from love sensed by poets and experienced by you and me. Similarly, education as measured by behaviourists is not a mirage. It exists all right. But it is not education in the sense we should be concerned with. It provides an inadequate conception of education. Fourthly, some things cannot be captured at all in behavioural terms. Can one imagine a behavioural account of musical appreciation that bears any resemblance to what people who appreciate music experience?

A further danger is that when behaviourism is dominant those things that do not lend themselves to behavioural accounts simply get ignored. This is ridiculous, if not terrible, in an educational context, where things such as critical thinking, autonomy and emotional stability are our goals. Furthermore, even on the most sympathetic view of behavioural objectives, there is a short term/long-term problem: observed behaviour tells us something, within the extreme limits being noted, about where we are now. It tells us nothing necessarily about the long-term efficacy of a programme. There is a straightforward sense in which we all owe something, for good or ill, to the schooling we had. Would tests in behavioural terms have indicated how valuable various parts of Bertrand Russell's education were in terms of fostering his indomitable critical spirit?[37] Behavioural objectives involve a narrow and mean-spirited approach to education, and preoccupation with behaviour may lead to a general lack of concern for other values. The more we conceptualise schooling in terms of producing specific behaviours, the less likely we are to think about such things as tolerance, humour, humaneness or cultural sensitivity, which may be crucial to a rounded and adequate conception of education.

These objections are not new, and those who are strongly committed to behavioural objectives have of course tried to meet them, but without obvious success. Popham (1968), for example, has striven to answer all the central criticisms. One can only say that he fails to reassure. He remarks that even for long-range goals we can usually find 'proximate predictors which . . . can give us a rough fix on the degree to which instruction is successful.' [38] But, in so far as that is true, intuition and judgement may equally give us 'a rough fix' on our success or failure. And if he is seriously claiming that behavioural indices, as measured now, can reveal the success of a particular programme in contributing to the future development of a tolerant, autonomous adult, then he is just wrong. Nothing that he has to say gets round the point that reduction of our planning to a systematic and detailed set of behavioural objectives is inherently trivialising and anti-educational; this is because the development of mind, the development of emotional and moral maturity, and the provision of a wide, but soundly chosen, set of experiences designed to encourage individual growth, with an emphasis on such qualities as critical spirit, self-direction, broad sympathies, insight and wisdom, which are among the important aims of a school curriculum, cannot be adequately defined in behavioural terms, cannot be reliably recognised by behavioural signs, and cannot well evolve in a setting that is predominantly bound by consideration of what can be immediately and readily observed.

Nor can Popham satisfactorily explain away the objection that such an approach stands in the way of spontaneity in the classroom and the opportunities teachers otherwise have for seizing on occasions, as and when they arise, and turning them to advantage. He cannot coherently deny the point that some subjects, particularly in the arts, may legitimately see the provision of certain kinds of experience, rather than the achievement of certain specific goals, as their function; not merely on the grounds that certain experiences may lead to certain objectives being met whether we can immediately see as much or not, but also on the grounds that certain kinds of desired response are necessarily personal and not characterisable in public terms. Thus, it may be that the desired response to reading a poem is that the individual should develop his own subjective attitude towards it, in which case, by definition, we cannot pre-specify any observable (or, in this case, non-observable) objectives. He has no adequate reply to the point that schooling takes place in a social context and has wider implications than would be taken account of with this approach: students' own achievements are to some extent affected by others such as parents and friends, and, in turn, have their effects on the outside world. Such interrelationships are an important consideration for the teacher, and they are simply ignored when we concentrate exclusively on the immediate behaviour of the classroom. He can hardly deny that such an emphasis dehumanises the business of education, in that it ignores all reference to characteristically human elements such as intention, appreciation, satisfaction and attitude. A more practical consideration, also ignored by Popham's defence of the behavioural objectives approach, is that the adoption of this approach may not be well-suited to the talents of teachers. Teachers are unlikely, for the most part, to have entered the profession in order to divide their day into a set number of time blocks, within each of which they are to concentrate on eliciting a small number of observable behaviours. Finally, Popham's defence does not show much appreciation of the possible political dangers of adopting such an approach. Schooling reduced to a behavioural objectives programme does not merely allow for a fair degree of monitoring teacher progress (its one putative virtue), it also opens the way for widespread government control of the enterprise through crude schemes of accountability.

Many critics of behavioural objectives have made similar points. Eisner (1969) has made much of the point that the nature of the arts is such that it is logically necessary that some of what one wishes to achieve be unspecified: a genuine aesthetic response cannot be standardised and prespecified, because of what is understood by an aesthetic response, namely something authentically personal. (Eisner therefore introduces the term 'expressive objectives' to be contrasted with prescriptive objectives; this is coherent, but could be misleading since, although they are indeed properly speaking objectives, they are not only non-behavioural, they are also non-pre-specifiable. The teacher knows that his objectives include that of eliciting some particular kind of response, but he does not have any particular specified response in mind.) It should be noted that Eisner's objection applies to any view to the effect that objectives need to be stated in terms of specified learner response, and not only to behavioural objectives. Sockett (1976) has suggested that the nature of science is more like that of the arts than some suppose, that it too involves unpredictable insights and creative responses, and that therefore here too one may want to value and encourage that which cannot be prespecified. Whether that is true or not, and perhaps at the level of school subjects it is a little disingenuous to blur the distinction between the arts and the sciences too dramatically, it clearly is the case that one may want to provide children with experiences that one expects to elicit some of a range of responses rather than prespecified objectives, as well as experiences that elicit some unobservable responses. In similar vein, Stenhouse (1975) is clearly correct to stress the value of the essay and of the exercise of judgement, as opposed to more precise measures in education, neither of which lends itself readily to a system dominated by behavioural objectives.

We must surely conclude that too great a preoccupation with prespecification of detailed objectives in general, and behavioural objectives in particular, is to be resisted. On the other hand, we clearly need objectives of some kind, at some point. As we have seen, all rational curriculum planning, and most curriculum planning in fact, does have objectives. For a rational curriculum proposes certain things for certain purposes rather than others. But these objectives may well be implicit rather than explicit, as in the case of the Farmington Trust material on moral education, as Whitfield (1980) has pointed out. They may be unspecific as to particulars; and they may be unobservable. Those who say that without objectives one doesn't know what to do, how to do it, or whether it's been done, are, therefore, correct. If the activity is purposive, there must be purposes, which is another word for objectives, and somebody somewhere must, in principle, be able to recognise that those purposes are being met in some shape or form. But it is not necessary that they should be directly observable or measurable objectives. They can be recognised by judgement, intuition or sense. They do not always have to be recognisable at the time by the teacher. And they do not have to be pre-specified in detail. The mistake has been this assumption: that they must be behavioural, detailed and pre-specified. One might very reasonably have a series of long-term aims, and teach one's lessons in the hope that some of them will be met. And although we shall certainly wish to monitor our success, in order to retain our confidence that some of our aims are indeed being met, the only logically necessary condition of a coherent teaching policy is some grasp of our aims conceptually. Nor is there any reason why one should not recognise some consequences of one's teaching as desirable, even though one had not anticipated them.

It follows from this that Stenhouse (1975) is mistaken when he writes that the best means of curriculum development is 'not by clarifying ends, but by criticising practice.'[39] He thereby introduces a false and unnecessary dichotomy, unless he is simply making an empirical generalisation to the effect that curriculum practice tends to be unmoved by theoretical discussion about aims and purposes, but does change when attention is centred on what particular people are doing. The dichotomy is false because criticism of practice can only be coherently carried out in the light of discussion of aims. If he is making the empirical claim, it should be said that he produces no evidence to support it; it seems probable that he is confusing the question of the best way to get teachers interested in considering changes in practice with what actually leads to changes in practice. It may well be that teachers tend to eschew what they fear as abstract theoretical discussion about aims of education, but that none the less large-scale, important changes in educational policy have largely come about not through teachers focusing on their practice, but through the community at large changing its thinking as a result, directly or indirectly, consciously or unconsciously, of educational theorising, good or bad, about aims. The inescapable conclusion that emerges from the argument is that, on the contrary, it is clarification of ends that is all important for the development of a sound curriculum. But what is needed is a clear grasp of some few basic ends or aims, derived from an understanding of the purposes of schooling, by planners and teachers alike, rather than a long shopping list of isolated and randomly chosen skills and behaviours. It should also be remembered that stressing the logical need for some appreciation of ends has nothing to do with a view about their place in the practical business of curriculum planning or lesson planning. As Taylor (1970) says, 'the important thing is that objectives are integrated with full weight into the total scheme, not that they should necessarily be the starting-point.'[40]

6. CONCLUSION

From the foregoing discussion the following points emerge, recognition of which should shift the focus and conception of curriculum planning away from its preoccupation with giving the appearance of a precise applied science. We do not know (in the proper sense of having adequate evidence to support truths in which we believe) very much about how to improve our organisation and presentation of material in principle; what we may reasonably claim to know is of marginal significance, and any general rules always have to be reassessed in the face of each new group of individuals. The reliability and importance of our empirical data in relation to curriculum have been greatly overrated. Certainly, we should seek to do whatever we can to check that what we think should happen and what we think is happening, are happening. But we should not distort what in fact cannot be directly observed by presuming that it can be, we should not assume that it must be possible to verify everything, either immediately, or even in the long term, and we should not assume that only empirical tests are valid tests, partly because they are less reliable than is popularly supposed, and partly because other forms of assessment are more reliable than is popularly supposed. (See also Chapters 6 and 8.)

What is required, both in order to assess and plan a curriculum, and in order to plan a strategy of instruction, is a thorough understanding of what we are teaching and why we are teaching it: a coherent grasp of the nature of the content we are dealing with, such that we can perceive its potential for serving clearly conceived ends, derived from our understanding of the purposes of schooling, when treated in various ways. If we have that, we are in a position to work out methods for facilitating learning of this material, in ways that serve these purposes, with particular children. The kind of psychological and instructional understanding that teachers need is not particularly well served by the very general and tentative claims advanced in educational psychology courses or theories of instruction. What they require is the ability to assess the capacities, needs, interests and readiness of individuals, such as can only be gained from experience of teaching children in schools. Textbooks on curriculum frequently abjure one to remember such things as that poor performance may be the result of low self-esteem, a broken home, or a lack of response to informal teaching methods. But, as it may equally well be due to arrogance, boredom, a complacent home or shortcomings in the teacher's personality, such rules of thumb, which is what they are, are of little use compared with the intuitive capacity to see that a particular child is suffering because he is the son of a broken home, or lacking in self-esteem. Of course, logically, theory lies behind such observation, but studying the theory in this case might not be time well spent. Knowing in advance all the factors that might influence a child's performance is neither necessary nor sufficient for recognising which *are* influencing it.

We come now to the question of whether questions of method should particularly concern curriculum planners and theorists. Since I have already argued that the very idea of curriculum design as an applied science is unconvincing, it will come as no surprise to the reader that I regard the idea of writing specific instructional steps into the curriculum as being highly questionable. But at this point a distinction should be noted between what I term 'technical how' and the 'essential how' questions.[41] Some methodological points arise directly out of the nature of, and purpose for teaching, the content. For example, if you are teaching history in order to elicit critical response, it follows that you don't want mere rote learning of dates, names and events; if you are concerned to give a sense of time and place, it follows that you would probably be wise to teach world rather than national history. Those sorts of implication about how one should teach I call 'essential hows', because they are determined by the essence of the lesson. Others, those I call 'technical', are questions about which of various means to adopt, raised without relation to our purpose. Should teachers use blackboards or overhead projectors? Should we employ computers? Should we discuss or encourage reading? Should we teach in mixed ability or streamed groups? Should we use work cards? In practice this distinction may sometimes become blurred, in that examples of essentialist hows may become technical, and vice versa, given changes in one's overall purpose. (Given some purposes, reading books would be essentially preferable to lecturing, for instance. Given a course in using computers, the use of them would be essentially required.) But in principle the distinction still holds. A curriculum outline that includes references to methodology that are logically implied by the overall purpose is acceptable. But, to go to the other extreme, is there any justification for a teacher-proof pack, a curriculum design that spells out in detail the techniques that should be used, the order that should be followed, the materials that should be used and so forth, for the most part making points about technical hows? I shall argue that such an approach to curriculum involves at best arbitrariness, since there *is* no correct way, in point of detail and technical hows, to teach most things, and at worst is inappropriate, for there may well be bad ways or inferior ways to teach courses, but whether a particular way is good or bad must depend upon particular circumstances which curriculum planners are in no position to judge. Perhaps the most common result of detailed centralised curriculum planning is that we are presented with what is merely an unimaginative and restrictive framework, which emasculates any potentially good teacher, in order to save children from the excesses of one or two bad ones. There is something bizarre about listing such things as use of 'anecdote', 'puns', 'riddles', 'bulletin boards', 'debate', 'epigrammatic definition', 'games', 'guest speakers', 'dictionaries', and 'team competition' under the heading of 'instructional techniques' in a curriculum outline,[42] not because it is wrong or silly to suggest that the teacher might use such stratagems, but because a teacher who needs to be given these ideas afresh with every curriculum outline, and who, by implication, won't use ideas that are not listed, is in more trouble than one can believe many are, and is not likely to achieve anything of value even with this back-up. And there is something positively pernicious about being more restrictive and specific, to the point of including in one's curriculum detailed instructions to use a pun at this point, get children to look up a word at that point, and to invite a guest speaker now. What to do at any given point in the classroom must always be a function of insight into the current state of mind of the pupils, allied to a clear conception of what one is trying to contribute to achieving and why.

In order to complete the argument for this point of view, it is now necessary to examine the evidence concerning teaching methods.

6 Research into Techniques, Methods and Styles of Teaching

It is a presumption shared by most educators that teaching makes a difference. I believe that to be the case. What I do not believe to be the case is that we are in any position to prescribe useful general rules about how teachers should proceed in order to achieve various aims, other than those that follow automatically from an understanding of what we are trying to achieve. There are two aspects to this thesis. First, I do not believe that research has in fact convincingly established any such general rules. Secondly, I believe that the reason for this is that it cannot hope to do so, rather than simply that research has been incompetently carried out. There are those, such as Egan (1983), who appear to believe that it is logically inconceivable that research into teacher effectiveness should yield any methodological rules. I think that that is incorrect, although some of the problems that lead me to argue that in fact research will never yield rules are logical ones. But in any case, for curriculum purposes, it would be enough to establish that we don't have any such rules. If that is so, the view that curriculum theory should concern itself with empirically-based prescriptions for practice is evidently misplaced, and the idea that curriculum planning should involve instructional prescriptions of a specific kind is to be resisted.

In this chapter I shall examine a number of pieces of research into teaching, carried out over a number of years and conducted in both Britain and the United States, in order to present and illustrate the argument. In so far as the argument is convincing, it should be apparent that it would not make sense for anyone to suggest that there are pieces of research I have not referred to that might have been more successful. I am arguing that in the nature of things, as they are, that cannot be so. Many of those who are centrally involved in, and who still believe in the value of, wide scale empirical research none the less accept that we have not learned a great deal from it: 'much of what we present concerns . . . what we genuinely *don't* know about teaching' (Dunkin and Biddle, 1974).[1] 'There is no established relationship between teacher behavior and student achievement' (Heath and Nielson, 1974).[2] 'Research has not yet linked teacher behavior with student achievement in a direct associative way' (Good, Biddle and Brophy, 1975).[3] However, whereas empirical researchers tend to believe that the answer lies in more research of the same kind but better done, such that acknowledged 'problems of instrumentation, methodology and statistics' (Berliner, 1976)[4] are sorted out, I wish to suggest that there are inherent difficulties with such research that cannot in practice be overcome, with the result that such research cannot hope to produce definitive and useful rules for teaching.

It is true that research to date has suffered from 'conceptual confusion' (Dunkin and Biddle, 1974)[5] and from categories, chosen for research instruments, which are 'given but minimal definition'[6] that might be improved upon. It is true that 'no studies of teaching have yet made use of representative samples'[7] and that that might in principle be corrected. It is true that steps might be taken that would improve the control of variables. But even then there would remain insurmountable problems that mean that such research could not provide us with reliable information about correlation on the finer points of teaching and classroom organisation, let alone about cause and effect, nor any worthwhile degree of useful guidance for practice.

I shall base the first part of my overview on Dunkin and Biddle's *The Study of Teaching* (1974) which reviews something in the region of 500 studies, both field surveys and experimental research, of various aspects of teacher effectiveness. I do this partly so that the reader may conveniently check for himself anything he wishes to, and partly because I wish to draw attention to a related theme — namely, the ability of empirical researchers to recognise all the particular weaknesses and problems in their line of work, while failing to appreciate the force of the indictment that they add up to. Dunkin and Biddle are moderate and fair commentators. They recognise more or less all the deficiencies that there are to be seen. Yet they remain confident and optimistic in defiance of the evidence they themselves adduce.

1. CLASSROOM DISCIPLINE

I shall begin by looking in some detail at the research undertaken, over a period of years and in slightly different contexts, by Kounin and his associates (1958, 1966, 1970) into classroom control and pupil deviancy. I have selected this for attention first because Dunkin and Biddle, who are quite willing to be critical when they see occasion to be, regard it as a 'strikingly original program'. 'We suspect that

Kounin's research holds considerable promise for the eventual improvement of classroom teaching,' they write: and they add that they 'regard these findings as impressive'.[8] We should expect, then, some pretty reliable data about the correlation between certain aspects of class management and certain pupil behaviours.

'It seems to us', write Dunkin and Biddle, 'that adequate management of the classroom environment also forms a necessary condition for cognitive learnings.'[9] It seems so to me as well, but that is hardly illuminating, being a matter of what is meant by 'adequate management'. By definition, given that classrooms are essentially concerned with promoting cognitive learning, management that fails to promote it is inadequate! Conversely, that which successfully promotes it is thereby shown to be adequate, at least in that respect. It ceases to be a matter of definition if one is more specific and says, for example, 'What I count as adequate management includes keeping children quiet'. But in that case it is not reasonable to assert that adequate management seems a necessary condition for cognitive learnings, for it has not been shown that keeping children quiet *is* a necessary condition of enabling them to learn. Clearly what we need to know, to make this observation significant, is what kind of classroom management is adequate to promote cognitive learning. But as to that, Dunkin and Biddle themselves say that of the three central traditions of research in this area that they review, the findings of one in relation to process-product are weak, the second (which is represented by Kounin) does not deal with product or student achievement, and the third consists of 'experiments' that 'are largely flawed'.[10] From which an impartial judge might be inclined to deduce that we are left with the truism that we want adequate rather than inadequate management, but that unfortunately research has not revealed what constitutes adequate management.

Before summarising the research it is necessary to point out that the typical manner of writing up research, standing at one remove, even in the calm and non-persuasive manner of Dunkin and Biddle, may be misleading. Although they are meticulous throughout their book in stating that cause and effect cannot be observed and is a matter of inference, the 'findings' they cite as impressive turn out to be assumptions about what the teacher 'should' do to gain certain effects, and not simply the recorded correlations. They claim further that the research shows that certain things, such as the clarity and firmness of the teacher's response to deviant behaviour, are 'simply unrelated' to success at control, and that 'we learn that desist clarity induced greater conformity among deviantly linked audience pupils'.[11] But strictly speaking these comments are inaccurate. We do not learn that greater conformity is 'induced' in certain circumstances. We gather certain data about correlations, from which we infer, possibly wrongly, even if the data are unimpeachable, something about cause and effect. Likewise, we do not 'establish' that clarity and behavioural change are 'unrelated': we fail to find a correlation that might incline us to infer a causal relationship.

Dunkin and Biddle also refer more than once to 'high reliabilities' for judgements on the part of the researchers and for the manner in which scores are computed, such that 'the greater the score' the more 'with it', 'smooth', or whatever we are focusing on, the teacher is presumed to be. This is reasonable in as much as 'reliable' here has a technical meaning. But the unwary will assume that this means that we may trust the manner of computing scores to tell us which teachers actually *are* more with it or smooth, and that the judgements are reliable in the sense of accurate. That is not necessarily so. 'High reliability' refers only to the fact that it has been found that different researchers tend to make similar judgements. They might be very poor judgements; and it is particularly worth bearing in mind that observers are usually trained for a research project, and therefore to some extent led to make similar judgements, and that their commitment to a certain kind of research is likely to lead them to base judgements on similar kinds of signs. Whether a high score actually tells us that a teacher is very smooth in classroom control depends not on the reliability of the system of scoring, which tells us only that a small group of researchers get the same scores using the same observational signs and methods of computing, but on the sense of the system. It is quite conceivable that an obviously ludicrous way of picking out and measuring some quality in a teacher should none the less have high reliability. (For a more detailed discussion of reliability and validity see Chapter 8, s.2.)

Kounin, as we have just seen, was not concerned with pupil achievement. In a research programme centred largely on deviant behaviour he and his associates, in three studies (one with kindergarten children, one with grades 1 – 6, and one with grades 1 and 2) examined discipline and control in relation to pupil behaviour.

For the initial study they formulated a series of teacher behaviours and pupil behaviours to be observed. The central focus of attention was what was termed 'the desist incident', by which is meant any identifiable action on the part of the teacher that is stimulated by pupil deviancy. These, it was found, could be spotted with high reliability — which is to say that the observers concerned tended to agree as to whether a teacher was or was not engaged in a desist incident at a given time. Desist incidents may take many shapes and forms, so the research then categorised certain aspects of any such incident that might be thought likely to modify the effectiveness of the act: clarity, firmness, roughness, child treatment, intensity and focus. The observers, therefore, were to concern themselves not simply with observing the desist incidents of teachers, but more particularly with assessing 'how much information the teacher provided in her desist'.[12] For example, it was to be noted whether the teacher simply said 'Stop that', or specified a person or the deviant act (desist clarity); whether there was much force or impact in the rebuke (desist firmness); whether there was a degree of temper apparent (desist roughness); whether the reprimand had 'attention-demanding properties and the potential to intrude into the awareness'[13] of students not directly addressed (audience pupils) (desist intensity); what the teacher made the burden of her response—for example, 'Stop doing *that*', or 'Get on with *this*' (desist focus); and 'how the child was treated in the desist. Does the child see the teacher as being for or against him in this incident?'[14] (child treatment). (Child treatment, intensity and focus were introduced after the first study, and roughness was dropped).

It is at once apparent that these categories may overlap, that it is a matter of judgement whether a teacher exhibits any of these characteristics, and that the observer's view of whether the child sees the teacher as being against him, may not be the same as the child's view. In other words, although the degree of specificity, systematisation and breakdown involved in this approach may make it seem more scientific than simply sitting in on a lesson and recording one's impressions, there is no reason to suppose that it provides a more accurate account of what is going on, or is in any way more free of varying individual opinion. The approach treats an organic whole as if it were a series of independently observable items of behaviour, and the items on which it concentrates, besides being artificial, are not directly perceived but judged to be in operation by a fallible observer. How fallible particular observers are will obviously depend more on their experience and intelligence than on the system of observation they are using.

Even at the level of recording what is going on, then, this programme of research is inherently vulnerable. This does not mean that it will necessarily produce a false account of what happens, but it does mean that we have no way of checking whether it does or does not. The matter becomes considerably more confused and unreliable when we turn to the further categories introduced by Kounin to shed light on the effectiveness of various teacher strategies.

The researchers were also interested in obtaining information relating to desist success, in terms of the students' response to desist incidents, ranging from immediate obedience through to open defiance. At one stage they were also interested in the reactions of other children besides the target deviant student. Following different kinds of desist incident on the part of the teacher, would the audience children carry on working, become more involved, be disrupted, or what? In connection with this, it was also considered important for the observer to make a judgement as to whether particular audience children were deviancy-free or deviancy-linked prior to the desist incident. Were they in some indirect way involved with the deviancy behaviour, perhaps as interested spectators, or were they pursuing their work in a single-minded way?

In later research (1970) Kounin was concerned with exploring the effects of what he termed 'withitness' and 'overlappingness' on the part of the teacher. 'Withitness' refers to the extent that the teacher is on the ball, picking up early signs of deviancy, picking out the right culprit, and so forth. A with it teacher is one 'with eyes in the back of her head', so to speak. This concept was operationalised in terms of a set of specific target mistakes (e.g. the wrong child reprimanded, perhaps an onlooker or a contagee rather than the initiator of the interruption). But whereas most categories in this research were employed against observations made at rapid, regular intervals, withitness was measured in terms of judgements based on observing a whole lesson or a whole day. Overlappingness 'refers to what the teacher does when she has two matters to deal with at the same time.'[15] A teacher is credited simply with some or no overlappingness, depending on whether she does or does not show a capacity for dealing with more than one matter at a time.

Two further items for observation were 'smoothness' and 'momentum', both relating to the overall flow of the lesson. 'Stimulus boundedness', referring to the tendency of the teacher to be deflected from the subject at hand by events in the classroom, 'thrusts', referring to the tendency of the teacher to burst in on children's activities with a statement, order or question, 'dangles', referring to the teacher's tendency to leave a subject hanging in the air to be resumed later, 'truncations', leaving a subject in mid-air and not returning to it, and 'flip-flops', terminating one activity, starting another then returning to the first, were coded, and teachers were judged high in smoothness if they indulged in few such interfering behaviours. 'Momentum' refers to keeping the pace of the lesson going and was measured by reference to two time-slowing behaviours: dwelling for too long on something, be it pupil conduct, instruction relating to a particular item or anything rather than the main point of the lesson ('overdwelling'), and 'fragmentation', which was 'coded when the teacher dealt with individual pupils . . . or props one at a time'.[16] In addition, attention was paid to 'group alerting', which is to say the extent to which the teacher keeps her pupils on their toes, and 'accountability', referring to 'the degree to which the teacher holds the children accountable and responsible for their task performances.'

It will readily be seen that these concepts are not directly and unequivocally visible. It is a matter of judgement whether a teacher is dwelling for 'too long' on something, whether a thrust effectively 'bursts in' upon the child, where a 'dangle' ends and a 'flip-flop' begins, or whether the children are really being kept on their toes. Individuals may reasonably hold different views on such questions, and an informed judgement would require, amongst other things, a good understanding of the teacher's long-term aims and her relationship with her pupils. Furthermore, an overall assessment of the flow of a lesson based only on these selected outward signals is by its nature relatively superficial. It no more equates to the general estimate that an experienced eye might form impressionistically, than an attempt to estimate the flow of a soccer game by adding up the total of a number of pre-specified moves would equate with the judgement of an experienced observer delivered on the strength of watching the game through.

Finally, 'valence and challenge arousal' and 'variety', meaning, respectively, direct attempts by the teacher to arouse interest in academic matters and variety of activity in the classroom, were also measured by scores assessed on the basis of a breakdown into eight features. Set against all these managerial concepts were two pupil behaviour categories: work involvement, assessed by making a judgement every 12 seconds as to whether a child is definitely, probably, or definitely not, involved in his work, and deviancy, assessed by making a judgement every 12 seconds as to whether a child is seriously misbehaving, mildly misbehaving or not misbehaving. One contextual variable was also catered for: children were coded as being involved either in recitations or in seat work, the former indicating a public role, the latter a private one. (Some of Kounin's research also coded grade level and emotional disturbance level of the children.)

By observing at regular intervals and categorising teacher and student behaviour in terms of the above categories, the researchers arrived at the following 'findings' or conclusions: pupil involvement was greater, and deviancy less, in the upper grades and among normal rather than 'emotionally disturbed' children. Work involvement was greater and deviancy lower in the context of recitation than in the context of seat work. Deviantly-linked children (those on the fringe of deviant activity rather than instigators of it) are more likely to react to desist incidents than those who are completely 'innocent', although the pattern of their reaction is not all that consistent. Desist clarity 'induces' greater conformity amongst deviantly-linked audience pupils (only), and desist roughness 'induces' behaviour disruption amongst audience pupils. Desist clarity, firmness, child treatment, intensity and focus were 'simply unrelated' to desist success, pupil work involvement or pupil deviancy. The later group management study (1970) produced 'far more promising findings',[17] we are told: withitness correlated highly with work involvement in recitation contexts, and with deviancy control in both recitation and seat work. Momentum correlated highly with deviancy control in a recitation setting. Likewise, though to a lesser extent, smoothness and group alerting correlated with work involvement in a seatwork setting.

Those are the reported 'findings'. How firmly established by this research programme should we regard these as answers to the question they are alleged to help answer? 'What should the teacher do to increase involvement and decrease deviancy for the groups of pupils in the classroom?' We should not regard them as established at all, for this programme of research has in no way got round the contingent and logical difficulties in its way and, because of its limitations, cannot be said to have furnished us with good reason to accept its conclusions, even if some of them happen to be true. This we shall see by considering the defects under six headings.

The claim being made, on the basis of the research, is that 'in general, for recitation, the teacher interested in provoking involvement should first of all demonstrate withitness, smoothness, momentum and group alerting. It would also help if she exhibited overlappingness, accountability, and valence and challenge arousal . . . In the seatwork context . . . the teacher should demonstrate seatwork variety and challenge. It would also help if she exhibited withitness, smoothness and valence and challenge arousal.'[18] If the aim is to avoid pupil deviancy and disruption, in the recitation context, the teacher should above all exhibit withitness and momentum. In the seatwork context the emphasis falls heavily on withitness. These seem moderate and plausible suggestions. But the research as such has given us no right to draw even those modest conclusions.

We shall begin with the more obvious, though not for that reason necessarily more insignificant, objections to the research.

Scope of Sample

This programme of research was confined to children of or below junior school age. The first study involved observing only 25 teachers of kindergarten level for 4 days; the second, 30 teachers of students in grades 1-6, spending half a day observing each classroom; the third, 49 teachers, with students in grades 1 and 2, for one full day. Thus, even if the findings were clear and secure, it would be extremely rash to generalise from them in view of the extreme smallness of the sample. To generalise to the secondary level would quite obviously be illegitimate.

Scope of Categories

No product criteria were involved in this research. That is quite straightforward, and we can hardly complain about it in itself since the programme deliberately omitted them. But, even assuming the findings to be reliable, it does limit the usefulness of the research, since we cannot draw any immediate conclusions about the value of these various behaviours on the part of teachers, in view of the fact that what induces work involvement and deviant free behaviour in children might not produce or lead to desirable educational achievements.

These are contingent shortcomings of this particular research programme, which might in principle be improved upon. We should not underestimate the very real practical difficulties in the way of working with large and random samples, while adding achievement or product categories to our already crowded and complicated observation schedule, but it is not written in heaven that it could not be done. However, we should not lose sight of the fact that *until* it is done, as it has not yet been done, our small-scale research does not warrant our leaping to the generalised conclusions that we do leap to.

The third objection is more devastating in that it is more difficult, if not impossible, to get round in practice.

Control of variables

Nothing has been done in this research to take account of other unmentioned factors that might well have a significant bearing on what, according to our observations, is going on. Perhaps one child responds to a certain kind of desist incident in one way, not because of the desist incident itself, but because he is used to a certain kind of behaviour from his parents; perhaps another reacts differently because he has a particular kind of relationship with the teacher; another because he is affected by the presence of the observer. Consequently, we are in no position to fully explain even that which we do observe.

This criticism of many empirical studies is by now very well worn and formally denied by few researchers. As a result it seems to have lost some of its edge. But in point of fact it is calamitous for the value of such research for, if only one or two possibly important factors are not taken into account, it makes drawing firm conclusions quite unwarranted. And the truth is that the list of factors not controlled in any piece of research into teaching runs, not to two or three, but into unnumbered hundreds; for, until somebody establishes otherwise, we must presume that any and every facet of each individual's nature, of each individual's background, of every context, and of every conceivable combination of those various facets, might be the sole or the crucial element in explaining what goes on. It is therefore not possible to state simply whether this problem is contingent or necessary. Certainly some variables that are not controlled in any given piece of research might in principle have been; others, such as the unique combination of this particular child with this particular teacher, interacting in this particular way, at this time in this context, cannot be, as a matter of logic. (The uniqueness of the combination may be the explanation of what happens on this occasion, and, if it is unique, it cannot be generalised from.)

In practice one might choose to take seriously repeated correlations of significance: if it appeared that shouting at students was invariably accompanied by high achievement on a particular test, and that such high achievement was never otherwise achieved, one would be inclined to infer a causal relationship. But such unambiguous and informative correlations have not been established throughout more than fifty years of research, from which one is inclined to deduce that there are not any simple and important rules that always govern the teaching situation. The more one is inclined to that conclusion, the more important it becomes for any research to do justice to the likely complexity of the matter, not by simply focusing on a few specific items, but by isolating them. The difficulties in the way of doing that, whether at bottom contingent or necessary, would seem *a priori* to be insurmountable, and they have certainly not been surmounted in practice.

Cause and effect

This research, in common with all such research, gives us at best correlations. It tells us that A accompanies B. As already suggested, if the sample is large and random and if, by further studies or if possible by controlled experiment, we can also see that B does not occur without A, we may reasonably infer some cause and effect. But in this case, and in most other cases, these vital conditions are not met. The samples studied by Kounin are exceedingly small and far from random. Because this research consists of field study, there is no attempt to see whether observed correlations are consistently related. At best we know that where these particular teachers were relatively 'withit' in a recitation context, their students were relatively involved in their work. We have no reason to assume that their involved students would not have been equally involved with teachers displaying less withitness, or that some of them might have been and others not, or indeed that it might not be that the involvement of students tends to promote withitness on the part of the teacher, or one of a hundred and more other possibilities. Perhaps fear of the headteacher explains both why these particular teachers strive to be withit and why these particular students are involved in their work. It does not matter whether these or any other suggestions strike us as particularly plausible. We are not, after all, considering the plausibility of Kounin's conclusions, but the question of whether they can be said to be based on something approaching the rigorous kind of study that we associate with claims in the natural sciences, and it is surely clear that they cannot be said to be so based, so long as so many alternative explanations are equally feasible.

This limitation on research into teaching is another that is formally admitted by almost all researchers, again with the practical consequence that it tends to be forgotten or set aside with the sting taken out of it. But again it would seem to be of the greatest importance: such research does not yield information on cause and effect and is therefore of limited use. Sadly, what often happens is that, while the limitation is formally acknowledged, the educational world proceeds as if it were not there. Thus Dunkin and Biddle, while stating clearly and correctly that since 'the studies were all field studies . . . it is possible that the cause-and-effect relationships between teacher behaviors and pupil responses assumed by Kounin, and ourselves, will eventually be found in error',[19] none the less, quite inconsistently and illegitimately, conclude by talking of it being 'established' or 'found' that desist clarity 'induces' work involvement, etc.

Conceptualisation
The limitations already referred to would seem to me to be sufficient to put paid to the idea that such research is establishing anything very important. However, we now come to what is surely the most serious deficiency, namely the conceptual inadequacy of the research programme, which will be seen on examination to be partly a

contingent matter, and therefore in principle capable of improvement, but partly a logical matter and as such impossible to improve on.

If research is to avoid some of the shortcomings already noted, it is clear that the concepts involved, the categories we are concerned with, must meet four criteria: they must be clear, they must be unambiguous, they must be observable, and they must be distinguishable. These are distinct qualities: a concept may be clearly articulated but still be ambiguous; it may be unambiguous and clear but not directly observable, and two clear observable concepts may be impossible to distinguish in practice. These are not demands that concepts necessarily have to meet at all times in all walks of life: it is not a crime to entertain an ambiguous concept of something that is not directly observable. They are demands that must be met by our concepts, if we are going to conduct research based on observation of separate items. Yet these demands are clearly not met in this research.

It is not clear, for example, what is meant by 'valence and challenge arousal.' Certainly we are given an account of what is meant (the attempt to arouse interest in academic matters),[20] but not every account given of a term is a definition (sometimes it is an explanation, or an example, for instance), and not every definition provides an adequate account. 'Existentialism', as we saw in Chapter 1, is correctly defined as 'the view that existence precedes essence', but that is scarcely helpful to those who want a real understanding of what 'existentialism' means. What is lacking here is a satisfactory definition of 'valence and challenge arousal' such that we may know clearly what constitutes an instance of the attempt to arouse interest in academic matters. What counts as 'an attempt', for a start? And must it be a good attempt, or perhaps a successful attempt? How does one judge a 'good' attempt? What counts as arousing interest? Does the student have to proclaim or show interest? And what counts as an academic matter? This would seem to be an example where a little more thought and work could solve the problem. We could arrive at a clear definition of 'valence and challenge arousal'. The fact remains that the research proceeded without it, so we do not have a very clear understanding of what precisely it was that correlated with various other things, when we are told that it was 'valence and challenge arousal'.

Many of the categories suffer from ambiguity or equivocation. Even if we know formally what is meant by 'overdwelling', 'thrusts' and desist 'clarity' or 'intensity', recognising instances is a matter of judgement rather than of unequivocal sighting. If we knew what 'valence and challenge arousal' meant exactly, we might claim with some confidence to be witnessing it, on a given occasion. But whether this teacher is overdwelling on something or engaging in a desist incident with clarity will be arguable, even though we know what the words mean. Therefore, the very claim that teachers engaging in these behaviours found themselves faced with students behaving in particular ways is uncertain. Were the teachers in question really overdwelling? Who knows? All we know is that the researchers in question judged them to be. Similarly terms such as 'focus', 'intensity' and 'clarity', though their meaning may be clear, are contingently negotiable. Not only will different individuals judge different utterances to be focused, intense or clear (and what matters is not whether observers, or you and I, agree that something is clear or focused, but that the children in question do), but the terms themselves do not indicate what degree of focus, intensity or clarity counts.

Some of the concepts in question are not only subject to this element of judgement because they involve degree or ambiguity, or simply lack of clarity, but because they are not directly observable. Whatever the problems involved, there is a sense in which whether a teacher is expressing herself clearly can be judged by observing her. Whether she is making herself *clear to the students*, however, is not so easy to observe, although there are some observable signs that may strongly suggest that she is not. (They are not very reliable, since students may understand without indicating that they do, or give the appearance of understanding when they don't. But some reasonable judgements may be made.) But how can one claim to see whether the child sees 'the teacher as being for or against him in this incident'? How does one directly observe the teacher's potential to intrude into the 'awareness of the individual children'?

To be fair to Kounin, he himself saw some of these problems in his categories for the first study and subsequently rejected them. But his later managerial concepts suffer in exactly the same way. It is a matter of judgement whether the teacher is making timing mistakes, to what extent he is stimulus-bound, or even whether he is making target mistakes, no less than it is whether he is overdwelling or fragmenting. Disentangling dangles, truncations and flip-flops is a daunting task in practical terms, since the observer has to judge retrospectively in order to see whether a topic has really been left in mid-air or is subsequently returned to. Deviancy may perhaps be relatively easy to code, but work involvement is obviously not, since it cannot be adequately characterised in purely observable terms: visible signs of paying attention or being interested are neither a necessary nor a sufficient indication of being involved.

Isolation

If such research is to tell us anything reliable and significant, it is also necessary that observed correlations should be between behaviours that, besides being clear and unambiguous, are distinguishable from other behaviours. To make anything of the information that A accompanies B, we need to ensure that both A and B are isolatable behaviours, and that they do not overlap with C, D, E, F, etc. For if A is defined partly in the same terms as C, and B partly in the same terms as D, we have no reason to suppose that the important point is that A and B occur together: it could be that it is the C element and the D element that actually correlated. The researchers themselves, as well as Dunkin and Biddle, uneasily acknowledge this point. The eight managerial concepts employed correlate with one another to a notable extent and force the question: 'Are we not in fact reporting the same finding several times?' Kounin tried to check out this possibility by using statistical devices to see whether some of the concepts maintained correlations, while others were held constant. But that reaction misses the point, which is not really that the various concepts might be identical (just different names for the same thing), but that they may in practice overlap. That is to say, the more reasonable fear is not that 'withitness' and 'smoothness' may be the same thing, but that a teacher in practice does things that contribute to both withitness and smoothness. This means that the technique of coding behaviour in only one category misrepresents reality.

The standard response to these various conceptual problems is to insist that in fact observers' judgements, notwithstanding the admitted difficulties in the task, have been shown to be reliable. But we have to remind ourselves what that means. It does *not* mean that they have been shown independently to be accurate or adequate perceptions of what is truly going on. It means that those people who regard this kind of approach as satisfactory and who (usually) are trained to interpret certain visible behaviours according to a particular schedule, tend to find it fairly easy to stick by the schedule. It means, for example, that people who agree to interpret 'being involved in work' in terms of the child keeping his eyes on a book, tend to agree in their judgements about whether children are involved in their work. It means that, having their commitment to crude behavioural signs in common, they tend to judge the same teachers to be 'intruding into the individual awareness of children'. Such proven reliability does not touch upon the fundamental point that the conceptual problems are such that those who adopt this approach do not do justice to the reality being observed.

The conclusion that must be drawn from the preceding observations is that what we gain from such field studies are uncertain judgements about correlations, which we have no reason from the research itself to suppose are causally related. (The judgements are uncertain, because we do not *know* that A correlates with B, given the conceptual shortcomings of this approach.) In principle we might none the less gain something from a proliferation of such studies, if we used them as a springboard for subsequent controlled experiment. Having arrived at the view that A correlates with B, which might be true, even though the approach employed is not well suited to giving us secure information except in the case of behaviours that are readily observable, we could then seek to set up controlled situations, in order to see whether A always and only occurs with B, from which in turn we might reasonably draw some conclusions about cause and effect. Unfortunately, in practice we can seldom carry out such experiments. To some extent we are inhibited by practical and moral restraints on what we can do by way of experimenting with human beings. (One cannot, for instance, very easily deprive one group of children of what are hypothesised to be good teaching techniques, just to find out whether they are thereby disadvantaged.) More importantly (because this also invalidates the use of statistical controls run through the computer), we are constrained by the self-same conceptual points that show the initial field study to be of doubtful value. One cannot isolate and control features of classroom behaviour that do not consist exclusively in clear, unambiguous, separate, observable behaviours. One can experiment to see what the cane does to the bottom, but not to the mind. One can experiment to see whether children look out of the window, when teachers ask questions, but not to see whether asking questions is a technique that enhances work involvement.

What, then, are we to make of the 'findings' of Kounin's research? We certainly do not dismiss them as being untrue. But what we discover when we look at them closely is that some of them are true but are not empirical points at all, and that others, which are empirical and may be true, have in no way been shown to be true. Withitness, we are assured, has been shown to be important. But since 'withitness' *means* such things as timing one's interventions with children well and directing them towards appropriate children, it is bound to be preferable to a lack of withitness. Of course, this is not to say that withitness will necessarily always turn a teacher into a success, because the study gives us no right to conclude that withitness is either a necessary or a sufficient condition of causing any particular pupil behaviours. This is partly for the basic reason that any causal relationship at all is a matter of inference rather than observation, but it is also because it is in the nature of a field survey without proper control of variables to leave us uncertain as to whether the same pupil behaviour might not have been exhibited in otherwise similar circumstances when the teacher displays little withitness, or as to whether such pupil behaviours might not be exhibited under different circumstances. Thus the observation that withitness appears to correlate less with the pupil responses in question in a seatwork context than a recitation context cannot legitimately be interpreted to show that withitness is less important in the former context. At best, it may merely suggest that the nature of seatwork is such that the teacher's behaviour is less relevant than it is in the more public recitation context. (This would seem to be true, because of what is meant by seatwork.) But it must none the less still be the case that in so far as a seatwork context involves interaction between teacher and students that interaction will be more profitable if the teacher is with it rather than without it! What would be worth knowing, if it could be known, is not the general truism that withitness is preferable to a lack of withitness, but what specific with it behaviours correlate with what specific student behaviours. But even if the field study furnished such specific information, we would not be able to generalise from it: the fact, if it were one, that in the few classrooms observed when a teacher did X students did Y, cannot be taken to show that doing X leads to Y in any situation, since we know so little about other factors involved in these and other situations.

Likewise, smoothness and group alerting, as defined, must be preferable to their opposites, other things being equal, because on virtually any view of the business of teaching, we want students to be alerted and to feel that there is some pattern to what is going on. The interesting and important questions would be what behaviours different children actually recognise as alerting and smooth, and how important these behaviours become when, as is always the case, other things are not equal. When, for example, a particular student comes from a broken home, dislikes the teacher, has no present interest in the subject, is used to failing in school, is in love, has an ambitious father, is thinking of his summer holiday, or is affected by any other one or combination of a hundred other factors, how then will he react to various specific behaviours designed to alert the group or to contribute to the smoothness of the lesson? To such questions we have no answer at all, nor could we expect to get them from such research.

Other 'findings' that are clearly essentially truths of definition include the conclusion that deviantly-linked children are more likely to react to desist incidents than those who are innocent, that desist clarity induces greater conformity among audience pupils, that desist firmness induces greater conformity among deviantly-linked audience pupils (only), and that desist roughness induces disruption amongst audience pupils. How could one expect otherwise? Given that desist incidents are by definition overtly directed at deviant behaviour rather than innocent children, why should the latter respond? How could a lack of clarity on the part of the teacher attempting to induce conformity be more effective than clarity in respect of *any* students, whether deviant or audience? Given that desist roughness implies making one's presence felt in a relatively crude and tough manner, is it surprising that it disrupts even audience pupils more than a low key intervention? And since firmness implies making it clear that one means what one says and is not to be taken lightly, it can hardly be wondered at that those on the edge of being troublesome (deviantly-linked audience pupils) respond more to firmness than to a lack of it.

At this point it may be suggested that it cannot be correct to regard the above conclusions as essentially truths of definition, since they do not appear to be necessarily true. There are exceptions. For instance, desist firmness was not shown to lead to greater conformity amongst all students, but only amongst deviantly-linked audience pupils, and in every other case there may have been some individuals who did not respond in the way that students generally did. This does indeed show that none of these claims is simply a necessary truth. They are not straightforwardly analytic in the way that 'all bachelors are unmarried' is analytic, so that it would be inconceivable that we should ever find a married bachelor. It is certainly not inconceivable that we should find some students who readily conform even when the teacher's desist behaviour is unclear.

However, it is still the case that these claims are essentially truths of definition. They are claims that involve a general analytic truth, overlaid and complicated by the fact that what counts as an instance of firmness, clarity, roughness, etc. may be disputed, and by other factors that may affect what is going on. Thus it is a matter of definition that a clear desist incident must be more effective than an unclear one in itself, but whether an actual, clear desist incident proves effective depends both upon the child, as opposed to the observer, finding it clear, and upon that clear message not being outweighed by other factors. The apparent exceptions therefore, far from indicating that we are dealing with general empirical truths, merely reveal the shortcomings in this kind of research. Nobody could conceivably discover that in itself withitness is not a plus when it comes to promoting work involvement, whether in a recitation or a seatwork context, and nobody could conceivably establish that desist clarity is not always preferable to lack of desist clarity in terms of desist success. The suggestion that desist clarity is shown to be unrelated to desist success is simply false. At best, all that has happened is that the observers in this particular research programme have come across some situations in which either the students did not find what the observers found clear, or clear desist messages have been outweighed by other considerations (or both). (For consideration of Egan's view that such considerations make successful research logically inconceivable. See below, s.4.)

The conclusions in respect of momentum and variety, though perhaps slightly more informative at the empirical level, particularly in the latter case, none the less serve to further illustrate the significant emptiness inherent in such research. We are told that 'the teacher interested in provoking involvement should . . . demonstrate . . . momentum' in the context of recitation, whereas momentum 'appeared to make relatively little difference . . . in the seatwork context'.[21] An instance of the general problems of conceptualisation comes to the fore here, in as much as the distinction between recitation and seatwork is never made very clear, and in practice it is very unrealistic to see classroom activity in terms of alternative distinct contexts: much of what goes on in the name of seatwork may also occur in the name of recitation. It is not possible to characterise any particular period of interaction as plainly one or the other, unless we use only very superficial signs. If, for example, we define seatwork as a situation in which children are expected to pursue tasks on their own, we can distinguish that from situations in which the teacher formally instructs the class (or individuals). But in those terms we cannot categorise passages of time in which students while working on a task are periodically helped in some way or other by the teacher, or those periods of time when the teacher addresses the class, expecting each individual to make something different of what he says in terms of their various tasks.

This is simply to say that most teaching is too complex a business to be realistically categorised as either seatwork or recitation. The view that momentum varies in importance in the two contexts is therefore suspect. But in any case, consider what is interpreted as momentum: a teacher scores highly in terms of momentum in so far as he avoids such slowing-down techniques as overdwelling or fragmentation. We have already seen that it is a matter of uncertain judgement as to whether a teacher is spending too long on a topic, too long on a pupil, is nagging too much, or being too repetitive (behaviours coded as overdwelling), as it is as to whether a teacher is breaking the flow of the lesson up in saying such things as 'Put your pencils away. . . . Now hand your papers to me' (fragmentation). But, in so far as behaviour really does cause momentum to be lost and the overall shape of a lesson to be lost by fragmentation, that *must* make it harder for children to become involved in that lesson. Involvement in a lesson is necessarily facilitated by teaching that lends pattern and flow to what is going on. Why then does it appear to the researchers to matter less in a seatwork context? Presumably because in that situation the students are by definition working on their own to a greater extent, and are therefore less affected by the lack of momentum in the teacher's performance. They maintain involvement by providing their own pattern and flow.

A teacher is judged to be offering variety to a high degree either as a result of engaging (or causing the children to engage) in a large number of slightly different activities, or by engaging in a few markedly different activities. The high correlation between teacher variety and work involvement in the seatwork context, as contrasted with the low correlation between variety and involvement in the recitation context, would seem to be a genuine empirical point. That is to say, one would not wish to maintain that it is obvious from what is meant by the terms involved that variety would be more important in one case than the other. One might argue that it is fairly well known to those with experience of young children that they do not tend to have the ability to concentrate on anything exclusively for a long period of time, and that some of the variety that is apparently lacking in the recitation context to no disadvantage is in fact being provided in more subtle ways than the observers' categories allowed for. Thus, in the seatwork context, where children are predominantly working on their own, interest has to be kept alive, variety provided, by the relatively crude and visible sorts of technique categorised in the research programme (change of content, introduction of new props, requiring the child to do something different); in the recitation context, it might be argued, interest still has to be fostered, variety still displayed, but this can be done more subtly by changes in the teacher's tone, gesticulation, direction, etc. It would thus seem that the hypothesis that the research actually supports is the relatively unhelpful one that, when children are to a large extent working at tasks on their own, it is important to vary the nature of what they are doing to some extent, since the teacher cannot directly sustain interest by his own performance. I describe this as 'relatively unhelpful' because it seems, to me at any rate, fairly obvious as a general rule, and one which is none the less of little practical use to the teacher, unless he knows what variations in the situation will maintain involvement levels for particular children.

Slightly different is the case with the conclusion that pupil involvement was greater and deviancy less in the upper grades and among normal rather than emotionally disturbed children. There is still an element of logical necessity about this, for some of the defining characteristics of emotionally disturbed children are the same as, or closely related to, the defining characteristics of non-involvement in work and engaging in deviant behaviour, particularly when we limit ourselves to observable characteristics. Essentially, and to a considerable extent, we classify children as emotionally disturbed, using Kounin's categories, when they show little involvement and considerable deviancy. But certainly, that pupil involvement is greater in the upper grades is not true by definition. On the other hand, how useful is this broad piece of information, even ignoring the point that it may not be a reliable observation and cannot legitimately be generalised, for all the reasons given? And why should we assume that it has anything to do with the focus of the research, namely management control? Perhaps children tend to become more involved in school work and less deviant in the classroom, as judged by crude behavioural signs, as they grow older, regardless of the techniques of the teacher.

Dunkin and Biddle rather curiously remark 'surely these findings are requisite. . . . If classrooms were not better managed at the upper grade levels and among non disturbed pupils, teacher efforts would be futile indeed'.[22] Why? In what way would the fact, if it were a fact, that teachers actually tended to be more effective at controlling deviant children than non-deviant children, or younger rather than older children, show that their efforts were futile? But in any case, as we have just seen, the research does not show that classrooms were 'better managed' at the upper grade levels. It suggests that behaviour is less deviant and work involvement greater, and offers no clue as to why this should be so. If we were to define good management independently (which is not done in the research programme) and to observe that such good management correlated with high work involvement and lack of deviancy in the upper grades more than the lower grades, we still could not legitimately assert that management of deviancy is better in the upper grades. It might, for instance, be that lack of deviancy in older children makes good management easier.

That work involvement was greater and deviancy lower in the recitation context than the seatwork context is the final 'finding' to be considered, and it handily allows us to summarise the main criticisms made. First, although this is far from being a tautology or an analytic truth, there is none the less an element of necessity about it. The nature of recitation as contrasted with seatwork is such that it implies a deliberate attempt to involve students directly, and by involving them provides one fairly obvious way of cutting down on deviant behaviour. Secondly, the finding is insecurely based, because the categories of seatwork and recitation overlap: much of what is done in one context might also be done in another, and we therefore cannot be sure whether a different emphasis in either context would not have produced quite different results.

Thirdly, these particular concepts were not adequately defined, so that it is not really clear what the researchers are referring to anyway. Had they defined recitation and seatwork clearly, it is possible that they might have done so in a way that clearly distinguished them. That would meet the second objection, but at the price of trivialisation. If, for example, we classify as seatwork any situation in which children are required to pursue a task individually, and recitation as any situation where children are supposed to listen to other members of the group (students or teacher) individually, then the 'finding' that students were more involved and better behaved in the latter situation would be partly necessary (passive reactions will be observed as involvement), partly tendentious (listening to someone cannot be reliably observed), and partly meaningless as a guide to practice, since nobody could seriously suggest that we have to choose between these approaches. There is a time for seatwork and a time for recitation, regardless of how well individual pupils respond to either approach. Fourthly, we have no evidence about a causal relationship even for the classrooms observed. Fifthly, we cannot generalise from the studies in question, since other schools, other students, other teachers, in short other situations, will be different in countless ways.

It seems undeniable, then, that Kounin and his associates notwithstanding the fact that they had the grace to reject their first study and try again with new techniques of observation and new categories, and that they appear to have been relatively conscientious and sensible within the limits of their approach, have furnished us with very little indeed that could be said to be generalisable, useful for the teacher, and established by their programme of research.

What has gone wrong is very simple: failure to appreciate the *implications* of the many difficulties that are formally acknowledged by most empirical researchers, and failure in particular to handle the conceptual difficulties even so far as they can be handled, allows researchers to continue to think that in time more secure and more useful information may be gathered. Dunkin and Biddle, well aware of some of the shortcomings in Kounin's research, none the less feel able to refer to its 'impressive findings', as if matters such as the fact that 'the relationships between [judgements as to whether activities counted as seatwork or recitation] and those involved in the code for 'variety' are not made clear'[23] did not invalidate conclusions involving any of those concepts. They feel that the 'findings' 'in sum . . . appear to support many of the recommendations that used to be made in wholistic methods of teaching courses.'[24] So they may, for that is to say no more than that the judgements and inferences of these researchers concur with what many other people have assumed to be the case. And some of these assumptions may well be true. Indeed, some, as I have been at pains to point out, *must* be true. The important point is that few, if any, of these assumptions have been *substantiated* by this manner of investigation.

There is a danger of confusion between 'systematic' and 'accurate' observation. This kind of research is more systematic in some ways than the appraisal of the experienced teacher. For instance, it involves more than one person looking out for the same things in similar ways, and the system involved is made public. But even so, it is not necessarily more systematic all told than the impressionistic scrutiny of one individual, and rather more crucially it is not necessarily any more accurate at judging what is going on. Whether the programme is reliable and discerning depends not on its being overtly systematic, but on the system in question being a good one for the purposes in question. And, as we have seen, it plainly is not. It probably is reasonable to say that teachers should be alert to questions of timing, variety, momentum, manner of addressing children and so forth. It would be quite unreasonable to say that this programme of research has established that teachers should do anything in particular. The original question, 'How does one manage a room full of energetic and impulsive pupils?', has not been answered. What we have are a series of unsupported inferences, based on individual judgements about matters predominantly unobservable in a small number of particular situations, presented with a barrage of tables and figures which may tend to obscure the fact that it is indeed individual perceptions we are dealing with rather than the degree of objectivity that we can often gain in the natural sciences. The individual perceptions are further limited by a manner of observing that predetermines that only a small number of things shall be observed in an artificial way. (On systematic observation, see Chapter 8, s.2)

In the light of the foregoing, it is interesting to look at the reasons that Dunkin and Biddle give for regarding this particular research programme as important. As we have seen, despite more than one reference to 'impressive findings', they do not claim that very much has been established. Rather, their commendation takes the form of listing the following strengths in Kounin's work: 'the concepts used are striking and original; the methods employed for classroom observation were sophisticated; reliability for coding judgements was high, and, above all, the relationships found between teacher and pupil variables were strong.'[25] But it will be noted that all of these comments involve complimenting them on their procedures; they completely ignore the question of whether the procedures are getting us anywhere. It is somewhat like praising the organisation of a soccer team that, by consistently following a recognisable pattern of play, loses every match. Besides, we should look more closely at the individual compliments.

Throughout their book, Dunkin and Biddle make much of the generation of new and useful concepts. But they do not seem to have any clear idea of what the usefulness of a concept may consist in. Furthermore, they themselves, while claiming in summary that 'the concepts advanced by Kounin were simply unknown to many of his teachers'[26] until he introduced them, acknowledge at one point in the body of the text that these are not necessarily *new concepts:* 'although the term "desist incident" may be new to us, we recognise the concept to which it refers as a familiar one.'[27] Now this is a very important distinction: new words for familiar ideas are not in general of any particular value; new ideas, on the other hand, may well have some value for particular purposes. But how many new ideas are in fact being generated by Kounin's or anyone else's research into teaching? Obviously how many of the words and phrases spawned by empirical research introduce ideas that are new to how many people is itself an empirical question to which we don't have the answer. But I find it hard to believe that what is meant by most of the vocabulary of research represents new ideas to many of the teaching fraternity. Certainly, I do not detect any new ideas in Kounin's observation schedule.

What may be true, which is quite different, is that the idea of looking out for and concentrating on particular aspects of classroom behaviour may be new to some of us. But then there is no particular merit in that, unless so doing can in some respect deliver the goods. The truth is surely that they are *not,* by and large, 'striking and original concepts', and they are *not* particularly useful, because they involve items that cannot be observed in isolation, that do not, as defined, adequately match reality, and that sometimes contain in their meaning something of the results that we claim to be looking out for. Finally, is there not a blatant inconsistency in congratulating Kounin on generating 'striking and original' concepts and criticising him for introducing concepts some of which 'are difficult to understand', as Dunkin and Biddle do?[28] If they are difficult to understand, can they truly be said to be striking and original?

To say that the methods employed were 'sophisticated' is misleading, since that is a commendatory term and suggests that they are well and appropriately designed as well as complicated. Complexity is not a vice, particularly when one is examining something complex such as a classroom situation. But, as Dunkin and Biddle admit when listing weaknesses in Kounin's research, a complex set of observation techniques is difficult to handle, and may therefore not be handled well, in which case its complexity is neither here nor there. Secondly, the important thing is not to be complex, but to match the degree of complexity of the observation methods to the degree of complexity of what is being observed. As far as that goes, Kounin's methods, along with most classroom observation schedules, are not nearly complex enough. As we have seen, they simply ignore numbers of possible variables, and the manner of categorising a concept seldom matches the complexity of the concept. As to whether they are well and appropriately designed, that can be judged only by estimating their adequacy for the task. It makes no sense to say, as Dunkin and Biddle by implication do, 'well, anyway, in themselves these are well designed methods of observation, regardless of the fact that they are not giving us any reliable information'. If even some of the criticisms I have made are accepted, then it follows that these methods of observation were *not* 'sophisticated' in so far as that implies well designed for the task in hand.

That reliability for coding judgements should be high is a necessary condition of regarding the judgements as sound. If five people observe the same behaviour and code it differently, we are obviously going nowhere. However, it is not in itself a sufficient condition of sound judgement. In the first place, the consistency of judgement between observers may owe more to such considerations as a common outlook or a specific training programme for observers than to the reasonableness or plausibility of the judgements. In the second place, in itself, consensus among observers is no more meaningful than consensus among, say, the body of experienced teachers. Consensus does not guarantee truth. We should therefore demand high reliability, and be glad that Kounin's research has it. But we should not be misled into thinking that this has much to do with the value of the research programme overall.

The final compliment, that relationships between variables were strong, is, depending upon how we interpret it, either irrelevant or untrue. It is irrelevant to the question of the value of the research, if all that is meant is that following on this flawed research a number of high correlations are claimed: irrelevant, partly because, given the flaws and weaknesses, they are not reliable correlations, partly because it is inferences about cause and effect that we are mainly concerned to establish, rather than unexplained correlations. If the claim is taken to mean, as I am sure that Dunkin and Biddle do not mean, but I fear that some of their readers might conclude, that certain causal relationships were strongly established, it is false.

2. CLASSROOM CLIMATE

It thus seems that even the specific compliments that two seasoned researchers pay to a programme that they rate highly are somewhat empty. Let us turn at this point to a rather more cursory examination of Dunkin and Biddle's review of research into classroom climate, about which they themselves are a great deal less sanguine.

Approaching the matter historically they first refer to the 1930s research of Lewin and his associates into the impact of autocratic, democratic and *laissez-faire* styles of leader behaviour upon groups of boys engaged in clublike activities. This study (Lewin *et al.*, 1939) suggested that autocracy was generally accompanied either by rebellion or by submission on the part of the boys, and by high productivity when the autocratic leader was present, but by a tendency towards destructive behaviour in his absence. Democratic leadership was said to inspire more 'task-orientated, cooperative . . . friendly', and independent behaviour especially in the leader's absence. *Laissez-faire* leadership did least for productivity, and tended to be accompanied by intra-group hostility. In almost every case the democratic style was preferred by the group.

Dunkin and Biddle have the following reservations about this research. The study involved no classrooms, where the situation might be different. The leadership concepts, being broad, encompass many aspects and it is impossible for us to get a clear picture of what particular features of, say, autocratic leadership are causing what child behaviour, if any. In particular, they point out, following comments of one of the group leaders, that there does not appear to have been an adequate attempt to distinguish warmth and indirectness of style; there is an implicit assumption, obviously untenable, that the two always go together, and that autocratic styles must be cold. To that we must add the by now familiar criticism that it is not only that it may have been warmth rather than indirectness as such that led to certain child responses, but it may also have been any one or any combination of countless other variables, social, personal or contextual, totally ignored by the research, that were causally significant. And yet again we must note that some of the major 'findings' seem in fact to be essentially logical necessities: if one is faced with an autocratic leader, defined as one who directs and controls, there is not much that one can do but submit or rebel; if leadership is defined as democratic, in the sense of encouraging the group to get on with things on their own, it is scarcely surprising that group members should be more cooperative and independent than they are when they are being directed to do specific things (autocratic), or neither directed nor encouraged *(laissez-faire)*. We should also emphasise the truism that the findings, if reliable, would still only be generalisations: the study did not show that in these particular cases all group members responded in the same way. No significant empirical discovery about how to treat children in classrooms in order to obtain certain results, therefore, has emerged from this study.

Reference is then made to Andersons's (H.H.) (1939) research into dominative and integrative teaching. Anderson perpetuated the mistake of identifying warmth and indirectness, so that the directive teacher is defined in terms of being cold and unsympathetic as well as being overtly controlling. The reality that a directive style of teaching might be accompanied by warmth and sensitivity, and indirective style by coldness and lack of sensitivity, and that control and direction may be exercised in subtle ways even by a seemingly indirect teacher, is totally ignored by the crudity of the categories. But given these crude categories, one would expect less positive response in general from children to what are identified as dominative styles of teaching, and the conclusion that dominative behaviour produced less pupil independence, spontaneity and participation seems more or less inevitable.

One point that should be made in passing is that Dunkin and Biddle illustrate disturbingly and well, throughout their book, the extent to which researchers have clearly been governed by ideological commitments rather than the dispassionate attitude of the ideal scientist. Anderson's description of dominative teaching is such as to leave us in no doubt about his prior commitment to integrative styles and to make it a foregone conclusion that dominative styles will produce undesirable responses. This is of course only a contingent weakness in empirical research, but the evidence suggests that it is none the less a very real one.

Withall (1949), meanwhile, approached the task by categorising seven distinct types of teacher talk, including such items as the provision of 'learner supportive statements that have the intent of reassuring or commending the pupil', and 'directive or hortative statements with intent to have pupil follow a recommended course of action'; the idea being that these more specific categories would give sharper focus to the notions of teacher-centred and learner-centred classrooms. But the definition of the categories largely in terms of teacher intention makes them quite inappropriate to the nature of empirical observation: one can witness an utterance and, by using judgement, classify it as being encouraging, peremptory, or whatever; but one cannot witness the teacher's intentions, nor see the utterances as the individual children see them. Furthermore, Withall's research is fatally flawed by being yet another instance of the failure to distinguish between a formal manner of teaching and a cold attitude towards children.

Ten years later another Anderson (R.C.) (1959) was, very reasonably on the evidence to date, fulminatng against the inadequacy of such research into teaching, and calling for its abandonment. The findings, he pointed out, were weak and contradictory, the research lacked rigour and was generally conducted in apparent ignorance of other research into similar things, and the operational definitions being used were imprecise. But Anderson did not go so far as to see or to say that in the nature of things such research must continue to be largely futile. Consequently, the effective rejoinder of the research band-wagon, just beginning to gather steam, was that we could sharpen our concepts, refine the methodology and improve the research designs, and all would be well. A key figure in the move towards a 'new deal' research design was N.A. Flanders.

Flanders (1970) approached the matter by drawing a contrast between direct and indirect influence. 'Direct influence consists of stating the teacher's own opinion or ideas, directing the pupils' actions, criticizing his behaviour, or justifying the teacher's authority or use of that authority.' 'Indirect influence consists of soliciting the opinions or ideas of the pupils, applying or enlarging on those opinions or ideas, praising or encouraging the participation of pupils, or clarifying and accepting their feelings.'[29] Now any experienced teacher, or indeed, one might feel, any sensible person, would immediately have three responses to this basic distinction between direct and indirect influences. First, few if any teachers adopt one or the other approach. A teacher needs to and does employ both direct and indirect influences, and furthermore very often they are being employed at the same time. Secondly, one cannot always tell what kind of influence the teacher is having from appearances alone. Teachers may be more or less subtle in putting over ideas, criticising or encouraging the opinions of children, and the children do not always all see what the teacher is doing in the same light as each other, or as observers. Judging what is going on is going to be an exceedingly tricky business sometimes: is that teacher response stating an opinion, clarifying Johnny's opinion, encouraging other children to form opinions, all three, or what? Flanders' own admission that 'anyone with teaching experience recognizes that there are situations in which an integrative pattern is less appropriate than a dominative pattern',[30] though its wording betrays a residual commitment to the former, does not go far enough. It is not simply that there may be a place for both approaches, but that the two approaches cannot always be, and very possibly should not be, divorced at all. Thirdly, in so far as teachers do effectively adopt one style or the other, there are certain predictable consequences that we hardly need to watch out for and verify empirically. Students taught by an indirect style should, by and large, show more signs of involvement and opinion-giving, and should feel that their ideas are worth having. Students taught by a direct style should show fewer signs of those things, but should show more signs of conformity to the teacher's demands and opinions.

But Flanders' own major influence has been through the development of a more specific observation instrument, the Flanders Interaction Analysis Categories System (FIAC), which, in modified form, is still alive and kicking in such recent research as the ORACLE programme, examined below (s.6). If we ignore detailed developments, FIAC basically provides ten categories for observation, seven of which relate to teacher verbal behaviour, four of those being classified as signs of indirect influence (acceptance of students' feelings, praise or encouragement, acceptance or use of students' ideas, and asking questions), and three being classified as signs of direct influence (lecturing, giving directions and criticising); there are in addition two categories for judging pupil verbal behaviour (student talk-response and student talk-initiation), and the tenth category is silence or confusion.

Granted that these categories are more specific than the broad terms 'direct' and 'indirect', to which they are supposed to give focus, it does not follow either that they are more satisfactory or that they are clearer and hence easier to handle.

In the first place, the price of greater specificity, it might be argued, is a less realistic way of looking at what goes on in the classroom, for these categories alone by no means exhaust all the dimensions of direct, indirect or combined styles of teaching. It does not matter what they may be; it is enough to recognise that a judgement about the directness or indirectness of a teacher based only on these categories may be incomplete and quite misleading.

In the second place, as the many subsequent modifications to the instrument indicate, these categories are no more free of problems of definition and judgement than the broader categories 'direct' and 'indirect'. What, for example, counts as teacher respect for a student's opinion? And how (which is a different question) do you accurately judge that it is being exhibited? When is teacher talk lecturing? May not criticism be imparted through encouragement, or vice versa? Is it always possible to tell whether a student is more properly to be regarded as initiating or responding to something? It is noteworthy in this respect that in 1960 the act of the teacher in repeating a pupil's answer was coded to count as acceptance of the pupil's idea *or* lecturing, depending essentially on whether the acceptance was judged to be authentic. In 1963 such repetition of an answer was to be coded simply as lecturing. In 1968, it was decided that 'when a teacher repeats a student's idea, indicating that . . . [it] . . . is one that should be considered rather than that it is the correct answer' it should be construed as using the student's idea, which takes us back to the first position in terms of scoring, although of course the authentic acceptance of an idea deemed to be valuable, and the use of an idea deemed to be in some way deficient, are rather different.

The mistake is to think that such tinkering with the coding is solving any problem. The point is precisely that repeating a student's answer might mean any one or more of a vast number of things, depending upon when it is done, how it is done, who it is done by, and whose answer it is done to. Trying to tie it down to one or two predetermined interpretations is totally absurd and inevitably leads to an artificial, oversimplified and distorted view of what is actually going on. And that is to ignore the further point that judging whether acceptance of an idea is authentic, or whether repeating it is designed to make use of it or to expose its inadequacy, is a difficult business that ought to lead to different judgements on the part of different observers. Here is a case where high reliability, far from being a virtue, ought to make us positively suspicious. If all of a group of observers are at one in judging teacher repetition of an idea to involve authentic acceptance, it is likely that they are working with very superficial signs (for example, he *says* he accepts it), for the reality is that teachers repeat students' responses for a wide variety of superficially undiscernible reasons.

The procedure followed in using the FIAC instrument was for observers to code behaviour every 3 seconds. The object of including student behaviour as well as teacher behaviour was that information should be gained about what student response follows what teacher behaviour, rather than merely a picture of teacher behaviour. However, it is evident that this approach will not give us any reliable information about cause and effect in classroom control. It will give us a view of particular teachers' and particular students' behaviours over a particular period. That view may conceivably be more or less accurate, but we shall not be warranted to rely on it, since it is limited by the small number of categories into which all behaviour has to be squeezed, it will be based to a large extent on the judgements of observers which may well be fallible, given the inherent difficulty in making them, and it will be specifically distorted by the unreal assumption that at any given moment the individual is engaged in one behaviour only. As to cause and effect, it can tell us nothing: even if the view of teacher behaviour and student behaviour could be relied upon, the fact of a student behaviour following on a teacher behaviour cannot in itself be construed as cause and effect and, until such time as somebody demonstrates the contrary, there is a strong *a priori* assumption that the effect of any particular teacher behaviour on students will depend partly on a host of factors, personal, social and contextual, that are completely ignored in this research.

Dunkin and Biddle acknowledge the conceptual confusion involved in FIAC. They point out, for example, that it is far from clear that the categories are mutually exclusive and, in particular, they note, for what seems like the millionth time, that there still seems to be an implicit assumption that warmth and indirectness somehow necessarily go together. The reason that it seems worth continually stressing this one example of conceptual inadequacy, apart from the fact that it does run through the research, is that it highlights the point that the fundamental problem in empirical research is that those involved in it seem not to understand that its chances of being profitable are, if not entirely, at least necessarily dependent on researchers acquiring some conceptual finesse of the sort demanded by philosophy. Whether, as I am arguing, it is impossible to adequately conceptualise human interactions in clear, distinct, observable terms or not, it is absolutely certain that so long as researchers cannot see obvious points, such as that a directive teacher might exhibit more warmth than an indirective one, they at any rate will be incapable of producing worthwhile research.

Dunkin and Biddle now turn their attention to a review of approximately 100 studies concerned with indirectness and/or warmth in teaching styles, most of which make use of what they themselves (enthusiasts for the game, let us remember) describe as 'methodologically primitive'[31] instruments based on FIAC. They are very fair in stressing the difficulties in combining or comparing these studies, given that they each employ different categories (different words, anyway, if not always different concepts), and different ways of measuring the overall directness of a lesson. But these points, though they certainly diminish the usefulness of such research taken as a whole, which it would have to be if we were to hope for some significant findings, need not concern us.

What, if we were to accept the various conclusions of these different research programmes and assume that they are compatible, would we seem to discover? Ignoring the crippling consideration that the manner of the research means that we have no reason to suppose that it has established its conclusions, are the conclusions that are none the less drawn of interest and significance?

We discover, or, to be precise, think we discover (i) that teacher behaviour is predominantly direct; and (ii) that pupils are not talking publicly for more than 25 per cent of lesson time.[32] These seem plausible findings, because 'directness' and 'talking' are broad and clear enough terms to allow us to accept the judgements of observers, without being too concerned about the problems of identification. We may reasonably argue about whether specific behaviours should be coded in one category or another, while accepting enough items to agree that the overall picture is directive rather than indirect. However, by the same token, we have to admit both that these findings did not require the relatively elaborate systematic research schedule that was used, and that they are of relatively little significance. Precisely because it is a broad picture of two fairly unambiguous things, it could as well have been arrived at by the straightforward unsystematic or impressionistic observation of anyone with some understanding of the business of classrooms. The methods employed do not make the view any more secure. And the significance of the picture is slight, since we know from the meaning of the term 'direct teaching' that it must involve a preponderance of teacher talk, and we do not know anything about the merits or demerits of either of these features of classroom life.

One study suggests (iii) a correlation between the social class of pupils and the indirectness of teachers.[33] But even if there regularly is such a correlation in classrooms (which has by no means been shown, given the limitations of the research), it could well be, as the researchers admit, that pupil achievement has some causal relationship with social class, and that it is the former rather than the latter that stimulates the indirect style employed by some teachers. Or it could be the ideological commitment of certain teachers that causes them to adopt a particular style, and mere chance that of those observed most had pupils from a certain class background; or it could be that ideological commitment to indirect teaching tends to go with ideological comment to schools in certain areas; or it could be that headteachers of schools in certain areas tend to believe that direct styles have failed with children of that background and try to encourage indirect teaching. Or, to get to the point, it could be explained in a hundred ways, and we have no way of knowing from the research which is most likely.

(iv) The presence of computer-assisted instruction is not shown to correlate with any change of balance between direct and indirect teaching.[34] That is my wording, which is both more accurate and more revealing of the nugatory nature of this observation than Dunkin and Biddle's. They call this another 'finding' to the effect that 'computer-assisted instruction does *not* change the balance.'[35] But that, of course, is an illegitimate conclusion from the absence of high correlation in limited studies. Indeed, it must surely be obvious to anyone, if they think about it, that, whatever is observed to be the case in some instances, computer-assisted instruction might or might not change the balance of direct and indirect teaching. What is the value of the claim, if true, that in a few specific situations it did not?

(v) The degree of indirectness exhibited by teachers varied in different subjects.[36] Again this is hardly surprising: to some extent different subjects lend themselves more or less to directness, and to some extent conceptions of subjects at particular times and places lend themselves more or less to directness. For instance, in the 1950s, when there was considerable emphasis on seeing English as a vehicle for self-expression, one would expect English lessons to have been relatively indirect, as they were. The important questions are whether such a conception of English teaching is educationally justifiable and what the effects of it may be, neither of which, for different reasons, can be handled by empirical field surveys.

(vi) Dunkin and Biddle think that 'the most interesting finding' may be that teachers tend to be more indirect toward classes of higher intelligence than toward those of lower intelligence.[37] The problem here is that to substantiate this finding we have either to accept some standardised IQ test as a genuine measure of intelligence, which, for very similar reasons to those being advanced against the credibility of empirical research into classrooms,[38] we cannot, or we judge intelligence in terms of observable signs of participation and involvement, in which case we are bound to think that there is more intelligence in an indirect context, which by definition encourages conspicuous involvement. Either way the finding can only become truly interesting, if we are in a position to approve or condemn it, which we are not. If the research could tell us whether, or under what conditions, indirect teaching was preferable in specific respects for children of higher intelligence, that would be interesting. But it cannot.

(vii) Indirect teachers tend to be valued or judged superior to direct teachers by other people.[39] This kind of finding is relatively secure, since even allowing for the fact that people are not always honest when giving their opinions to researchers, whether one values someone or not is a relatively easy matter to determine. The explanation of this finding is presumably to be found in the fact that during the period of the research we are considering progressive ideology was in the ascendant in North America. Most people were led to believe, rightly or wrongly, that indirect teaching was good teaching. Naturally, therefore, most people judged indirect teachers to be superior. Whether this should be of any interest to those trying to determine what *is* good teaching, as opposed to what is thought to be, is another question.

(viii) Indirect teachers tended to score higher on the National Teachers' Examination history and philosophy examination.[40] Here again there seems little reason to doubt the claim, but it is a little difficult to know what to make of it. Of course, it had to be the case that of a given group of direct and indirect teachers, the direct would tend to score higher, or the indirect would tend to score higher, or there would be no appreciable difference. We have no particular reason to assume that this is other than a random result. On the other hand it might not be, in which case we would need to consider the nature of the examination carefully, to see whether there are any features of it that might explain its apparent congeniality to indirect teachers. But even then it is far from clear what relevance this might have to the effects and value of indirect teaching.

(ix) Indirect teachers are said to have greater ego strength, and (x) to be less authoritarian than direct teachers,[41] both of which are clearly inevitable consequences of the definition of indirect teaching. Behaviouristically-minded observers do not classify teachers who appear to need to dominate and instruct as being other than lacking in ego strength and authoritarian.

(xi) Teacher indirectness correlates highly with the cognitive level of classroom discourse.[42] This is not a tight necessary truth, but it seems a commonsense expectation, given that indirectness is defined and judged in terms of a strong degree of classroom discourse. It is true that it might none the less be relatively poor discourse, though one might reasonably expect practice to improve facility, if not necessarily quality; but, given the operational definitions of teacher directness employed, it is inevitable that teacher directness should fail to correlate highly with classroom student discourse, regardless of quality. What we must avoid doing is assuming that indirect teaching has hereby earned a plus; no reason has been given to applaud the active display of classroom discourse at any particular cognitive level, and there are besides severe conceptual problems in the way cognitive level is measured in such research.

(xii) Indirectness 'appears to effect the amount of pupil-talk',[43] or, as we should say, indirectness appears to correlate with the amount of pupil-talk, as it must do given what is meant by indirectness. Similarly, the claims (xiii) that it is reported to 'raise the amount of pupil-initiations',[44] (xiv) that it is associated with greater pupil achievement,[45] (xv) that it is associated with greater creativity,[46] and (xvi) that it is associated with lower pupil anxiety,[47] are all, to a greater or lesser extent, conceptually necessary. Indirect teachers are *defined* as the sort of people who encourage pupil-initiations, stress individual achievement, inspire creativity and seek to diminish anxiety. Again, whether these are good things to do, or whether what they regard as creative or an achievement really are such, are further questions.

I am ignoring claims pertaining to the effects on teaching practice of being trained in the use of FIAC, because, even though the evidence suggests that such training may prove effective in making teachers more indirect, as it relentlessly emerges that adopting an observational strategy in terms such as FIAC has little to recommend it, and as we recall that no reason at all has been given for preferring an indirect style, there seems no reason to want to train people in such a way. I am also ignoring all those findings that Dunkin and Biddle summarise as 'are (and are not) to be found'. That seems a curious way to refer to conflicting conclusions. If one study finds no correlation between X and Y, and another one does, it would seem more reasonable to conclude that no steady correlation was observed, rather than to suggest, for example, that one study reports indirectness 'to *raise* the amount of pupil responses' and another 'to *lower* the amount'.[48] Given the lack of control of countless variables and the illegitimacy of claiming to have *seen* cause and effect (as opposed to inferred it), no study should be claiming to find that indirectness either raises or lowers the amount of pupil responses.

However, since it may seem to the reader that this particular example involves conceptual necessity again, and that it is curious that any study should report lack of correlation between indirectness and pupil responses, since the former is partly defined in terms of generating the latter, this is a good opportunity to recall the particular nature of the conceptual tie-up in some of these findings. I am not suggesting that indirectness is as inevitably tied to initiating or encouraging student responses as triangularity is to three-sidedness. Indirectness is a broad notion, defined in terms of a number of features and involving an overall estimate. A teacher may therefore be categorised as indirect even though one thing he does little of is encourage student responses, provided he meets the various other criteria to a significant extent. Therefore, we may observe indirect teaching failing to correlate with student responses. But only on occasion. If we consistently found an absence of correlation, then it becomes clear that encouraging student responses cannot be part of what researchers mean by indirectness. But in point of fact we know that it is, and therefore we do find for the most part a correlation between the two, and it is not an empirical discovery but an essentially conceptual point. What of course we would like to get are some consistent, reliably observed correlations between useful and plainly non-conceptually-linked behaviours. But we have now summarised all the superficially noteworthy findings from a 100-odd studies, covering a 20-year period, and can see that there is no such correlation amongst them.[49]

One study, and one study alone, reported a correlation that might seem to support the assumption of a negative relationship between direct and indirect teaching.[50] That is to say that the assumption, which lies behind almost all the studies in question, that direct teaching takes the form of high amounts of lecturing, directing and criticising and low amounts of praise, acceptance and questioning, while the exact reverse is the case with indirect teaching, which seems a singularly obtuse assumption, is not borne out at all by the evidence. (The fact that one study supports it is neither here nor there: obviously there may be some extreme teachers who fit the stereotypes exactly and, if one has the misfortune to encounter them, one will see the concepts as having a negative relationship. But there is no necessary reason why they should, and not much practical likelihood of encountering the extremes.)

3. TEACHER WARMTH

The studies on teacher warmth, when this is distinguished from teacher indirectness, follow a similar pattern. If the concept of warmth is broken down into the more specific concepts of providing praise, accepting students' ideas and teacher criticism, as is the manner of most of the research, it is said that we gain the following information. First, six fairly straightforward claims are made about praise. (i) Teachers use praise sparingly; (ii) they give praise more to higher achieving pupils or to those to whom they feel more attached; (iii) they give praise especially to white pupils from whom they expect high achievement, and (iv) to black pupils from whom they expect low achievement; (v) they tend also to praise students from whom they expect future high status social positions; (vi) use of praise appears to vary with the social class status of the school's location.[51]

There are slight elements of predictability, if not necessity, about some of these conclusions. For example, praise that is deserved has some kind of a conceptual link with high achievement, and part of the way in which we judge whether a teacher feels attachment towards particular students is by monitoring the tendency to praise them. None the less, there is no reason why these should not be relatively secure claims, since they relate to relatively clear and observable concepts. Observers should be able to provide a reasonably accurate account of whether teachers do or do not engage in praise to any great extent, and to what extent they provide it for relatively discernible groups, even allowing for the fact that sometimes what appears superficially to be praise may not be praise either in fact or in the judgement of the persons supposedly praised, and vice versa. Such claims about the general tendency of teachers could only be reasonably based on wide field surveys, and the information they provide has usefulness in terms of building up an accurate picture of what does currently go on in classrooms. Educators need to be aware of such phenomena as those recorded.

However, the usefulness of even these claims only goes so far. Assume that this is what is happening, the all-important question remains: What are we to do about it? For the research, as we should be coming to expect, has little it can legitimately and unambiguously say about the effects of such practice, and nothing about its acceptability. (vii) The 'findings' concerning the association of praise with student achievement and (viii) student attitude, even if they could be trusted, are contradictory, as they were in the case of directness.[52] (ix) It is said that teacher praise is associated with a more positive self-concept, but that is clearly to be expected from the nature of praise, which by definition involves attempting to boost the self-concept.[53] (x) It is said to be associated with lower pupil non-verbal creativity,[54] but quite apart from the problems inherent in defining and judging such creativity, this tells us nothing about the nature of the relationship between the two and nothing about what we should do about it. (Do teachers perhaps seek to inspire those they deem to be low creatives by praise? Does praise perhaps stultify creativity? Is it one or more of countless other possible factors that explain what is going on, perhaps different factors in different cases? Who knows?)

Dunkin and Biddle report that greater acceptance of pupils' ideas (i) 'appears to raise the amount of pupil initiations'; (ii) 'is unrelated to pupil achievement'; and (iii) 'occurs with lower pupil anxiety and greater pupil creativity'.[55] The first of these claims, despite being cautiously phrased, is another example of the illegitimate shift from correlation to cause and effect. The studies in question did not perceive acceptance *raising* the amount of initiations: they perceived acceptance and initiation going hand in hand. It is conceivable that teachers respond sometimes to initiation by being more accepting. In any case the conceptual tie-up here is very strong: accepting ideas necessitates initiation of ideas, and clearly students will grow tired of initiating ideas that are not accepted. As to the second claim, we must remember that this means only that a high correlation between acceptance and achievement was not found in these studies. 'Unrelated' has to be understood as a technical term meaning precisely and only that. We must avoid the temptation to think it has been shown that acceptance of ideas has no effect on achievement, although of course it is quite possible that it doesn't. (There would, in any case, be a question as to what counts as achievement, and in respect of what, to be answered. If the object were to increase the achievement of students in the public handling of their ideas, it would be hard to believe that some degree of acceptance would not be desirable. But that in turn would raise again the question of what kind of acceptance. Acceptance of ideas can be a subtle business, by no means always readily observable by one who does not know and understand particular teachers, children and their long-term relationship). The third claim must be viewed with suspicion as being essentially conceptual. Students who are encouraged to furnish ideas will tend to do so, and their confident provision of ideas was no doubt interpreted by observers as a sign of low anxiety. Whether such acceptance correlates with anything approaching genuine creativity remains unknown; the creativity discerned by the observer is *defined* in such terms as the furnishing of ideas.

When we turn to the use of criticism by the teacher it is suggested (i) that it may tend to be employed more with boys than with girls; (ii) that it is more common in schools in lower-class locations; (iii) that lower achievers receive more criticism; (iv) that teachers who criticise tend also to 'have lower scores on the attitude of indifference to pupils'; (v) that criticism is associated with lower pupil achievement motivation; (vi) with greater pupil fear of failure; (vii) with lower self-concepts; (viii) with greater dependency; and (ix) with lower pupil anxiety.[56]

The first claim is another example of a relatively secure one since boys are readily distinguishable from girls, and criticism, though not by any means entirely straightforward, is a great deal more easy to define and recognise than, say, interest, indifference, creativity or intelligence. It is also a finding, as I think it may reasonably be called for once, not without interest, for it will be recalled that boys also seemed to receive more praise. This suggests that boys in general elicit more positive responses from teachers than girls.[57] Needless to say, whether there is any good reason for this, or whether it matters, remain further questions, but none the less it is information worth having.

Given that, for whatever reason, we have evidence of correlations between lower social class and lower achievement, we should not be surprised to find the second and third claims together, and it can scarcely be regarded as surprising that lower achievers tend to receive more criticism. The ninth claim has interest, because it seems superficially counter-intuitive. If praise to some extent lessens anxiety by definition, one might have expected criticism to raise it. So, of course, it would have to, if criticism were a genuine antonym of praise, as is sometimes assumed. But here we see the dangers of any such crude black-and-white conceptualisation. The truth is that criticism is not necessarily a violent destructive assault, not necessarily the precise opposite of praise, and it need come as no surprise to us that criticism may decrease anxiety. Perhaps it is a direct attention of many possible sorts that basically reduces student anxiety. But whatever the reason, and we do not know what it is, it is worth knowing that at any rate some of what is judged to be teacher criticism by some observers does not necessarily provoke anxiety.

The other claims relating to criticism are conspicuously conceptual rather than true empirical discoveries. Whatever tests one uses to measure teacher rejection and indifference, no matter that they are liable to be crude and superficial, they are bound to relate in some way to the signs used to judge a teacher as being critical. To criticise is to some extent to reject, and is not, whatever else it is, to be indifferent. Naturally criticism is associated with lower pupil achievement, because by and large that is the context in which teachers resort to criticism. Equally naturally it is associated with greater fear of failure, lower self-concepts and greater dependency. Prevalent teacher criticism *means*, amongst other things, teacher dominance (though there are also other ways of achieving this), emphasis on mistakes, and pointing out limitations in student powers.

What, then, do we gain from the various studies into the classroom climate that have been reviewed? We get a limited amount of fairly secure information about the tendency of teachers' behaviour towards various definable groups in terms of sex, race and class. The possible importance of this information cannot be doubted, but its immediate use can be. For what are we to do with it? No immediate conclusions for practice follow, since it is not a function of the research to show whether these tendencies are good or bad in themselves, nor what effects or causes they have. It would no doubt be disingenuous to suggest that such differences of treatment for, say, boys and girls are arrived at for good reasons in most cases, but it is certainly possible none the less that there are good reasons, in the sense either of explanations or justifications, for such differences. For the rest we have a very large number of extremely weakly-based correlations, the vast majority of which are truisms dressed up as empirical discoveries. The correlations are weakly based, primarily because they rest on inadequate conceptualisation, but in addition the studies involved, though selected as a reasonable sample of such research, are agreed to have had many other weaknesses and shortcomings by those such as Dunkin and Biddle who value the enterprise. The studies tell us absolutely nothing directly about cause and effect.

Before summarising the reasons why these inadequacies were inevitable, and not simply the consequence of researchers doing the job badly, I want to focus on an oddity of Dunkin and Biddle's position which partly explains why I have kept up a running commentary on their comments on this body of research. Throughout their review, although they do themselves misleadingly undercut some of the force of their view by summarising studies in terms of 'findings', and by referring to cause and effect, implicitly or explicitly, when they should confine themselves to correlations or associations, they are in fact very critical of the bulk of the research. They say that researchers have not 'generally concerned themselves with contextual influences on teaching behaviour',[58] which is by any account a grave indictment. They acknowledge that correlations are generally and wrongly being interpreted as 'cause and effect relationships'.[59] They acknowledge that there are many 'contradictory findings'.[60] They repeatedly have occasion to point out that unwarranted conceptual assumptions are being made, including some almost crazy ones such as that warmth and indirectness necessarily go together, or that criticism is the exact opposite of praise and receptiveness. They recognise that 'the biggest problem [is] conceptual confusion';[61] in particular, categories are given minimal definition and assumed to constitute single facets for no obvious reason. More generally, in relation to all the research they review, they say 'we too are concerned with the inability of the research so far conducted to answer a number of crucial questions concerning teaching', 'much of the research . . . doesn't provide adequate answers.'[62] They quote the Committee on the Criteria for Teacher Effectiveness of the American Educational Research Association (1953) without dissenting: 'The simple fact of the matter is that after 40 years of research on teacher effectiveness . . . we can point to few outcomes that a superintendent of schools can safely employ in hiring a teacher.'[63] They write that no investigation has 'ever been able to provide much evidence that rating scales [e.g. for assessing the sensitivity of teachers] can be used validly.'[64] 'No studies of teaching have yet made use of representative samples.'[65] And most of the research consists in field studies, which, they are well aware, cannot yield information about cause and effect.

And yet, despite all of that and all the individual criticisms of particular pieces of research, they feel able to turn round in one of their summarising chapters and assert that not only has observational research 'produced information of value to teachers, but in some ways that contribution is a massive one', and, generally afire for 'the empirically-based information that represents the science of teaching', conclude that 'at long last we are beginning to know what is actually going on in the classroom, as well as *what produces and results from* classroom events'[66] (my italics).

How on earth can they do it? How can they square that conclusion with their devastating criticisms? How, after all that they have said, can they believe either that we are beginning to know about what 'produces and results from classroom events', or even that future research is likely to provide such knowledge? The answer is, in fact, simple and takes us to the heart of the matter. Dunkin and Biddle perceive many of the problems in research into classrooms, but there are two points that they either do not see or that they do not face up to. The first is that the practical constraints on such research are to some extent insurmountable. The second is that the 'conceptual confusion' they refer to is partly the consequence of logically unavoidable conceptual problems.

The research that is reviewed in this and other chapters is, I think, shown to tell us very little indeed that is secure, genuinely empirical discovery, and of direct use to the teacher. The reasons for this, that are acknowledged by Dunkin and Biddle and many other workers in the field, include (i) the fact that the conceptualisation has been in various ways poor; (ii) the fact that the research has not been conducted with the open mind free of ideological prejudice that is necessary for a genuinely scientific endeavour; (iii) the fact that the studies have invariably been small-scale and not conducted with random samples; and (iv) the fact that field studies cannot yield information about cause and effect, while experimental research is faced by various practical constraints, and there has in fact been very little of it. In view of these limitations, it is unwarranted to conclude that research to date has put us on the threshold of knowledge.

But steps could in principle be taken to rectify those shortcomings in future research. What we cannot do is to get round the problems that not all concepts can be adequately characterised in observational terms, and that the sort of control necessary for a truly experimental situation cannot be achieved. If we wish to arrive at general laws about teaching, certain information about cause and effect in the classroom, then we need to be able to identify unambiguously, and to isolate and control, various aspects of teacher and student behaviour. This, for the most part, in the nature of things, we simply cannot do. Of course we can define and isolate some things, such as teacher's age, student's sex, or school's intake; but those are not the concepts that are crucial or central to teaching and education; and, in any case, so long as other important variables cannot be controlled, our knowledge even of these relatively straightforward things is necessarily incomplete. It is not in the nature of things possible to define even such relatively clear and familiar concepts as praise, criticism and desist-incidents in purely uncontentious observable terms, still less concepts such as self-esteem, acceptance and warmth. What counts as praise, acceptance or warmth is not a function simply of what is done, but also of the spirit in which it is done. This means that whether the teacher is exhibiting warmth in relation to a pupil is a matter of judgement rather than physical observation, necessarily, and that what matters is the perception of the student, not the observer or even the teacher. I am not *being* warm to you, unless you feel the warmth, no matter what I do. And, partly because of the nature of these concepts, partly because of the way human beings and the world are, it is not in the nature of things possible to isolate or control most of the factors that may be presumed to have some kind of bearing on a classroom situation. One cannot simply control everything except teacher praise in order to see what effect it may have: the teacher exhibiting it will always be a particular individual; the students receiving it will always be particular individuals. The interrelationship may be unique.

Nor would one wish to discover what praise in and of itself does, even if one could, since in a real classroom praise never does exist in and of itself. What we ideally need to know is what this kind of praise, from this teacher, with this child, in this situation, does, and that kind of knowledge has nothing to do with scientific laws. The most that we can hope to get from observing classrooms are some generalisations about relatively observable behaviours, of varying degrees of certainty. But generalisations are quite distinct from general laws, and they are not pointers to practice, for the teacher should never act on a generalisation, since for all he knows the children he faces, or some other aspect of his situation, are exceptions to the generalisation.

4. CONTEMPORARY DEBATE ON EMPIRICAL RESEARCH

Considerations such as those raised in the preceding sections have led some, such as Smedslund and Egan, to make the very strong claim that empirical educational research is necessarily pointless. Smedslund (1979) argues that psychology (and we may extend the argument to research into teacher effectiveness) involves a running together of 'the analytic and the arbitrary', that which is true by definition and that which is only of particular or local significance, and hence is arbitrary rather than a constant that is generalisable.

Egan (1983) illustrates this in the context of education by imagining that a hypothesis is set up for empirical examination to the effect that 'presenting lists in an ordered way would be better for learning than presenting them in an unordered way.' The empiricist thinks he should go and look to see whether this is regularly the case. But, says Egan, embedded within this hypothesis is an analytic element, something that is a necessary truth: a list that is ordered in some way has to be better for learning than one that is not because of the conceptual link between learning and order. Learning a list that literally has no pattern, shape or order for one is a logical impossibility. Learning implies understanding, and that in turn necessarily involves giving some kind of shape to what is learned. Mind is such that it necessarily orders, and cannot conceive of what is literally not ordered. Even what is dismissively called rote learning involves imposing some sort of pattern, even if only one of sound, in order to memorise. Meaningful learning by definition involves ordering. There is no need to experiment or observe in order to find that out.

The important question therefore becomes what counts as ordered or what types of ordering prove effective. But it is apparent that different arrangements may appear ordered to different people. A list of numbers that is random to me may have pattern or order for you, because it is your telephone number. This is where the arbitrariness comes in. When we conduct our research with ordered and unordered lists, we perhaps find that some children learn some lists better and others other lists. This cannot be anything to do with the lists being ordered or unordered in any absolute sense, because, as we have already seen, those that are learned must be ordered. Any variations must arise out of different perceptions of what is and what is not ordered. If some children can learn this list more easily than that, but for others the reverse is the case, this must be because the former group sees order where the latter does not, and vice versa. But this means both that in practice researchers who do not grasp the point will make mistakes, imputing ability to learn an unordered list to children who in fact see an order where the researcher doesn't, and that any conclusion from such research lacks any general significance: arranging a list in this particular way is not shown to be a good thing in general, for, from the fact that these children saw order in this arrangement, it does not follow that others will.

Egan goes on to supplement this logical point by offering some illustrations of purportedly empirical discoveries, which in fact are essentially analytic in the manner that, as we have already seen, many claims made about teacher effectiveness are. For example he cites Hilgard's (1956) claim that psychologists have established empirically that 'brighter people can learn things less bright ones cannot', and that 'a motivated learner acquires what he learns more readily than one who is not motivated.' Egan has little difficulty in showing that these are in fact essentially analytic claims that require no empirical verification and have in no way been 'established' by psychologists. They simply had to be true. Bright people are defined partly in terms of their ability to learn things that others cannot. If it were to come to a question of what things bright people can learn that less bright ones cannot, we can move one of two ways: either we define brightness in terms of A, B and C, and catalogue items D, E and F that they learn better than others, in which case we have an empirical finding, but one that could only be generalised if we agreed on the definition of brightness in terms of A, B and C, and found that all such people learned D, E and F better than other people; or we define brightness in terms of learning D, E and F, in which case it is a matter of definition.

The basic point that there is a great deal that is analytic and a great deal that is arbitrary, in the sense of only locally significant (where the local significance arises from the researcher or those who are the object of the research, or both), is obviously correct, and the research we have examined has revealed countless examples of it. However,

Egan surely goes too far in suggesting that empirical research in education is thus inevitably futile. He seems to feel that the chances of a case such as that cited above, where researchers define brightness in terms of A, B and C, and consistently observe bright people thus defined learning items D, E and F better than others, are negligible — that researchers will inevitably fail to clearly distinguish the concept they are examining (brightness) from the effects or correlations they refer to. The evidence suggests that in the past they have so failed, and there is reason to believe that arriving at clearly isolatable and observable concepts is a great deal more daunting a task than is usually appreciated. But I cannot see that it is necessarily impossible. It surely is not impossible to formulate some hypotheses about human interactions that are not simply analytic and that, while they involve arbitrariness in the sense of a particular view of what is ordered (or whatever) that might have been different, can none the less be articulated reasonably clearly so that empirically-derived conclusions may reasonably be drawn. For example, one could reasonably investigate the hypothesis that 'teachers give less attention to girls than to boys.' Egan tends to dismiss such examples as mere number-counting, but descriptions of the extent to which things occur are not to be dismissed simply because nothing automatically follows from them. We need some straightforward data about what is happening, in order to advance to any kind of further theorising or prescription. Furthermore I do not see, in principle, why certain correlations should not be empirically established and give rise to reasonable inferences about cause and effect.

To summarise this important recent contribution to the debate about the research into teacher effectiveness: it is true that much research has involved a fusion of analytic and arbitrary elements; it is true that much will necessarily continue to do so. But it is not true that nothing of a genuinely empirical nature could in principle be established. What stands in the way of that is the impossibility of observing and isolating most of the central concepts in the field of education. But some concepts could in principle be handled in a manner adequate to the task.

It is important also that we should not rebound the other way, and accept the view of Sanders (1978) that the time has come to assume that the sort of teaching techniques researchers study have no effect on the sort of measures of achievement they use. (Although I would agree that they tend to operate with impoverished conceptions of teaching and achievement.) Dunkin and Biddle remark at one point that they 'assume that the activities of teachers are reasonable, natural, rational events.'[67] That seems plausible enough, at any rate if we replace the word 'are' with the phrase 'may be'. But they go on to say that 'they have discoverable causes and effects.' That, of course, does not follow. If there is cause and effect, it is not necessarily the case that it is discoverable by human ingenuity. On the other hand, the fact that it has not been discovered does not necessarily mean that there is no cause and effect. Sanders' argument is that research into teacher effectiveness has not established any relationship between teacher and student achievement. On the other hand, we have the view of those such as Coleman *et al.* (1966), Jencks (1969) and Schletchty (1976) that student achievement is essentially dependent on student ability and socio-economic background. He therefore wishes to conclude that 'differences in teacher behaviour (other things being equal) do not account for . . . differences . . . in achievement.'[68] And he concurs with Johnston (1975) in the view that the skills of a teacher are such as any competent adult should be able to perform and that all that is needed for improvement of practice is 'greater poise and efficiency.'[69]

But as an argument this plainly won't do. The premiss that research has not established any clear links between teacher behaviours and student achievement is correct. But, for exactly the same reasons, research has not established that ability and socio-economic status are the sole determinants of achievement, or that they causally effect it at all. Nothing has been established. Nor is the suggestion that 'teacher behaviours (other things being equal) . . . do not account for . . . differences . . . in achievement' at all helpful, given that in the school situation other things never are equal. The view that the behaviours required of a teacher are nothing out of the ordinary may well be correct, but Sanders ignores the possibility that what makes a successful teacher may be crucially a matter of sound judgement as to when to do what. Granted research has not helped us, and in all probability will not help us, to determine when to do what, what follows is at most that research into teacher effectiveness is not getting us anywhere, not that the teacher behaviours researched into are not very important.

One final aspect of contemporary research should be noted and that is the interest shown by some in Aptitude Treatment Interactions (ATI). Paradoxically, the importance of this movement lies in the fact that it unwittingly spells out the case for taking emphasis off research into classroom interaction. The initial impetus for such research came from an appreciation of the fact that the classroom does not consist in specifiable acts that lead inevitably to certain effects, but rather in a series of interactions, such that the effect of an act might differ depending on the circumstances in which it is performed. Rather naively, Cronbach (1975) subsequently came to observe that 'interactions are not confined to the first order; the dimensions of the situation and of the person enter into complex interactions.'[70] Snow (1977) goes further: such are the complexities of a classroom that what we learn from observation will be 'quite specific, limited in both time and place.'[71] This is really a quite astonishing admission for a researcher who believes that 'instructional theory *is* possible.'[72] For that which is 'quite specific, limited in time and place' is, by definition, not theory in the scientific sense, which is concerned with formulating laws that transcend particularity. Of course, if Snow or anyone else wishes to call this specific account of particular classrooms 'theory', or to say that 'instructional theory' is a special kind of theory, we have no call to stop him. The important point for us to note is that researchers who see their task as only consisting in attempts to describe particular classrooms, forgetting all the problems inherent even in doing that, thereby lend support to the view that the formulation of general rules about the effectiveness of teacher behaviour is a lost cause.

5. TEACHING STYLES AND PUPIL PROGRESS

Two major British studies of the effects of teaching practices on student learning have focused on junior schools.

Neville Bennett (1976) and his associates observed a number of classes taught by teachers using what the project determined to call different 'styles of teaching'. The progress of the children in the different classrooms was measured in three areas over the period of the research by means of standardised tests used at the beginning and end of the period. The areas were English, reading and maths. The conclusions of the research team were that the children taught in a formal style made the most progress in maths and English, and the second most progress in reading. Those taught in an informal style made the second most progress in maths, and the least progress in reading and English. Those taught in a mixed style made the most progress in reading, the second most progress in English, and the least progress in maths. The class that was judged to have made the most progress overall, however, was taught by a teacher classified as informal.

Before we turn to criticism of the nature of this research, it must be acknowledged that there is a further, distinct problem with such projects, which is not directly the responsibility of the research team, and that is that their conclusions are typically treated in a quite uncritical and non-understanding way by the general public, including educational journalists and television and radio reporters. Bennett himself might well believe a great deal less in the worth of his conclusions and in the certainty with which they have been established than summaries of his research in newspapers might suggest.[73] It is none the less a very serious further problem that, typically, research that inadequately and weakly suggests that something could be the case is taken at large to have shown that something is the case. On this particular occasion an interesting side-feature was the way in which a number of traditionally-inclined individuals and newspapers took the research to have established the value of formal methods, while those of an opposite persuasion drew the opposite conclusion. (Liberals felt it showed the value of the middle way.) The truth is that it did not *show* anything, because of the inherent weaknesses necessarily involved in such research. At best it could be said to have suggested certain things.

The main reservations about Bennett's approach are as follows:[74] many important variables were not controlled (one might say that that alone is sufficient to make the research forgettable, since the variables not adequately catered for include such important things as differences in home background of students, differences in experience of the teachers, and differences in home support for the students). The standardised measures of progress used are themselves open to criticism of the sort being directed against research generally and therefore cannot be uncritically assumed to be *bona fide* measures.[75] They cannot even be assumed to be measuring the same thing in different pupils, but they certainly cannot be assumed to be unquestionable detectors of educationally significant achievement for all the reasons referred to above, and now being reconsidered. Whether a particular test truly measures progress is largely a conceptual question about what constitutes progress. The research is set up in such a way as to assume that it is short-term consequences that matter when it comes to evaluating teaching styles, whereas it might well be argued that long-term effects matter rather more. The sample, which involved thirty schools, is far too small on which to base conclusions.

Some of the above weaknesses, as has been pointed out before, are undoubtedly logically removable, and therefore must be accounted as weaknesses in this particular piece of research rather than endemic within research into this kind of matter (and it is the latter that is of prime concern to us). It is not in the nature of things impossible to take a large sample, to concentrate on longer-term effects, or even to take some sort of steps to control some of the variables. However, since our ultimate concern is with finding out what we can reasonably expect to establish with confidence about curriculum matters, these contingent shortcomings should not be underestimated. They are there, presumably, not because Bennett and his colleagues don't know their business, but because though not in the nature of things *logically* impossible to get round, they are in the nature of things extremely difficult, if not impossible, to get round. And, of course, if they are not got round, the conclusions of the research are of no interest to us.

But the major shortcoming of this research lies in the fact that it is crucially dependent on its basic categorisation or classification of teaching styles, and that classification is inadequate both for contingent and necessary reasons. Bennett, having, for good reasons,[76] begun his research with eleven different styles of teaching in mind, in the event operated only with the three mentioned: formal, informal and mixed. The absurdity of this procedure (in terms of any hope of producing reliable information) should be, but manifestly is not, evident to all. If one operates with very broad categories, such that many facets of performance are contained within each one (which in turn is a necessary consequence of operating with few categories), then it is almost certain that there will in practice be no clear instances of any category. No individual, that is to say, is likely to display all and only the characteristics of the broad definition of a formal teacher. Rather, individual teachers will tend to be relatively formal or informal in certain respects, or on balance. Nor does adding a third category which is avowedly a mix between the two solve this particular problem. It will still not be possible to pick out many, if any, teachers who clearly belong to one of the categories. The problem is intensified if, in addition, the characteristics of the various styles are not adequately clarified or not readily perceivable. Working with Bennett's definitions, it is quite possible that you or I would classify some of those whom he regarded as formal teachers as either informal or mixed. And very obviously that could make a great difference to the conclusions that we would be drawing from the same data. There is then the further problem that in working with these broad definitions we are that much further away from establishing any detailed cause and effect, even were our data reliable. Even if there was no question about whether Bennett had established, at least for his sample, that formal teaching is more effective when teaching mathematics, that style is so broadly conceived and involves so many practices that may also be involved in informal or mixed styles of teaching, that we do not have much of a clue as to what precisely it is about this general package known as formal teaching that might have had the effect in question. (If indeed it was something about the teaching rather than, say, the ethos of particular schools.)

In short, it does not seem very profitable to think about teaching in terms of styles, models or types, all of which imply some distinguishable job-lot or package of procedures. Whereas it may seem appropriate to classify cars or dresses in terms of styles, it would be unwise to think in terms of styles of loving or living, save to make the crudest and most general of observations; unwise, because, apart from the difficulty of really knowing about people's styles of love or life, it seems implausible to imagine that there are a small number of distinguishable styles, to one or other of which each person must more or less approximate. The differences between people roughly classed together are probably at least as important as the similarities, and any attempt to classify lovers is therefore almost certainly a distortion of the truth. It may have its uses; it may be appropriate and reasonably accurate to classify some people as relatively submissive and others as dominant for certain purposes, but it is unlikely to prove an adequate account of their characteristics as lovers overall. When all is said and done, Kieran and Susanna are not Tristan and Isolde. Teaching is surely in its logic rather more like loving than it is like an automobile. At any rate, there is absolutely no *a priori* reason to suppose, as is implied by talking about styles and models, that what is important in the teacher's performance is caught in any of the various styles and models that have been produced. It might have nothing to do with the fact that she adopted what was classified as an informal style that led to one teacher achieving more progress with her children overall in Bennett's sample. It might have had nothing to do with her teaching at all; her success might have been due to something like a more sympathetic smile or more patience.[77]

The objection to introducing students of education to the idea of models of teaching and such like is that these broad, package-deal concepts tend to lead to stereotyping. We cease to look at, recognise or even think of the individual nuances. We lump everybody into one of five or six boxes. One of my main concerns here is to make the point that these broad models, styles or categories are bad research tools, but they are also misleading in the wider context of educational theory. Not only will empirical researchers fail to satisfactorily establish much of interest while they operate with broad concepts, but educationalists generally will cease to say very much that is interesting about teaching while they hide, in their casualness of thought, behind broad models of Socrates and the like.[78]

Stenhouse (1975) preferred to talk of strategies of teaching, which is certainly preferable, but I would argue that we need to be more specific still. We have to think of teachers as being particular individuals, doing particular things in particular contexts, and try to research into these particularities. We have surely all had the experience of being familiar with two people who are seemingly and by any general categorisation very similar, but one of whom we like and one of whom we do not. What it is that causes our different reactions may be difficult or impossible to say, but it certainly might not be locatable in some potentially observable difference of behaviour. In the same way, any experienced teacher knows that factors that make a difference in teaching may be slight, unobservable in any systematic way, and seemingly nothing to do with teaching as depicted in the theorists' style or model book. What Jones and Blenkinsop do may be more or less indistinguishable, but successful in Jones' case and not in Blenkinsop's, while Smith, doing the opposite to Jones, is no less successful. Knowing that, as we do, how could any practising teacher take seriously the clumsy attempts of some educationalists to inquire into teaching methods? It is as if one were being asked to look at conservative, *avant-garde* and liberal types of person in order to establish which type was the most kind. The problems involved in defining 'conservative', '*avant-garde*', 'liberal', and 'kind', in classifying people as one or other, in seeing whether their actions were kind, and in drawing any legitimate conclusions about cause and effect, would seem to render the enterprise pointless rather than complex.

6. ORACLE

More recent than Bennett's research into teaching is the Observational Research and Classroom Learning Evaluation Project (ORACLE), conducted from the University of Leicester. Part of this 5-year project involved the study of junior classrooms, focusing on children between the ages of eight and ten years, and was concerned with describing organisation and the patterns of student and teacher behaviour in the classroom, and with the effect of these on student achievement. Steps were also taken to observe aspects of the transition to middle or secondary schools in a longitudinal study, but I shall not comment on that part of the research.

The style of the first two volumes which presented the findings of the research (*Inside the Primary Classroom,* 1980, and *Progress and Performance in the Primary Classroom,* 1980) is distinctive in certain ways. It is presented throughout, rather curiously, in opposition or contrast to the Plowden Report on primary education, which appeared in 1967 and was noteable for its commitment to individualised learning, open classrooms and progressive education. The oddity of this juxtaposition lies in the fact that Plowden was frankly prescriptive rather than descriptive. It did not purport to have researched rigorously into what was going on in classrooms, so much as to recommend what should go on. And, although it may be true that its proposals enjoyed a certain notoriety, it is also the case that the inadequacies in its argument were quickly exposed (Peters, 1967). Its central concepts, such as progressive education itself and discovery learning, were simply not sufficiently clearly articulated or, indeed, apparently, worked out. Perhaps more important, its basic and probably reasonable premiss, that educational development comes about as a result of 'the complex and continuous interaction between the developing organism and its environment,'[79] does not lead directly to its conclusion that individualisation of the educational process is essential, if that is taken to mean that the teacher must constantly treat each child in an individual way. What follows from the premiss that teaching will have different effects on different children is that the learning process in each case will necessarily be unique, *whatever the teacher does*. Whether the teacher needs to approach each individual in a distinctive manner will depend upon whether a particular approach is or is not well suited to gaining desired educational ends with different children, notwithstanding certain differences between them. It certainly does not necessarily follow that uniquely individual teacher treatment is required, feasible or sensible in all situations.

Repeated references to the fact that Plowden recommendations are not much in evidence in the schools therefore appear somewhat irrelevant. It is true that some educationalists, such as certain contributors to what were called the Black Papers,[80] also often referred to by ORACLE, have sometimes written as if all is chaos in our classrooms and have attributed this to the use of progressive methods. But in the first place this is a minority view, and in the second place what such people actually tend to be complaining about is a lack of commitment on the part of schools to a certain fairly specific conception of education. The ORACLE report never reveals what its own conception of education may be, but nothing that it says and nothing that it measures would seem particularly relevant to the question of whether the schools are or are not producing the kind of end-product that such Black Paper contributors want. (I think we may concede that ORACLE shows that, at any rate in its sample, chaos and anarchy are not rife.)

The ORACLE research is also noteable for its repeated references to the inadequacies of Bennett's research into primary teaching. Here the contrast is legitimate, since Bennett purported to be doing the same kind of thing, and most of the specific criticism of Bennett is well founded. But then, since Bennett's research *was* inadequate, there is not much significance in the ORACLE claim to have produced some different findings. However, by constantly setting their own research against these somewhat straw men (an acknowledgedly weak piece of prescription and an undeniably weak piece of empirical research) they are enabled to invest their own conclusions with a good deal more seeming significance than they perhaps have. Certainly, the repeated insistence by ORACLE that its research and findings are 'very important' and 'extremely significant' gives the impression that they do protest too much.

The research methods employed included systematic observation, impressionistic descriptions of classrooms, reference to timetables, and questionnaires. When it came to assessing student achievement a variety of tests were employed, supplemented by teacher-based assessments and certain structured exercises, which served both to moderate or check teacher assessment and to help train teachers in making their assessments.[81] Abbreviated versions of the Richmond tests were used at the beginning and end of the research period to monitor individual increases in competency at basic skills in English and maths. Study skills, such as the ability to draw a block graph, make a map of the classroom, or make the model of a clock face were also tested. In addition, a rather more ambitious attempt was made to monitor progress in 'listening with concentration and understanding, creativity and inventiveness and acquiring information other than through reading.'[82]

The first question to be asked is how reliable these various instruments and tests are. That they have proven reliability in the technical sense that the various people concerned with using them came to exhibit uniformity of judgement is not denied and, indeed, is scarcely surprising, since, on ORACLE's own admission, observers were trained to categorise responses in similar ways, and teachers were encouraged to modify their personal assessments in line with standardised tests.[83] The question therefore is whether the various ways of describing events and measuring achievement were reliable *as means to painting an accurate picture*. In some cases, the answer is clearly, yes. The Richmond style of test is not foolproof, since a child with a very rich vocabulary might by chance be ill-equipped to deal with the specific items presented to him in a test, he might be feeling unwell, etc. But, by and large, to test specific reading skills or aspects of reading ability (e.g. vocabulary) and mathematical competency directly, as these tests do, seems a sensible enough procedure for seeking to measure actual gains in achievement. It is a further question, however, whether these tests are getting to the heart of what we want to know. ORACLE explicitly links its use of the Richmond tests to the aim that children should 'read with understanding' and be able to read 'fluently and accurately'.[84] What precisely one means by these phrases is obviously highly negotiable. But it seems fairly clear that what a 9-year-old child *might* achieve in these respects, and what many of us would hope he would achieve, is not being realistically tested by his capacity to identify synonyms for thirteen words (each to be selected from a list of four words), and to show comprehension of short passages by selecting the correct answer from those given (generally concerned with the ability to 'recognise and understand stated or implied factual details and relationships').[85] Yet, that is all that these tests sought to examine.

When we move on to the other teacher-based assessment tests, even more serious problems quickly appear. Judging whether a block graph or a model of a clock face is well or adequately drawn is not a straightforward matter without agreement on what counts as a well-drawn block graph or clock face. The researchers' answer is, of course, to gain agreement, but that is only agreement amongst those involved in the programme of research. Whether you or I would agree is a further question (and one that cannot be answered, since we are not privy to the material and the actual judgements made on it), as is the question of what precisely competence in these specific study skills should be taken to betoken. There is no obvious reason for the outside world to accept that improved ability to draw a block graph, a map of the classroom or a model of a clock face, by the criteria evolved by the research team, which are not even fully available to us, is telling us much about pupil progress in study skills generally. When we are dealing with recorded differences in achievement between pupils of something in the order of a maximum of 5 per cent, and generally much less, then, bearing in mind all the possible factors that might variously account for the differences, even if they are accurately measured, the whole exercise seems relatively trivial. But the more immediately important point remains that to estimate a 9-year old child's achievement purely in terms of such things as his ability to draw a map of the classroom seems to involve a very impoverished conception of what children might hope and be expected to achieve. One would not be surprised, for example, to find one of the Black Paper contributors complaining that part of what he means when he claims that the schools are not doing their job is that these are the kinds of measure of achievement that people think important.

When it comes to more complex concepts, such as creativity, the weakness of this approach becomes manifest. Creativity is a normative concept. That is to say, it is something that all agree necessarily has some worth. The question of what it is therefore becomes of some importance, since we do not all agree on what does have worth, and we do not wish to find ourselves trapped into approving of things just because they are labelled 'creative'. We want to be sure they are truly creative. Now there is in fact a vast literature on the concept of creativity, most of which convincingly establishes that there is no obvious connection between creativity and so-called creativity tests, and of all of which members of the ORACLE team appear to be entirely ignorant.[86] Their means of testing creativity was to present children with a circle and a V shape on a piece of paper (0>), and to ask them to draw a picture incorporating the two. Marks were then awarded for originality and appropriateness. Originality was assessed simply by reference to the frequency of the response (the more unusual within the group, the more original). Appropriateness was marked according to a scheme evolved through discussion amongst the teachers, the main feature of which was that both shapes should be fully incorporated into a single picture. It is not clear whether children were explicitly instructed to do this. It is not clear therefore whether we are dealing partially with a matter of understanding instructions, or whether we are arbitrarily decreeing that a composition based on two shapes, but not linking them directly, cannot be very creative. Besides which it is far from obvious what counts as fully incorporating both shapes in their entirety in a single picture. Would this count for example?

What we are actually assessing turns out to be the ability of the child to incorporate two full shapes into a single picture, in a way that as few as possible other children do, with further marks being awarded according to the subjective judgement of a panel of teachers on appropriateness. What this has to do with creativity in any real sense is not clear. (There is no evidence at all that standardised creativity tests, of which this is a simplified and slightly confused derivative, correlate with subsequent development and display of creative talent.) More to the immediate point, does it matter whether a child can be judged to have done well at this task, never mind what we call it? Is it an important test of pupil achievement or progress? It hardly seems so to me.

What must concern us in considering the value of this research for curriculum theory and practice is whether any of its conclusions about the effects of different teaching styles on pupil progress deserve to be taken seriously, when the measures of pupil progress are either direct tests of such things as vocabulary, numeracy and rudimentary comprehension, which do not adequately represent achievement in respect of the goals of understanding, fluency and comprehension actually sought, or extremely tenuously related to the complex matters they wish to assess. Certainly it would be valuable to know whether children taught in this way or that thereby develop greater creativity and inventiveness, a greater capacity to listen with concentration and understanding, and an enhanced ability to acquire information both through reading and other channels. But quite apart from problems about inferring cause and effect, and quite apart from the problem of what creativity and so forth actually are, it is surely self-evident that children between eight and ten years of age do not usually become *markedly* more creative or more understanding *in general* in the course of a single term. What they do is acquire particular partial new understanding, new bits of information, new specific abilities, habits, and so on. What we therefore need to know is whether in the short term under view the foundations are being well laid for the ultimate development of the qualities in question in something approaching a full sense. Testing whether children can make a picture out of shapes, identify the sounds of different musical instruments on a tape and recognise pictures of the said instruments, and answer questions relating to a series of pictures that have been shown, would hardly be adequate to that task, even if the subjective element involved in judging whether responses are appropriate, correct or good could be removed. It should also be noted that the tasks to test listening with concentration and understanding were deliberately designed to require a minimal reliance on the ability to read and write (in order not to handicap children with 'conventional learning difficulties').[87] But this divorces the tests still further from the sort of achievement we are actually interested in, since one obvious and very important aim of schools is to develop facility with the written language. Why should we care whether a certain style of teaching does correlate with children's ability to recognise the sound of musical instruments, if what we are trying to do is get them to master the English language, for example?

A similar problem arises with the instruments for observation of classroom events. The authors themselves acknowledge the vulnerability of timetables (which do not always accurately represent what actually happens) and questionnaires (which people do not always fill in honestly, sensibly or with full understanding. Sometimes indeed questionnaires are framed in such a way as to make it difficult to give a truly informative answer: one ORACLE question asks the teacher to respond 'yes' or 'no' to the question 'do you give weekly tests?' Such a question necessitates that those who give twice-weekly tests, two-weekly tests and no tests at all, all have to respond 'no', which hardly helps in producing an accurate picture of what is going on in the classroom). They seem to feel that by using many different instruments the individual weaknesses of each one are somehow cancelled out, so that a true overall picture emerges. That of course is not so. Ten different inaccurate accounts of an event or a situation do not necessarily add up to an accurate one. (Even common denominators may be innacurate representations of reality.) They are just as likely to confuse the issue beyond redemption.

However, the main feature of ORACLE is its reversion to the kind of systematic observation pioneered by Flanders' Interaction Analysis Categories System (FIAC). Using this approach, observers build up a picture of classroom activity by recording at 25-second intervals the behaviour of teacher and children according to various predetermined categories. The observation schedules employed by ORACLE concentrated on the interaction between particular target pupils and teachers, between target pupils and other pupils, on the activity and location of target pupils, on teacher activity and location, and on teacher utterances. These broad categories were broken down into such items as 'target is focus of teacher attention', 'target attempts to be focus of attention', 'target in audience', 'target interacts with teacher', 'adult reacts negatively to behaviour', 'adult interacts with whole class', 'target ignores attempted initiation [by another pupil]', 'target waiting to interact with teacher', 'teacher privately interacting elsewhere with another pupil', 'teacher recalling facts', 'teacher offering ideas [open or closed]', 'teacher making statement of facts', 'teacher telling child what to do', and 'teacher praising work'.

The only reason offered for adopting this approach is that it is systematic. It seems to be wrongly assumed that since this manner of observing is constrained by a clear system, which is undeniable, it must somehow be more reliable as a pointer to truth than any manner of observing that is not so constrained in advance. As we have seen, that is clearly not necessarily the case. The question is whether the system is good (which will depend upon factors such as its lack of ambiguity and the recognisability of the items) and appropriate to the task — that is to say, whether it makes sense to see the complexity of the classroom in terms of some seventy allegedly discrete units of behaviour, formulated beforehand. If we wanted to know whether an individual at a dinner party consistently communicated with one particular person, it makes some sense to look out for specific behaviours at fairly frequently regular intervals; if, on the other hand, we want to arrive at an overall description of the dinner party on its own terms, to give some account of its ebb and flow, its dynamics, it probably doesn't. But in any case the ORACLE observation schedules are not well designed to get at the reality of the classroom, simply because the items are often artificially distinguished, inadequate to fully describe what actually happens, do not focus on what is educationally important, and either require subjective interpretation on the part of the observer or, where that problem is minimised by training observers to see things as the researchers require, are liable to be inaccurate.

There is no obvious reason, for example, why a teacher should not be *both* giving private attention to an individual *and* interacting with the class, or *both* praising work *and* offering ideas and stating facts. If it be said that the observer must decide on the most appropriate of mutually exclusive categories, then we are obviously faced both with subjective judgement and a distortion of reality. A teacher who subtly raises all his questions by means of praising work or effort would not appear in the record to have raised any questions at all. Then there is the question of whether the categories adequately cover what may be happening in the classroom and whether what is covered is of particular educational importance. What about the teacher's ability to evoke enthusiasm, the question of whether children are stimulated, interested, appreciative, taking things in, gaining new insights and so forth — all ignored by ORACLE? True, these kind of happenings would be even more difficult to monitor, but they might be rather more important (on the face of it they certainly seem to be, if our concern is with judging whether we are making good progress in educating people), and they might be what is predominantly going on. This survey, after all, is supposed to give us an accurate picture of life in the classroom, but to do that, it must not only accurately convey a part of what is going on (which it seems far from likely that is). It must also capture the whole. It must therefore, if we are going to accept the approach at all, select the categories that are crucial to the enterprise.

Furthermore, failure to include such items also serves to distort any subsequent inferences about cause and effect or the process-product relationship. It is conceivable that all the alleged differences in outcome can be directly related to something such as teachers' varying abilities to present ideas clearly and to evoke enthusiasm in different situations, an explanation that is arbitrarily ruled out by the systematic exclusion of any such categories from the observation schedule. The third and most obvious shortcoming of this approach is that the various items still have to be interpreted before they can be observed. Some admittedly are simple enough to interpret ('teacher out of room' is straightforward enough, and not liable to lead to discrepancy of judgement amongst observers); but some are not. Whether a teacher is engaged in praising a child or otherwise reacting positively is not always self-evident. Furthermore, what matters in terms of drawing conclusions about process-product is whether the child feels he is being praised, and not whether the observer thinks he is or even whether the teacher intends to praise. One does not need to have much experience of life to know that it is a quite common occurrence for an individual to fail to see that he is being complimented, criticised, etc., even when it seems relatively obvious to others. What constitutes 'negative reaction' on the part of the teacher is clearly subject to fallible judgement, as is the question of whether a target is 'non-involved'. We should note also that the manner of such research places the fallibility of observers beyond our scrutiny. Since we were not there, we have absolutely no way of knowing whether the judgements were absurd or sensible. This leads to the unfortunate consequence that even if the observers were in fact extremely astute and accurate, we have no way of knowing it. We therefore have no good reason to trust their 'findings'. (Replication by other researchers, even if it took place more often and with more encouraging results than it does, would scarcely help since, by the same token, we do not know that it truly does replicate previous research.)

There are two responses to this line of objection that are put forward by ORACLE, neither of which, however, is able to invalidate it. First, it is pointed out that there was substantial agreement in judgement amongst observers. But this is nothing to the point, particularly when they have been trained to make similar judgements; no more is Marxism shown to provide an adequate explanation of events by the fact that a number of Marxists will see things in the same way. Nor, incidentally, does the fact that the category 'not listed' (i.e. a behaviour not specifically coded) was rarely used show, as is claimed, that 'the category system proved to be . . . inclusive'.[88] It *might* indicate that; but equally it might arise because the observers strained to fit every behaviour into the category system they had, because they lacked imagination, or for a number of other reasons. Therefore it does not 'show' anything. Secondly, operationalising the concepts in relatively specific observable terms (e.g. 'looking out of the window' is given as an instance of 'being distracted'; 'the teacher writing on the blackboard' is coded as 'silent *interaction*'!)[89] is plainly inadequate. Although these behaviours are relatively easy to recognise, they suffer from the defect of drifting away from the categories in question: one may look out of the window while concentrating hard, and it is difficult to see what interaction is necessarily taking place when a teacher is writing on the blackboard.

I would not suggest that such an inventory may not give us a reasonably accurate picture of such things as time spent by the teacher in talking, time spent addressing the whole group rather than individuals, or amount of time spent in direct communication between individuals and teachers. But that is merely to say that this formal and systematic approach is really only suited to estimating matters of directly and uncontentiously observable and measurable behaviour. What it clearly does not necessarily give us is a reliable or full picture of what is going on at stated intervals, or a sufficiently subtle description of the lesson overall. It cannot legitimately claim to be discovering 'precisely what is happening in these classrooms'.[90]

There are other general points to be made about ORACLE's methodology. The claim that it is a large-scale study, involving well over 1000 days in the classroom, conducted by observers who were all experienced teachers, is slightly disingenuous. The research team involved some who had never taught at all in any school, and the observers included some who had absolutely no experience of teaching in a primary classroom.[91] Consideration of the details of the research as conducted shows that since each class in the survey was observed for nine days (three days for three terms), and each day was broken into two 55-minute sessions, giving a total of 18 sessions, and since each target pupil was monitored for 4½ minutes per session, the total amount of time spent observing students was 81 minutes. Similar computation shows that each teacher was monitored for 5 hours, 43 minutes. Add that the 'large scale' consisted of 58 teachers in only 19 schools, and that the sample was in no way random, and any idea that there was a full-scale, intensive review of a representative sample of primary classrooms must surely begin to evaporate.

Of course, it does not necessarily follow from the foregoing that what ORACLE has to say is false, only that relying on it is problematic, and that its claim to have unearthed 'a mass of objective data'[92] must be understood to mean no more than that the data were derived in the manner and by the techniques described. Since it has been shown that the manner of research is seriously flawed, that it certainly involves a great deal of subjective judgement both by the research designers and by the observers, and that, more specifically, there is good reason to criticise both the limited nature of the categories as a whole and some of the particular items, it is transparently clear that the data are not particularly objective in the sense of well-founded, reliable or beyond individual interpretation, and that the picture provided is not necessarily any more accurate than the impressionistic view of an unsystematic observer would be.

We turn now to the alleged 'findings'. (The quotation marks and the use of the word 'alleged' are demanded by the inadequacies in the manner of arriving at the conclusions.) The interesting thing here is that, even if there were good reason to rely on them, which, as we have seen, there is not, they are by and large an insignificant lot. As regards the description of the process, we are told that if we extrapolate a typical teacher from the data and a typical student (itself a highly suspect move, since there may be reasons, good or bad, why teachers behave differently in different situations with different pupils, and no teacher is typical), the typical teacher 'spends most of her time in a teaching session interacting with her pupils',[93] while the typical child spends nearly two-thirds of his time working on his own. This asymmetry is described as 'a striking feature of the junior school classroom'.[94] It is again said to be 'striking' how little individual attention the teacher gives to pupils, and the conclusion that 'the bulk of the pupil's interactions with the teacher is as a member of the whole class. Only a small proportion of such interactions are experienced by the pupil as an individual' is yet again described as 'the first striking finding of our study'.[95]

But in what way is this striking, and to whom? In the first place, the general nature of the information is not new ('One of the best-known series of generalisations stated about teaching is the so-called law of two-thirds posited by Flanders (1963). According to this 'law' two-thirds of the time spent in classrooms is devoted to talk, two-thirds of this talking time is occupied by the teacher' (Dunkin and Biddle, 1974).) In the second place there is a certain inevitability about it, if the teacher is going to make any attempt to interact with pupils impartially to any great extent. In the third place, the important question is whether this matters, whether it is of any use for any discernible purpose. It is not striking, unless it is either unexpected, which it evidently isn't, or important for some educationally significant reason, which it has not been shown to be (nor will be, when we consider ORACLE's claims about process-product connections).

Further 'findings' of the study in respect of classroom process are that the typical pupil is actively engaged in preparation for, or some aspect of, direct participation in a task for about 74 per cent of the time, teachers do not appear to invest significantly greater time giving attention to low, high or medium achievers, nor to have more contact or pay more attention to any particular age group, or to either sex to any significant degree, though (again in line with much other research) boys apparently receive slightly more attention than girls.[96] Thus, 'in all three areas of analysis' (achievement, age and sex) 'teachers distribute their attention across the class roughly equally. This is an important finding'.[97] But why, even if we could be confident that this was true of the sample, and that it could be generalised from (which it cannot be, the authors themselves admitting that their sample is not 'representative of primary classrooms as a whole',[98] let alone secondary classrooms), is this important? Only if we can produce some reason to believe that it matters in respect of achieving some educational aim does it even become interesting, let alone important. But, in the event, the 'finding' is not even related to their own tests of achievement, let alone to any adequate educational criteria.

A negative correlation between size of class and the amount of teacher attention is reported. That is to say, the larger the class, the less individual teacher attention each child receives, despite the fact that teachers of large classes appear to try to compensate by spending more time interacting either with individuals or groups than with the whole class. This is to be expected: the larger the class, the harder to give individual attention, even when one tries, because of practical problems of discipline, control and motivation, and because one doesn't want to leave anybody out. Once again we are told that 'these are all important findings which cast a good deal of light on the inner dynamics of the primary classroom'.[99] In fact, they are not entirely reliable findings, nor are they generalisable and, for all that has been said so far, they are quite meaningless details about the time teachers spend addressing themselves to various children. They do not describe the 'dynamics' of the classroom any more than an account of the number and movement rate of pistons in an engine describes the dynamics of the engine.

Information recorded relating to the organisation and management of classrooms includes the claim that most classrooms observed grouped children around tables, and that only about one-fifth of the teachers organised children in homogeneous ability groups for mathematics or languages. This is said to be a different finding from that of the HMI survey (1978) into primary schools.[100] But as the latter asked teachers what they *claimed* to be doing, while ORACLE determined by its own criteria what the teachers they observed *were* doing, there is no direct comparison. Children, though predominantly organised in groups, none the less generally worked individually. Then 'we have another striking finding. The typical interaction is very largely only with pupils of the same sex.'[101]

The typical pupil appears to spend 28.5 per cent of his time on mathematics and number, 36.1 per cent of his time on language, 10.9 per cent of his time on art and craft, and 24.4 per cent of his time on general studies, findings which more or less coincide with the impressionistic conclusions of the HMI survey. It is suggested that the teacher spends only 3.3 per cent of her time on spoken English, but here we have a clear instance of the problems of definition and judgement. Since we have already been told that the teacher spends most of her time talking and interacting, the conclusion that only 3.3 per cent of time is spent on spoken English must involve a very restricted view of what counts as 'spending time on spoken English'. It may be reasonable to work with a restricted definition, and it may be true that in some specific sense only 3.3 per cent of time is spent on it. But since our interest here is in developing language skills, we must surely recognise that general talking and interacting may be just as significant a contribution to that end. We could not, for instance, reasonably conclude that it is clearly a disgrace that only 3.3 per cent of time is spent on spoken English. Discrepancies cited between these findings and the Bullock Report (1975) are therefore quite meaningless, since what Bullock counted as time spent on oral work and writing was not the same as what is meant by ORACLE (and what either mean is not at all clear to the rest of us).

Of teacher-pupil interaction, it is reported that 12 per cent takes the form of questioning of one sort or another, 44.7 per cent the form of making statements, and 22.3 per cent the form of silent interaction. Here the element of subjective judgement by observers becomes more pronounced. First there is the basic question of categorisation. A teacher utterance of the type that offers imaginative suggestions such as, in the context of creative writing, 'the house might be old and creepy with cobwebs and dust and a musty smell,'[102] might just as well be classified as a disguised question as a statement, or as telling a child what to do as a task statement. Secondly, whether a task statement is thought-provoking or stimulating to children is obviously not directly or uncontentiously observable. And the same applies to 'perhaps the most important finding', to the effect that 5.3 per cent of teacher observations have 'substantial cognitive content'.[103] The point is that judgements of this kind require a thorough overall grasp of the lesson and its place in the wider context of the class life, a thorough awareness of the state of mind of the children in question, and a thorough conceptualisation of cognitive content, none of which is catered for in the ORACLE approach.

Obviously no conclusions can be drawn about how we ought to proceed in the classroom from this data as it stands, even if it were reliable. For that we would need some evidence about the effects of these various arrangements and practices. Now in fact most of these findings are ignored when we turn to the ORACLE volume concerned with process-product findings. There is, for example, no attempt to relate the finding that the typical pupil interacts very largely only with pupils of the same sex to anything — no attempt to suggest a context in which its alleged 'significance' might become apparent. Similarly, there is no attempt to relate the practice of making utterances with substantive cognitive content to any outcome. All we are being told, therefore, is that as a result of observing 58 teachers, in a certain rather restricted manner, 5.3 per cent of teachers' utterances are judged, by people who may know little about primary schools and nothing about some of the subject-matter, to contain 'substantial cognitive content'.

In order to tackle the issue of process-product relationships, ORACLE classified the teachers in one of the six styles: 22.4 per cent of them were *individual monitors,* meaning essentially that they had a high level of one-to-one interaction with pupils, did a lot of talking and asked questions mainly of the factual rather than the probing or open-ended kind. They also do a lot of marking; 15.5 per cent were *class-enquirers,* those who engaged in a high degree of class teaching and asked many questions and made many statements introducing ideas and problems; 12.1 per cent were *group-instructors*, those who go in for considerable interaction with pupils as members of groups and whose teaching is largely didactic, their main emphasis being on information rather than, say, problem-solving; 10.3 per cent were described as *infrequent-changers*, those who, for one reason or another, changed their style, but perhaps only once, during the course of observation; 15.5 per cent were *rotating-changers*, teachers who employed a formal arrangement for bodily shifting groups of students around to meet different curriculum requirements; and 24.2 per cent were *habitual changers*, meaning those who engaged in a high degree of not formally planned switching between class and individual instruction.

The alleged findings about the process-product relationship include the following. It is said that there is no best buy amongst teaching styles overall, that while 'the class enquirers were the most successful in mathematics and language skills, it is the pupils of the infrequent changers who make the greatest gains in reading. However in language skills the class enquirers enjoyed no overall superiority from [sic] either the group-instructors or the infrequent-changers. In mathematics the progress of pupils taught by infrequent-changers did not differ significantly from that achieved by the group taught by the class enquirers.'[104] The least successful style would appear to be that of rotating-changers. There is something about a class-based approach that appears to pay dividends where maths is concerned. In basic skills of English there is little significant difference between class teaching, group teaching and infrequent-changers. For high achievers, class-enquirers seemed to have the most effective approach, followed by individual monitors who were otherwise relatively unsuccessful. 'One case where class-enquirers emerged as the most successful teachers was in their pupils' ability to pose suitable questions.'[105]

It is gratifying to hear that there is no best buy, because nobody who thought about the variety of contexts, people and subjects being taught could ever have reasonably supposed there was, and indeed the only impetus for so believing came from earlier empirical researchers. Some of the other findings too seem *a priori* reasonable. Adopting the style of a rotating-changer, given that that term implies a high level of disruption in the classroom, surely does not seem a very sensible way to approach teaching, given the problems of concentration and discipline that it can give rise to. The difference between class-enquirers and infrequent-changers is said to be slight, but this may be because the latter were class-enquirers part of the time. It seems predictable that high achievers should be able to cope effectively with an enquiry-approach, since if there is any correlation between achievement on the tests employed and general educability, such students will be more responsive to open situations. The fact that students of class-enquirers were relatively competent at posing suitable questions is presumably a direct consequence of the fact that they have been encouraged and allowed to pose questions. The conclusion that different subject-matter may favour different approaches is likewise supported by reason: the nature of studying maths is decidedly different from engaging in creative arts, as defined, and one would no more expect a similar approach to be profitable than one would expect a cricket coach to proceed as if he were teaching physics.

So none of this seems very surprising. But it has not been proved to be the case or demonstrated by research, and it is not very helpful. It has not been proved, partly because of the shortcomings in acquiring data about child and teacher behaviour, and partly because of the inadequacy of the tests of achievement, both of which have already been referred to. But it has also not been proved partly because of the inadequacy of the categories of teaching style, and partly because of general problems about inferring cause and effect.

Essentially, these styles take us back to the days of broad generalisations. These are categories that may place individual teachers with crucially different characteristics in the same basket, as 'clever people' may exhibit their cleverness in very different ways or as fruits, while being fruits, may be remarkably different from one another, so that pinpointing what, if anything, causes what effects is going to be exceedingly difficult. And different observers might have classified the teachers differently or the same observers might have classified the teachers differently on different evidence. (Compare s.5, above). (To be accurate, since this is a *post eventum* classification, we should say that data derived from observation on a different occasion or by different observers might have yielded different classifications.) For example, few people are unambiguously class-enquirers, as defined, at all times. Some will for the most part act as class-enquirers, some will arguably but not certainly act as class-enquirers, and some will sometimes appear to be class-enquirers, but not always. The observation that 15.5 per cent of the sample were class-enquirers therefore needs to be understood for what it is: not the observation that as a matter of fact 8.99 teachers were adopting exactly the same stance throughout the period of research, but that nine teachers, despite proceeding differently from one another in various ways, specifiable and unspecifiable, and despite individually varying their own pattern and pace to some extent, and notwithstanding many other differences between them that may or may not be significant in respect of effective teaching (e.g. warmth, humour, sensitivity, awareness, clarity), can be roughly grouped together by a few rather imprecise criteria. Anybody who then, accepting a correlation between group-enquirers, thus categorised, and students making progress on the particular measures of achievement in question, drew any conclusions about cause and effect, would obviously thereby open himself to a certain amount of ridicule.

Furthermore, the relationship between the different elements in the accounts of the various styles seems to vary. Sometimes there is a logically necessary relationship: the bodily moving of students according to different subject requirements seems to be an essential part of the definition of a rotating-changer. Sometimes the connection appears to be contingent, but indirectly logically implied: the fact that individual monitors do a lot of marking seems to arise, for fairly predictable but not inevitable reasons, out of what they are defined as, rather than to be part of the definition. For the most part the elements seem to be contingently related to one another. Why, for example, should individual monitors, as otherwise defined, necessarily be didactic? This further confuses the chances of making anything of any correlation between process and observed product. Perhaps individual monitors are found to correlate highly with student achievement X. But is that a consequence of a one-to-one relationship or of being didactic (assuming it has anything to do with either)? Since the two could easily be divorced, this is a question of considerable importance.

We turn now to the question of inferring cause and effect. An inference about cause and effect is reasonable in so far as a correlation is observed repeatedly in controlled conditions. But in such research as this replication is minimal and, far from being controlled, literally hundreds of variables are not even thought of. Who is to say, for example, that some one or more of the children in the ORACLE survey were not materially affected in their performance by factors such as their liking for the teacher, the support they received at home, the clarity of the teacher's exposition, their respect for any teacher, a nagging toothache, a general lack of confidence, a desire to do better than their best friend, a liking for a particular subject, things they have seen on television, their ability to read, a chronic inability to sleep, the desire to make use of a new pen, and so on and so forth? And yet such possibilities were not even considered by ORACLE. Furthermore, in every individual case the effect of a particular variable may be different, because it combines with a different set of other factors. Thus even something like home support may work productively with one child and counter-productively with another, or serve to help a particular child in respect of one subject and not in respect of another. It is possible, and in fact quite likely given the number of variables at work (each of which, however long the list, could be further subdivided; there are, for instance, numerous different types of home support) and the vast number of combinations they give rise to, that each interaction between teacher and pupil will be literally unique. How can one hope to replicate and control unique events?

ORACLE's attempt to answer this fundamental objection to the nature of such research is the well-worn one of carrying out statistical exercises controlling the variables one by one. But this completely misses the point which is not that it might have been this factor rather than that, that causes the outcomes in question, but that hundreds of factors are not even being considered and that it might have been a different and unique set of factors in each case. (More realistically, perhaps, that several different explanations might account for the same outcome with different children).

Let us for the moment keep the matter ludicrously simple and quite unrealistic by imagining that there are only five conceivable factors that could account for pupil progress, and that those five factors are entirely unambiguous and observable. Let us say that the variables are style of teaching, sex, age and socio-economic status of the child, and the nature of the subject being taught. Even if, working on these assumptions, by some miracle we found that girls *always* do better at maths when taught by style A, regardless of age and socio-economic status, we could not legitimately conclude that style A should always be adopted in teaching maths to girls. For it may be that, although age and socio-economic status appear to be irrelevant, since there is no marked correlation between either one and achievement, what has happened is that some girls have done very well because the style of teaching somehow harmonises with their age, and others because it somehow harmonises with something in their socio-economic background. It therefore might be the case that style A would be a poor one to adopt with, say, a very young, rich girl, despite the fact that it appears to have worked well with girls, old and young, rich and poor.

Now of course, as soon as one states the possibility, the empirical researcher can argue that all that needs to be done now is to test this new hypothesis: does style A work well with young, rich girls? But the point is that in any given piece of research there are countless possibilities that they never do in fact think of and test. And now we have to face up to the reality: given the number of possible variations there is no way anybody is going to be able to control and test for all possibilities. Nor indeed are researchers going to be able to think of some of them, so long as they continue to construe a negative correlation as evidence that a certain factor is not significant. If, that is to say, they see that there is no obvious tie-up between a particular age and achievement at maths, and therefore conclude that age is not significantly related to achievement, they are hardly going to be disposed to conduct experiments to see whether it is after all. If, contrariwise, they see the point of what I am saying and don't treat negative correlations as an indication of no significant relationship, their whole approach becomes suspect: they collect correlations in the awareness that whether they are positive or negative may be neither here nor there.

Besides, continuing now in realistic vein, we do not get miracles. We do not discover that all girls do best at maths when taught by style

A, and the like. We get figures of this order: 60 per cent of girls do well at maths with teaching style A, 40 per cent with teaching style B. Such a finding plainly implies that, whatever the actual causes of these effects, style A does not *necessarily* suit girls. So what are we supposed to *do* with the finding? Ignoring the fact that figures of this sort obtained from observing 20 or so classrooms might easily turn out to be reversed if we studied another 20 classrooms, what teachers need to know is what it is best for them to do with particular classes. They are receiving no help on this question at all from such research.

If we now bring back into consideration the fact that we are not dealing with five readily identifiable factors, but at least several hundred far from readily identifiable factors, the vast majority of which are not even being considered by the researchers, it becomes clear that we are necessarily getting nowhere. There were 489 target pupils in the ORACLE study and, although we know how each one of them performed on various tests at the beginning and conclusion of the study, we do not have the beginnings of a confirmed or demonstrated idea of what explains their various individual rates of progress.

To this it may be said that, although it is true in principle that there are many explanations of pupil progress and that each child might make progress, or lack of it, for different reasons, that is not very plausible in practice. Common sense suggests that this or that are likely to be significant factors in a way that other things are not. In some cases, I quite agree. For example, it seems to me highly unlikely that those researchers who set out to examine correlations between teachers' eye colour and pupil achievement were on to anything likely to be important,[106] and I think ORACLE's suggestion that different subject matter may be suited to different styles of teaching eminently sensible. But if we bolster and modify the research by common sense and *a priori* reasoning, then the whole enterprise falls flat. The point of empirical research is supposed to be to *demonstrate* something, to confirm or falsify the hypotheses of reason. This it totally and utterly fails to do, if it is admitted that the particular findings are arrived at by a process of common sense interpretation of inadequate data.

There is no contradiction, therefore, in my saying that I think some of ORACLE's conclusions, though of very little practical significance for the teaching enterprise, are probably true. I think it highly likely, as already indicated, that teachers need broadly to modify their manner of teaching with different subject matter, that too much routine and formalised shifting about of children is distracting, that 'class-directed activities' are liable to prove useful in 'cutting down the amount of distraction',[107] and indeed that some variant of class teaching involving a fair amount of thought-provoking questioning (roughly corresponding to ORACLE's class-enquirers) is likely to prove, generally, most effective for pupil progress in mathematics, reading and language.

But there is more than a smack of tautology about those findings. (Disrupting seating arrangements is disruptive; directing the whole class minimises lack of direction and attendant distraction; engaging the whole class, by whatever means, and provoking thought in them would be part of most people's definition of successful teaching, but particularly so if the tests of achievement are going to involve children in open-ended and relatively undirected activities, as some of ORACLE's tests do.) In other words, one can argue that such conclusions are *a priori* reasonable, if not actually analytic. What we cannot do is say that the ORACLE survey has done anything to confirm them empirically. It is simply not the case, for *all* the reasons given, and not simply the impossibility of establishing specific cause and effect, that the ORACLE research has *shown* that to teach maths successfully you need to adopt the style of group enquiry, or anything else about the process-product relationship.

7. CONCLUSION

This chapter has given detailed consideration to a number of programmes of research into aspects of teacher and student behaviour. The research covered in the first three sections all emanated from the United States and it is drawn from a period of fifty years. It is ironic, not to say sad, that at a time when the overall contribution of such research has come to be seriously and tellingly criticised, even by those with considerable experience of, and commitment to, the field, the manner of such research is being belatedly and uncritically adopted in England in such projects as ORACLE. It is clear from the evidence we have scrutinised that what has and is being done by way of empirical research is inadequate to tell us anything secure and important about how teachers ought to proceed in the classroom. It is also clear that the major shortcomings of such research are its conceptual inadequacy and the inappropriateness of systematic observation techniques to the subtleties of human interaction. It is not true that nothing of any significance for education could in principle be examined and verified. But what is true is that most of the crucial and interesting concepts in education, not only have not been, but could not conceivably be, adequately framed in isolatable and observable terms, and therefore cannot be satisfactorily empirically researched. In order to furnish something of value, empirical research will need to confine itself to noting correlations between unambiguous, essentially observable concepts. In the present state of our ignorance, curriculum theory has no right to draw on alleged rules of teaching, and no cause to demand that students scrutinise the body of meaningless conclusions.

Part III:
CURRICULUM DEVELOPMENT

7 Curriculum Implementation

1. THE RELATIONSHIP BETWEEN PLANNING AND IMPLEMENTATION

Curriculum design is concerned with the manner in which a curriculum proposal should be set out or presented; students of curriculum design are interested in establishing a more or less rigorous account of what kinds of factor, and in what degree of detail, need to be included in a curriculum submission. (See Chapter 3.) I have suggested that in practice this concern with setting out one's stall in terms of what needs to be included as a matter of good curriculum design in some absolute sense, regardless of subject or other differences, shades imperceptibly into a concern for setting out one's stall in such a way as to sell one's product, regardless of its educational merits. We thus find students of curriculum design moving from consideration of what a teacher needs to know in order to make proper use of a curriculum proposal, to consideration of what the teacher and others need to be told in order to persuade them to adopt it.

Perhaps this tendency to run together the tasks of fully explaining a curriculum and successfully marketing it is partly a consequence of one point that almost all curriculum specialists seem agreed upon — namely, the difficulty in practice of actually succeeding in implementing curriculum innovations as intended. Kelly (1975) has produced figures relating to science education in Britain which suggest that, some five years after the working-out and widespread advertising of a new curriculum, 20 per cent of schools at which it is aimed may remain unaware of it, while only 10-20 per cent of them will have actually adopted it. Furthermore, some of those schools that have adopted it will not have done so in a manner faithful to the original intentions of the planners.

This last point is scarcely surprising if trust can be placed in Fullan and Pomfret's (1975) observation that sometimes teachers cannot even identify the main features of a curriculum programme they are attempting to implement. In general, as Taylor and Richards (1979) say, the evidence overwhelmingly suggests that most teachers in Britain proceed haphazardly in their overall programme of teaching, rather than in response to coherent curriculum planning or theory. (The situation is necessarily different in North America, where in many areas central direction of curriculum is stronger.) For every curriculum development which is successfully implemented, such as the Nuffield Latin Project in Britain, or the spread of New Maths in the United States (though even in these cases many individual teachers in adopting the curricula in question made major changes to them), there are many that never get as far as the schools, and many that, when they do, alter beyond recognition from the original design. (Reference to the successful implementation of the Nuffield Latin Project and the New Maths curriculum should not be taken to imply that these were necessarily desirable innovations. We are concerned only with the point that a few curriculum proposals do gain acceptance, not with the question of their value. Nor should reference to the more central direction of curriculum in North America be interpreted to mean that North America has solved the problem of curriculum change. It may be relatively easy for the long arm of provincial government in British Columbia to impose a new curriculum on teachers. It does not follow either that the curriculum will be faithfully implemented or that it deserves to be.)

Some of the reasons for this state of affairs are not hard to locate. It has been suggested many times (e.g. Waller, 1938; Lortie, 1975) that teachers are in general conservative by nature. And there are considerations that are liable to make individual teachers antagonistic to change: there is little incentive in the form of career advancement, or other external rewards, for them to innovate; change would require considerable investment of time and energy on their part. Attempting to engineer change exposes one in a variety of ways to the rebukes of headteachers and School Boards, the cynicism of colleagues, and the possibility of failure. There are material obstructions in the way of progress, such as inadequate resources, ranging from lack of time and shortage of materials or teaching aids, through to lack of cooperation and support from colleagues, headteachers or government, not to mention the suspicions of children and parents. The pernicious credibility gap between theory and practice, which is to say the false but entrenched belief that theory is somehow divorced from practice (spawned in large part by a long history of poor theory), also upsets the prospects of curriculum innovation to some extent, as does the fact that some curriculum projects don't serve either the school or the university too well, as they try desperately to serve both. (The phrase 'image manipulation' has been coined to refer to this process of trying to stress one aspect of a curriculum to one audience, and another to another — trying, for instance, to make the proposal look 'practical' to teachers, and 'academic' to fellow academics.)

It can hardly come as a surprise to curriculum theorists that many hours of hard work go for nothing. What is more surprising is that curriculum experts tend to assume that this is obviously a *sad* state of affairs. But is it necessarily so? There is, as we have seen, an implicit assumption in much curriculum design and development that things, or at any rate some things, need changing. Indeed that assumption seems to be logically demanded by the idea of development, if not of design. And to that assumption is very often added the further implicit one that constant change is more or less inevitable and desirable. But both of these assumptions, particularly the latter, are far from self-evident. (We should note also that it seldom seems to occur to anyone that changes might legitimately involve reversion to older plans and practices: change does not necessarily demand novelty.) But even if the notion of curriculum development necessarily implies a need for change, the notion of curriculum theory certainly does not, and it might conceivably be the case that curriculum theory suggested no need for curriculum development. One might, as a curriculum theorist, be concerned to understand, explain and estimate the worth of current practice and, conceivably, one might conclude that all is well at least at the theoretical level, so that any failures should be seen as failures of carrying out curriculum prescriptions rather than failures in curriculum planning.

I doubt whether anybody does think quite that, but it is important to resist jumping from the observation that the majority of curriculum innovation planned outside the school does not get successfully adopted in the schools, to the conclusion that that must be a bad thing. At least some curricular proposals deserve to be rejected for a number of good reasons, such as that they are ill-thought-out, badly presented, don't serve the ideals of schools or teachers, or are impractical or unnecessary. There is no merit in change, unless it is believed that it can clearly bring more desirable results or more rapid results, and it is arguable that that would seldom be the case with the curriculum innovations that are proposed. It is further arguable that some innovations have, in the event, merely proved disruptive and demoralising to teachers and children alike, while others have completely changed the nature of the contribution a subject makes, without the schools necessarily being aware of it. That would seem to have been the case with modern techniques of language teaching that, for better or worse, make the nature of studying a foreign language a completely different kind of experience from what it used to be, and therefore require a completely different justification. To learn to speak a language for the purpose of daily communication (which is the emphasis of modern techniques), is very different from studying a language in order to understand something about language as such, which was the emphasis of earlier styles of instruction (Barrow, 1981).

We have to guard against reacting to the realisation that much curriculum design in the past has got nowhere in practice, by placing too much emphasis on selling it in the future. Assuming that we are concerned with worthwhile curriculum planning, we have to be careful that the laudable desire to see our curriculum become reality, does not become confused with attempts to present it compellingly or to sell it, in such a way that devices for implementation become aspects of design. It is understandable that some curriculum designers should come to the conclusion that 'the process of implementation is one of persuading people to make certain decisions' (Pratt, 1980),[1] but the dangerous implications of that view should not be glossed over: persuasion may take a number of forms, from rational argument to beguiling bewitchment, and the only kinds of implementation technique that deserve any place in the planning of curriculum are rational ones. In the context of politics we are familiar with the idea of many proposals, some of them rationally based, others the product of ideology, foolishness or self-interest, being tarted up, watered down or otherwise modified, precisely in order to attract votes or please the electorate. Whatever the merits of such activity there, we certainly don't want it here in the context of education, where we have a plain duty to seek out good reasons for doing educationally worthwhile things. So, although it is undoubtedly true that getting school teachers on your side by consulting with them, involving them in the planning, or by pandering to their whims, getting political support, and being funded by government sources, are effective devices for being taken seriously, and thus enhance the chances of implementation of one's curriculum, they are things that belong there — to the stage of implementation — if they belong anywhere, and not to the stage of design or planning.

A distinction needs to be drawn between concern for implementation in the sense so far discussed, and concern for implementation in the sense of putting a particular curriculum into practice. The former is a broadly political question of getting people to take up a curriculum proposal; the latter involves concern with explaining one's proposal in a way that teachers can make sense of and put into practice. The two may be related, in as much as teachers are more likely to be impressed by what they understand and regard as feasible, but they should not be confused. When outlining a rationale for one's curriculum, and when outlining the curriculum proposal itself, one should of course seek to do so in a clear, coherent and logically persuasive manner. What one should not do, unless we frankly admit that we are in the business of substituting honeyed words for sound argument, is incorporate into one's curriculum outline buzz-words that, while being vague and confused, are known to appeal to teachers, or references to popular but incoherent aims, and fashionable but unproven activities, simply in order to render the proposal attractive. The question of what is politically persuasive has to be kept entirely separate from our thinking about the curriculum itself. It is no argument against the desirability of a Grand Design for curriculum that teachers may resent having one imposed, just as it is no argument for specifying behavioural objectives that teachers may welcome them. If teachers are to be involved in planning curricula it must be because they are well qualified to do so, and not because it will keep them sweet. A persuasive curriculum is not necessarily a good one; a curriculum that fails readily to gain acceptance is not necessarily a bad one.

2. IMPLEMENTING CURRICULUM

In the remainder of this chapter my concern will be with what can be said about implementing curriculum change, or selling the product, *on the assumption that we have already produced a rationally defensible proposal.* Considerations of implementation should only be allowed to affect design when nothing is at stake in terms of the curriculum rationale.

A common and useful distinction is that between the formal adoption of a curriculum and what actually results when it has been adopted. Another distinction may be drawn between curriculum *diffusion*, referring to the manner in which a curriculum comes to be taken up or adopted, and curriculum *dissemination*, referring to the means adopted to try and ensure that it is taken up. Whatever words are used to mark those distinctions, it is important to recognise both that the means adopted to try and promote a curriculum are not necessarily the means whereby it actually comes to gain acceptance, and that formal adoption of a curriculum does not necessarily mean that it will be realised in a way that its originators intended.

A number of models of dissemination have been proposed, including the social interaction model, associated particularly with House (1974) and Havelock (1971), the centre-periphery model, the proliferation of centres model, and the shifting centres or learning systems network model, all three outlined by Schon (1971). But we need to beware of being misled, either by the reference to models or by the titles of the models themselves, into thinking that we are faced with clear and rigid alternatives. Although some of them fit certain aspects of curriculum dissemination fairly well (for example, new practices in England have for the most part been introduced in terms of the social interaction model), 'there is a good deal of overlap between these schemes and models' (Kelly, 1977).[2] The major distinction of importance is between some form of external impetus towards change in the schools, as reflected in the social interaction model and variants of the centre-periphery model, and some form of school-based curriculum development as reflected in Havelock's problem-solving model (1971). The precise-sounding and somewhat mechanistic titles of the various models are no more than labels designed to focus attention on particular aspects or emphases of a complex and far from systematic reality. The models represent artificial distinctions on a continuum between a view of implementation that involves imposing change directly from the top, through one that involves working through various more local agencies, to one that involves encouraging change to emanate from particular school situations.

Adopting the social interaction model means no more than seeing educational systems as 'complex networks of social relationships',[3] which they indubitably are. What one says next depends upon how precisely you see those complex networks. House (1974) conceives the educational network of social relationships as being comparable to an urban rather than a rural social setting, and hence more prone to influence by factors of size than by factors of distance. Just as large centres of population are thought to carry a message more effectively in respect of social change, in an urban context, so House feels that school innovation is most successfully engineered through concentrating on certain prominent schools. The centre-periphery model, as its name implies, envisages a central agency, such as the NFER or a School Board, distributing curriculum plans and ideas to potential users via local centres in various areas. The proliferation of centres models involves the idea of local centres taking on a more autonomous role, so that curriculum development is a more localised business, while the learning systems network model posits a number of shifting centres of curriculum innovation not based on existing local centres such as teachers' centres, but brought into being by interest in particular curriculum ideas. These models possibly do have some use as starting positions for consideration of what paths of curriculum change might be followed. But a model, any model, is essentially a hypothesis, to be discarded once it has been introduced in order to make a suggestion (see Chapter 3,s.4).

Models should not be used as if they were prescriptive theories. It is not, for example, an established fact that the best or the only way to successfully implement a curriculum, is to place it firmly in a number of large and notable schools. House's model merely serves to introduce that idea. No doubt that is one way to proceed, but it is certainly not a guarantee of success and there are other ways to choose from. Curriculum theorists need to understand what exactly happens when particular proposals are introduced in particular ways in particular settings. They need to advance rapidly beyond the stage of formulating models, since a model will necessarily be oversimplified, and more or less inappropriate to particular situations. To cling to it as other than a short-hand way of summarising one specific possibility is bound to be misleading. And if anyone were to be led to adopt a model as the correct one, and to act on it exclusively, that would be positively harmful. For it is not true that curriculum dissemination does take precisely any one of these forms, nor that it should. The word 'model', with its connotations of certainty, clarity and being a representation of reality, is being used for what are no more than unrealistically crude, uncertain and unclear accounts of possible ways of curriculum dissemination. For those reasons, I do not think that it is particularly profitable to conduct an extended examination into models of curriculum dissemination. What is required by the student of curriculum is simply an awareness of the agencies and considerations that may affect the attempt to implement curriculum.

The list of people and factors that may affect the outcome between initial stages of planning and ultimate implementation is long. If I wish to see my physics curriculum adopted, there are numerous people who may need to be persuaded of its value, including government ministers and their subordinates, local government officials, education authorities and School Boards, school inspectors, headteachers, teachers themselves, and parents. These people need to be won over and, in varying degrees, induced to act in, or at least comply with, the ways required by my proposals so that they do not unwittingly sabotage the curriculum. In practice, probably at least as significant in preventing successful curriculum innovation as any overt objections from those in power or deliberate shop floor sabotage, is unintentional failure at the level of adoption. That is to say, the distortion of a plan by those who do not fully appreciate its point, and as a result actually achieve something different from the planner's intentions.

It is this last consideration that particularly inclines some people to argue for teacher-proof curriculum design or, more weakly, for very precise specification in curriculum planning. It has also led some, such as Stenhouse (1975), to argue, in a seemingly contrary way, that effective curriculum change can only come about with teacher-participation in research and design. One can quite understand the thinking here, but these are none the less clear examples of cases where considerations of implementation seem to get in the way of planning. The idea that simply because teachers would take research in which they were involved more seriously they should therefore necessarily be involved in it, is to be resisted, even though, other things being equal, it would certainly be worth involving them. It is to be resisted as a principle, because there is no evidence to show that curriculum research or design involving teachers is in any way necessarily any better or as good as non-school-based research, even if it were true that it is more readily accepted. What is the value of greater success at getting research and design accepted if the work in question is no good? Similarly, teacher-proof curriculum design would be most valuable, if it were the case that designers necessarily know how to produce sound and worthwhile curricula, and that teachers know nothing. But neither is necessarily the case. Insisting on centrally (or even centre-peripherally) imposed changes in the schools, as a principle, would be equally foolish.

The truth is that there are no correct or easy answers to the question of how change should be implemented (that is why the models are misleading and unhelpful). To some extent the manner of dissemination that will succeed will vary culturally, as a result of different traditions and expectations. A ministry directive in Ontario will be more acceptable to teachers than a ministry directive in Leicestershire, because that is more in line with the way of things in Ontario. But what is required is a flexible approach to implementation, perhaps with some emphasis on area organisation so as to make full allowance for local conditions, and so as to encourage local participation. If it is standard procedure to operate through a centralised state agency in Tennessee, there is no obvious inherent objection to continuing in that way, requiring curriculum proposals to go via that route. On the other hand, if Oxfordshire has a tradition of curriculum research based on schools, why should it not continue in that tradition? We do not require a fixed policy on the route whereby curriculum change should be introduced. What we require is that local expectations should be taken account of, that where there is an attempt to introduce new curricula from outside the schools, it should be brought to the schools by way of local figures and agencies, and that where schools are interested in and competent to handle curriculum change, they should be free to engage in it. That seems a matter of plain common sense.

The crucial points remain that a curriculum proposal should be a well-planned one and that its adoption should be undertaken with understanding. The question of who should be involved in planning it cannot be answered by picking out particular groups. The qualifications for being involved are interest and the ability to make a clear and reasoned case for a proposal. Successful adoption can only come about through a reasoned articulation of the nature of the programme, set against understanding of what facts we may have relating to children and schooling.

Beyond that, selling the curriculum is indeed a matter of psychological and diplomatic political manoeuvring. But it is easier to sell a well-thought-out plan to those with requisite understanding than it is either to sell such people an ill-thought-out plan, or to sell the well-thought-out plan to those without understanding. In just the same way, good hi-fi equipment sells itself to those who know about hi-fi. Free gifts and sales techniques only need to be added if the equipment is poor, or the customers are ignorant.

This, I think, suggests something supremely important: emphasising the ways of implementation, particularly if that leads to tampering with planning in order to make the product more saleable, or even regarding packaging and selling as part of the remit of the planner, is a misconceived emphasis. Rather, we should concentrate on educating the teaching force, and others concerned with education, so that it is more receptive, not to the idea of curriculum change itself, but to understanding and thinking about the nature of curriculum and schooling. Teachers should, so to speak, be encouraged to ponder over the earlier chapters of this book rather more than over this one. This approach may lead on occasion to involving teachers more in research and design, but it is not necessary that it should.

The solemn truth is that at present some attempts at curriculum implementation involve little more than a poor plan, drawn up with the meticulous detail of a plan for a rocket, but serving no discernible educational end, being thrust at people in positions of some power, such as education authorities or headteachers, who would not be well placed to judge a good curriculum proposal if they were invited to, who then in turn impose it on teachers who may be in a similar position, and who in addition have no desire to change their ways. Yet research into the efficacy of curriculum implementation seldom, if ever, takes account of this, but proceeds as if the quality of a proposal and the competence of those involved had no bearing on the question of successful implementation.

To improve the planning of curricula would obviously be a good thing in itself and must be the first priority; but it must be conceded that that would not be enough in itself to ensure improvement in school curriculum, for the reasons given. To educate or re-educate educationalists of all sorts, however, would be enough to ensure discrimination between good and bad research and good and bad proposals, and, if it were so successful as to lead to good planning, it would solve most of the problems of implementation. The reason that medical innovation is relatively successful, while industrial innovation runs less smoothly, has got less to do with varying strategies of implementation, than with varying degrees of understanding. Doctors can more readily see the desirable innovations in medical practice than the industrial workforce can in industrial practice. So long as the educational workforce has as little understanding and consensus on the nature of the whole enterprise as it does, it resembles the industrial workforce more than the medical workforce, and getting changes adopted must predominantly be a matter of the blind finding ways successfully to coerce the blind. Once the workforce becomes proficient at gaining some genuine understanding of the nature of the enterprise, implementing will become a matter of rational dialogue.

3. UNDERSTANDING CURRICULUM CHANGE

Much research in the area of curriculum implementation is less concerned with putting forward strategies for achieving successful change than with understanding what goes on at present between the drawing board and the death or adoption of a programme. That is, in principle, an important and useful service just as, in principle, research into what goes on in classrooms is important and useful. However, exactly the same reservations must be entertained about the former as the latter, and for exactly the same reasons. Research into implementation cannot claim to have succeeded in revealing any certain laws; it cannot even claim to have been conducted satisfactorily, given the complexity of the business, the human element involved, and the conceptual problems, which result in it having proved impossible in practice to generate any reliable generalisations about cause and effect, other than commonsense observations or truisms.

We may be told that 'changes arise because the society is discontented with the ways schools function' (Orlosky and Smith, 1978),[4] but this scarcely needs stating, let alone researching. Or, in more detail, it may be argued, as by Doll (1970), that the four factors that most obviously effect curriculum change are the drive for power on the part of individuals or groups, money, in the form of generous grants for particular proposals or the interests of business (for example, in marketing a certain reading course), developments in our knowledge, and the needs and concerns of people. Such commonsense observations hardly bear on the questions of why one particular programme takes off in one area and not in another, why another programme doesn't take off at all, or what we should seek to do to ensure the successful implementation of a good curriculum proposal.

When it comes to more specific questions, such as how we are to determine the appropriate moment to introduce change or how we are to select appropriate schools or teachers, not surprisingly, in view of the nature of the problem and the research, we do not have any clear answers. For these reasons, and because of the extensive treatment I have given to the subject of educational research in the previous chapter, there seems no justification either for summarising the 'findings' of research into implementation, or for laboriously working through case studies to illustrate yet again how little that is both generalisable and important can be gleaned from them. If the reader is inclined to suspect laziness on my part, he should bear in mind that, given the necessary reservations about all such research, to offer a list that includes A's conclusion that X, B's finding that Y, and C's observation that Z, is a positive disservice. However much we formally acknowledge that these are insecure claims, they will tend to add up to a certain kind of picture or view — one which in fact there is no warrant for adopting, even if it happened to be to some extent true. Far more profitable would be that we should all *think* about the multiplicity of factors and the incalculable number of different combinations of these factors that may effect our chances of successful implementation.

But in so far as the reader cares to read a book such as MacDonald and Walker's *Changing the Curriculum* (1976)[5] and does thereby acquire some suggested information about curriculum change and implementation, the above discussion should serve to reinforce the point that any such tentative knowledge should be used only to explain and understand what does currently happen. We have no right and no reason to treat this gathering of information about what goes on as a preliminary exercise to prescribing means that *should* be adopted to achieve ends. What does happen ought not necessarily to happen, and some things that do not happen perhaps ought to happen. For example, perhaps the most obvious conclusion to be drawn from the observation that marketing forces are influencing curriculum is that this should be fought against; while the widespread absence of rational adoption of sound curriculum ideas should not deter us from pressing for it.

It is indeed important that we find out, if we can, whether certain curriculum proposals are partly defeated by, say, the opposition of headteachers. But it does not follow that we should forthwith devise ways of getting round headteachers. (Still less does it follow that such head-circumventing strategies should be built into curriculum design.) After all, headteachers may sometimes have been wise in obstructing particular programmes, eithei because they lacked value, or because any number of local circumstances make it inappropriate for their schools to innovate in that way, at that time. The reason that, despite the difficulties, we do ideally need to understand the processes whereby curricula come to be adopted or rejected is not in order to prescribe successful ones, but in order to find out the points at which we should be particularly keen to ensure greater understanding. If, to retain the example, we find that headteachers tend to be the main obstacle to curriculum change (for good or ill), the moral is not that they should be circumvented or included in the planning, but that, if headteachers are so powerful, they ought to be better educated than they are.

It is, in honesty, difficult to see what we can hope to do to spread a little more understanding about education and curriculum in government circles, but we can certainly work hard both to publicise and realise the view that a necessary condition of curriculum buoyancy (a better word than 'implementation', since it allows that good curriculum might not involve implementing new curricula at all) is better teacher education. It is not clear that teachers necessarily ought to be directly involved in curriculum design or development (it is certainly the case that one does not necessarily need to be a practising teacher to be involved in curriculum development), but it is clear that, for a variety of reasons, teachers need to understand the central issues of curriculum theory. The more the ideal of a better-educated teaching force can be approached, the easier and more reasonable it becomes to leave curriculum planning flexible, and to leave the question of adoption to the good sense of the profession, without necessarily requiring teachers to be involved in designing curricula themselves.[6]

8 Curriculum Evaluation

A.V. Kelly (1977) remarks that 'without some kind of evaluation any curriculum innovation becomes meaningless and probably also impossible'.[1] This chapter will consider various aspects of evaluation before returning to consider the sense in which, and the extent to which, this may be true. Certainly, as has been reiterated throughout this book, and as is one of the few things generally agreed by curriculum theorists, questions of evaluation are inextricably interwoven with questions of planning, implementation and development. The way in which we implement curriculum may affect the nature of the content to some degree. The manner of teaching may affect the content imparted, and may itself be affected by the demands of assessment. In the same way, our planning may to some extent determine, or be determined by, how we evaluate, and how we teach may affect how we choose to evaluate, or vice versa.

How we evaluate is related to what we are evaluating. There is more than a suspicion that, just as some have been tempted to let considerations of ease of implementation affect the nature of curriculum planning, so some have put the cart before the horse here, and made certain kinds of curricular proposals rather than others, because they can be more readily evaluated. This seems to me plainly wrong. Even if Kelly is correct in saying that without some kind of evaluation innovation becomes impossible, that would only entail that we produce curricula that can be evaluated in some way. It does not entail that the tail should wag the dog, or that a criterion of good curriculum planning should be ease of evaluation.

It is important to bear in mind at the outset the distinction between *informal* and *formal* evaluation. Informal evaluation refers to the straightforward judgement of the teacher (or other interested parties) based on observation; in most situations it is an option that is plainly open to us, likely to take place anyway (teachers just do tend to estimate how things are going), and surely to be encouraged. Nor would I dispute that there is value in the practice of formal evaluation, which refers to any systematically organised and publicly scrutinisable means of evaluating. But it must be borne in mind, or so

I shall argue, that things are not necessarily worthless because they cannot be evaluated formally, or even informally, and concern for evaluation should not be allowed to lead to domination of content by evaluation requirements.

A school might take various steps to encourage politeness, kindness, tolerance, enthusiasm or love of a subject in children, without feeling able to evaluate success in any formal way. But the fact that evaluation of success in such aims does not go beyond the impressionistic observation and judgement of teachers cannot be thought to render the pursuit of such aims pointless. A teacher might be concerned to develop appreciation of poetry in students, and conceive of this as something that cannot actually be monitored or measured. But it is not necessarily an objection to his engaging children in various experiences designed to evoke appreciation that he cannot be sure of his success or lack of it. A parent may have no way of knowing whether taking his children on holiday to foreign countries, encouraging an interest in music, or telling them stories, is having any particular long-term effect, but still feel it worthwhile to do these things. Why should schools not encourage activities and experiences that they have *reason to believe* might be valuable, without any certain way of establishing this? There can be good reason to believe in the value of an activity, even in the absence of any means of establishing success. It may, for instance, be argued that the nature of literature and the nature of emotional maturity are such that it is very likely that, through wide reading of literature, people will develop more sophisticated emotional awareness; it may then be reasonably concluded that initiating children into literature is desirable, even though we acknowledge that we do not have any empirical proof of literature bringing about a change, particularly here and now.[2] Conversely, teaching people to stand on their heads is not invested with any greater educational value just because success can be easily evaluated.

As with implementation and planning generally, we must resist the temptation to put form before substance, or to let concern for our procedures outweigh concern for worthwhile experiences. We must first work out what our curriculum ought ideally to contain, and how it might be taught in ways that serve our purposes; only then should we devise strategies for implementation and evaluation, and we should ensure that these do not do violence to our original aims.

1. ASSESSMENT

Two things that we have to be clear about are what we are trying to evaluate at any given moment, and for what purposes we are doing it. There are a number of distinctions worth drawing attention to here. First there is the question of the object we are evaluating. This might be the curriculum itself or some aspect of it, the curriculum plan or presentation, our own teaching performance, or the work of students. Since curriculum evaluation is in fact generally thought of as comprising the first two of these, it is probably wise to refer to the last mentioned as assessment, and to qualify evaluation of teacher performance explicitly.

About the latter there is little to be said that has not been covered in our consideration of research into teacher effectiveness. The individual teacher concerned to monitor his own progress faces all the problems of disentangling quite different kinds of factor possibly relevant to his ultimate success or lack of it in the classroom, and the consequent difficulty of locating cause and effect, that have been noted. This is not to say that he should not be concerned with evaluating his contribution. Indeed, one might argue that part of what it means to be a responsible teacher is to show this concern for the quality and effects of one's performance. But the individual teacher will have to rely on his judgement, and live with the fact that his conclusions are at best tentative. The most important consideration will be that he should have a very clear idea of the nature of the educational enterprise in which he is engaged, and of the particular contribution that his lessons are intended to make.

There is no inherent objection to his having some very specific and perhaps behavioural lesson objectives. But equally there is no necessary reason why he should have them, and in certain cases he should not have them. He should not attempt to constrain his lessons within a framework of behavioural objectives where the aims he is pursuing are not naturally and readily characterised in behavioural terms; and he should not confine himself to specific objectives when his real purposes is to contribute directly or indirectly to certain broad ends. Thus, a teacher who sees his course in history as an attempt to provide understanding of historical method and its problems, understanding of historical processes, and the development of a critical and questioning spirit, may well, from time to time, have lessons that allow of some specific and monitorable student performances being observed. (Students may be called upon to show that they know a finite list of possible contributory causes to an historical event, for example.) But he should not seek to determine success or failure overall in such terms. A critical questioning spirit, particularly since our course may be making a long-term indirect contribution to its development, cannot satisfactorily be assessed by monitoring specified performances on a lesson-by-lesson basis. What is required is a clear notion of what is involved in the critical spirit, a sensible view of appropriate teaching strategies derived from that clear conception, and generalised judgement as to the progress being made.

Assessment, as the term is now being used, will be concerned with estimating the standard of student response or level of student achievement, either in itself, in terms of individual progress, or as related to other students. Such assessment may take various forms, including the use of multiple-choice tests, a variety of more traditional types of written examination, practical work, the writing of essays, and oral discussion. It may also be used for various other purposes, such as to categorise students, to motivate them, or to exercise a form of control over them.

Whatever our particular purposes, certain general observations may be made. Flexibility is required here, as everywhere else, partly because our knowledge is so slight and uncertain, but more importantly because the varying combinations of literally hundreds of factors make each situation virtually unique. Different subject-matter, different educational aims, different immediate concerns, different classrooms, different students and different teachers, may all be variable factors that combine differently to make it sensible to adopt different assessment procedures. A good way of assessing the historical understanding of sixth-formers (grade 12) is not likely to be a good way of assessing the numeracy of elementary school pupils. The way to approach the question of what form of assessment is suitable for particular situations is to consider carefully what a specific form of assessment involves, and whether that suits what one is trying to achieve, rather than to seek to evaluate particular forms of assessment in terms of reliability in the abstract. It would be foolish, for example, to think that, because a certain form of multiple-choice examination is said to have proven success (as it has been suggested that four items to choose from represents an optimum number of items), it would necessarily be suitable as a means of assessing philosophical competence. Multiple-choice tests, at best, only test response to material as taught, and leave little scope for the student to adapt, to think autonomously or to present sustained argument. Since those are likely to be some of the aims of a course in philosophy, the multiple-choice test is likely to be unsuitable in that context. And one should not automatically assume that, if one wants to know about intelligence, one needs a standardised intelligence test that is well-thought-of. A well-thought-of intelligence test may be well-thought-of for reasons that have nothing to do with the concerns of a particular teacher. It may be well-thought-of because successful performance on it is alleged to correlate highly with some other performance valued by those who think well of the test; but that other performance may not be valued by this particular teacher. We need rather to consider that a particular intelligence test is heavily based, say, on requiring students to recognise a number of words, and to ask whether that is what we really want to know about our students.

The general observation that we should not allow the model of scientific investigation to dominate education has its application here in the form of a specific plea for the value of the essay as a means of assessment. Obviously, there are subjects and occasions where the essay is a relatively unsuitable mode of assessment, but one might well argue that all students should have some experience of essay writing, and that it can be a very appropriate means of assessment.

A standard objection to the use of essays is that they are very difficult to mark in a systematic way. As a matter of fact, that isn't necessarily true. If anyone wants to be systematic about essay marking he has only to break the essay down into various categories, such as use of punctuation, introduction of ideas and variety of vocabulary, and then to award points in accordance with performance in the categories. But would that be a sensible thing to do? Why should it be an objection that essays are usually not marked systematically? Is there any strong case for system in this context?

As we have seen (in Chapter 6) systematic procedure, in the sense of procedure in accordance with predetermined steps, is not necessarily desirable. A system is only as good as its steps are appropriate. Ideally, we require some form of rational procedure all the time, but that is rather different. One can proceed, whether marking essays or doing anything else, more or less rationally without necessarily having a fixed set of predetermined steps. It does not seem appropriate to assess essays in terms of fixed categories of readiliy observed features, such as the number of ideas introduced, the number of metaphors introduced, and the number of unfamiliar words used, because these are not crucial to the writing of a good essay. They are not essential parts of what an essay is. It *is* appropriate to assess an essay in terms of coherence of argument, clarity and force of imagery and such like, because they *are*, or may be, constituent parts of a good essay, but these by their nature are qualities that have to be judged impressionistically, since they are a function of the whole rather than isolated observable items. (Force of imagery is not simply visible or invisible; it has to be estimated by reference to the context.) Essay marking should, therefore, be rational, in that it should be undertaken with reference to certain stateable and definable qualities; and it can be rational in that sense. There is no obvious reason, however, why it should be systematic in the sense of marked by reference to immediately visible and predetermined items. (It has been claimed, incidentally, that marking essays by means of itemised schemes is not consistently more reliable than impressionistic marking (Coffman, 1971).)

Research supports what individual experience suggests — namely, that individual teachers can make startlingly different estimates of the worth of an essay (Starch and Elliott, 1912, 1913; Godshalk, Swineford and Coffman, 1966). But this hardly seems a sufficient objection to their use. In the first place, the research does not fully allow for the fact that different people assess essays differently because they are looking for different things. It would be unfortunate if one teacher's estimate of an essay was taken to be an objective assessment of the student's overall worth. But, when the essay is used as a means for individual teachers to assess students in the context of their own courses there need be no problems, particularly if the student is aware of the criteria of evaluation; and there is no reason why the judgement of teachers should not be as objective, in the sense of free of bias and based on specific criteria, as any other form of assessment. It is simply a mistake, a logical mistake and therefore beyond empirical challenge, to imagine that forms of assessment that leave little room for disagreement amongst markers are necessarily superior. If they leave little room for disagreement, this will either be because they concentrate on matters where people do not disagree, which will often mean trivial matters, or because they unwarrantably and dangerously reduce complex matters of judgement to uncontentious categories that do not do justice to what is allegedly being assessed. Sound assessment does require clear criteria. It does not necessarily require instantly recognisable categories.

The main advantage of the essay as a means of assessment, where it is appropriate, is that it requires the student to do something that is extremely important in itself, arguably one of the most important things in a child's school experience, namely to handle language not merely in order to communicate in the rather sloppy sense of 'to interelate with others' that the term generally carries in educational discourse, but to express ideas clearly and to forge coherent arguments or, with different kinds of essay, to evoke ideas effectively. This is a clear case where the nature of education can and should dictate the methods of assessment, rather than the science of assessment be allowed to dictate the nature of educational experience.

A further distinction to be noted is that between *norm-referenced* testing, which is designed to rank students in relation to each other, and *criterion-referenced* testing, which is designed to assess pupil mastery of content. (One might design a test to serve both functions at once, though in practice it might be difficult to do so without detriment to one or other objective.) Criterion-referenced testing does not do away with the problem of establishing norms or making value judgements about students. In order to decide on what criteria to use, one has to form a view of what students generally can be expected to achieve at the level in question, so that criterion-referenced tests have implicit norms of student achievement. None the less, they are distinct kinds of test, and criterion-referenced tests have the advantage that students are less likely to feel that they are competing with one another, or that beating others in tests constitutes success, or that the test is somehow a measure of overall worth; it places the emphasis firmly on the idea of coming to grips with the subject-matter. It is also likely that the adoption of criterion-referenced tests will incline teachers to more concern with appropriate tests, since they will be consciously looking for indications of the mastery of subject-matter, rather than simply affording an opportunity for students to sort themselves in to some sort of order. Nor are there any obvious functions of norm-referenced tests that cannot be catered for, if desired, by criterion-referenced tests. For example, some teachers may feel the need to use tests to motivate students, to vary the pattern of lessons, to exercise control, or to monitor their own progress in teaching, and criterion-referenced tests could perform these functions. In fact, one might say that the important distinction is between poor tests used simply in order to rank students, and tests that are appropriate to the matter in hand.

One curious phenomenon associated with norm-referenced testing that deserves mention is the normal curve distribution. Some have held the view that a good test should result in a distribution of students following the pattern of the so-called normal curve, which is to say that there should be a few students at the top, a few at the bottom, and the majority spread out in the middle. There is a *prima facie* logic about this: if it is an appropriate test for a group of students, then it should not be so easy that everybody gets top marks, or so difficult that everyone gets low marks, and, on the principle that the majority of people are neither very clever nor very stupid, one would expect the largest number of students to be in the middle.

Just how warranted this general principle that the majority are moderate performers is, is hard to say. At first blush, it looks as if it must be so: surely very clever people are by definition a minority for, if everyone or most people were that clever, we would not think of them as being very clever. But whether this is actually so depends upon what is meant by being 'very clever'. It is possible to define 'very clever' as 'especially clever', in which case, by definition, the number of very clever people must be small. But it is also possible to define very clever people in terms of achievement in respect of clearly stated criteria, in which case there is no necessary reason why everybody should not be very clever. (Psychologists interested in intelligence testing generally assume that intelligence is normally distributed in the general population. That is to say, they assume that its distribution follows the pattern of the distribution of physical attributes such as height and weight. It is very important to recognise that this *is merely an assumption*.) In view of this ambiguity in the meaning of 'cleverness', actual research into the distribution of cleverness amongst the population at large is not very revealing. As so often, either the research has unnecessarily empirically validated a necessary truth, or the empirical claim is of no use until we have a clear specification of, and agreement on, the criteria for extreme cleverness.

In any case, when we turn to the classroom situation, there is no reason to suppose that a particular group of students will follow the alleged pattern of the distribution of cleverness at large. It is not necessarily the case, therefore, that a test that allows the majority of students to do very well, a few to do moderately well, and a few to do badly, is necessarily a bad test. It may be a good test, in as much as it calls for and accurately assesses performances of desired sorts, and one that merely incidentally reveals that this group of students consists predominantly of high achievers in this subject. Certainly, what is quite ridiculous is the practice of demanding that the ultimate grading of students for a degree or a course should necessarily follow the pattern of the normal curve, so that in any given year there should always be a few first class and a few third class degrees, while the majority are awarded steady seconds. As an external examiner, I have many times encountered the argument that a borderline student should be given a second rather than a first class degree, *because* the normal curve demands that we don't have too many first class degrees. It is hard to imagine a worst argument.

There seems no reason then to commit oneself exclusively to any particular form of assessment. Many forms will have their time and place. The normal curve should be ignored. Norm-referenced testing should perhaps give way to criterion-referenced testing. But, beyond that, the question of whether and when to use essays, tests, formal examinations, multiple-choice, oral examination, and so forth, is essentially one to be answered by the individual teacher, by reference to the nature of what he is trying to teach, and the nature of various types of assessment.

2. CURRICULUM EVALUATION

If we now return to curriculum evaluation, it will be apparent that the nature of evaluation may be affected by the question of what is meant by curriculum. What we are seeking to evaluate will differ as our conception of curriculum differs between that of prescribed content, that of intended or achieved learning outcomes, and that of provision of a set of experiences. Equally we must not confuse evaluating the layout or presentation of a curriculum proposal with evaluating the proposal itself. In each case different factors are involved. The former requires us to think in terms of such things as clarity, accessibility and appeal to those who will make use of it. The latter requires that we think in terms of things such as educational value, coherence and practicality. We also have to bear in mind different uses that we may have for evaluation. We might be evaluating a curriculum in order to facilitate decision-making or to help administration in some way, or we might be evaluating it in order to see what pupils can achieve through it, or to see how easy it is for a school to adopt a particular curriculum.

The most important distinction is perhaps that between evaluating the *worth* and the *effectiveness* of a curriculum, that is to say, between assessing the extent to which a curriculum is effective on its own terms (i.e. successful at meeting its own ends), and estimating the worth or quality of a curriculum experience overall. One curriculum proposal might be very well organised to meet its stated ends, but educationally rather worthless. Another might be a mess in terms of organisation on its own terms, but none the less offer a worthwhile experience in the context of schooling.

When it comes to evaluating the worth of curriculum, we have to rely on our reasoning and judgement to some extent, taking account of a clearly articulated set of aims, which need not be those of the curriculum designer. This may seem paradoxical, but it is not. The quality of the design of a curriculum obviously will be partly a function of coherence between proposals for procedure and the stated ends. But the worth of a curriculum is a matter of it meeting desirable ends, and not necessarily the intended ends. Our judgement must also take account of the effects of a curriculum in practice rather than its presumed or intended effects, although it is important to remember that a curriculum that fails to meet desirable ends in practice may require only a change in the teacher's approach, or application at a different level, rather than an entirely new content.

We cannot directly observe, measure or otherwise empirically test the worth of a curriculum. Whether a particular curriculum is a good one has to be *thought* about, and it involves estimating the events of the classroom or the presumed consequences of classroom activities in the light of our aims and purposes. It follows from this that the task of curriculum evaluation cannot be left in the hands of mere technicians, by which I mean people whose talents are confined to the technicalities of evaluation techniques. Adequate curriculum evaluation, when it is concerned with estimating the worth of a curriculum, presupposes a sound grasp of the concepts of schooling and education.

A good curriculum design or plan, considered on its own terms and without reference to the quality of the curriculum it proposes, though less important and less interesting, is a more complex matter. Assessing its quality as a design does not have to include reference to the desirability of the aims proposed. A good plan may lead to a monstrous crime. To be good as a plan or design, a plan needs to be effective in enabling people to carry out the requirements of the plan. Reasoning, however, is still involved, along with observation. For a good plan is one that is clear, economic and easy to understand and act upon, and these are partially matters of judgement and require conceptual competence. We need therefore both to examine the plan in the abstract and to watch what happens when it is used, although in the latter case we have to beware of confusing faults of design with faults of implementation. A curriculum design might appear to have been poor because teachers were unable to implement it successfully, but that might conceivably have been the fault of the teachers.

Evaluation of curriculum design, because it is often undertaken at early stages in order to help improve the design, is sometimes referred to as *formative* evaluation (Scriven, 1967). This may be contrasted with *summative* evaluation, which is to say evaluation of a curriculum design deemed to be complete and translated into action. It is summative evaluation that most obviously runs the risk of failing to keep the distinction between evaluation of curriculum design and evaluation of curriculum worth clear. Even apart from considerations of worth or educational quality, a good design does not necessarily give us a good curriculum. For a curriculum may be well presented in a formal sense, but what it clearly and helpfully enjoins teachers to do may fail to deliver the goods on its own terms. It may be clear, coherent and manageable, but ineffective. This leads to what is for many people the main focus of interest: the business of devising techniques to evaluate the effectiveness of curriculum on its own terms, to see, for example, whether critical thinking is enhanced by this curriculum as its design intends, or whether quadratic equations are mastered as a result of that curriculum, as the plan maintains they will be.

The techniques for carrying out this kind of evaluation are varied, but they are almost all forms of observation. Occasionally, experimental research is carried out, which is to say that hypotheses are tested under something approximating to laboratory conditions, difficult as that may be with human beings; but for the most part here, as elsewhere in empirical educational research, the approach is descriptive. Evaluators seek to produce data relating to what goes on when a curriculum is adopted, noting, where possible, correlations between teacher behaviour in accordance with the design and student behaviour in accordance with the stated ends, from which they may seek to deduce some kind of causal relationship — the purpose being to see whether the curriculum does indeed produce the intended consequences or effects. The manner of observation may range from very informal (simply looking on) to very formalised routines such as those of systematic observation. (It will be recalled from the examination of systematic observation in Chapter 6 that this requires that an observer ticks off at rapid and regular intervals the type of activity in which students and/or teachers are involved according to a pre-specified list of categories.) Besides the direct observation of the researcher, interviews may be conducted with teachers and students, or questionnaires sent out, in order to gather other people's perceptions. In addition, standardised tests for particular things such as reading level or creativity may be administered. Very often standardised tests are used to provide an independent check on performance: students may be tested before and after the adoption of a curriculum, or a control group and a group that has been introduced to a new curriculum may be tested, to see whether any progress is being made that might reasonably be attributed to the curriculum.

Whatever the techniques used, we clearly remain on the level of individual perceptions of what is going on, whether they come from observer, teacher or student, whether they be free-floating or regulated by an observation schedule, and whether they be directly or indirectly gathered. This is true even of the standardised tests. It is all too easy to think of them as objective, reliable and uncontentious measures of progress, beyond the hazards of subjective judgement. But a reading test, creativity test or intelligence test only directly provides information about the set of performances or behaviours involved in doing the test. The child is observed to think of more possible uses for an old shoe box, when presented with a particular creativity test, after adoption of a new curriculum, than before. Or a child involved with a new curriculum is observed to spot a higher proportion of odd men out in a specific item on an intelligence test than a child experiencing a different curriculum. But it is a matter of interpretation on somebody's part, whether it be the designer of the test or the user of it, as to what these performances actually signify, let alone whether a higher score actually indicates progress or development. It is not a matter of simple observation, and it is very far from being objectively and uncontentiously certain that such children are creative or intelligent, if that means anything more than able to think of uses for an old shoe box or able to spot odd men out. With such evaluation, therefore, we are still at the mercy of the now familiar obstacles to educational research: subjects may behave atypically when being observed, people may, for a variety of reasons, not tell the truth when recording their opinions, they may not understand the questions in the manner that the researchers intend, they may not mean what the researchers think they mean when they refer to concepts such as creativity and intelligence, the observation schedules may be inadequate in a variety of ways to the task of mapping reality, and the whole enterprise is necessarily a prisoner of that degree of interpretation or judgement that inevitably accompanies perception.

The main thing that has to be avoided, as was the case with curriculum design and research into teacher effectiveness, is the mistake of confusing the systematic organisation of data collecting with accuracy of reporting. It is not necessarily the case that more formal procedures or more systematic techniques are more reliable pointers to truth. Given the crucial importance of this matter, I shall look once again at three of the central terms involved in arguments about the rival merits of systematic and informal techniques of observation and evaluation: reliability, objectivity and validity. The reader who feels that he has had enough of that may care to advance straight to the following section.

Much testing and many research designs can and do give us precise numerical readings for reliability and validity. Reliability is expressed as a correlation between $+1.00$ and -1.00 (the higher the score, the more reliable the instrument), and most research reports publish a precise reliability reading for their procedures. The ordinary connotations of the words reliable and valid, combined with this practice of asserting positively a proven high reliability and validity scoring, naturally incline some people (not, no doubt, experienced researchers themselves) to imagine that, where research instruments have such high scores, we are dealing with a proven instrument for extracting the objective truth, especially when it is further explicitly claimed that the test or observation schedule is an objective measure. This, however, is highly misleading.

Reliability does not refer directly, if at all, to the reliability of a test or observation schedule as a predictor or pinpointer of truth. It refers to the consistency of the test under different circumstances (usually to consistency amongst observers/testers). If a test has been demonstrated to give the same results whether boys or girls take it, whether it is marked by teacher A or teacher B, or whether it is taken on Monday or Friday, then in those respects it is said to have high reliability, meaning no more than that the results do not appear to be affected by those particular considerations. A reliability score is, in other words, essentially an indicator of certain variables being seemingly irrelevant. That of course is important in its own way. If we are not concerned about differences between teachers or want to eliminate that variable as a possible factor influencing events, it is desirable to have a test with a good reliability score in that respect — a test that appears to be unaffected by teacher differences. And indeed reliability must be a *necessary* condition of a test or an observation instrument that is going to get at the truth. For if a test can be affected by irrelevancies such as which teacher is doing the marking, or the time at which it is taken, it cannot be an accurate test of pupil performance as such.

However, it is clearly not the case that reliability is a *sufficient* condition of a test being accurate or pinpointing the truth. Our test may be unaffected by differences of time or in markers, but still be recording nonsense. It may still be a very poor test of what it purports to test. This might be because the respects in which it has high reliability are actually not very important, or because the reliability is the result of something other than the sound construction of the test. Thus, a high reader reliability, which is to say a clear indication that a procedure for essay marking is unaffected by who is doing the reading, might conceivably arise as a result of some common error on the part of all the readers, or by trivialising the procedure. It might, for example, be achieved by requiring all readers to mark essays by length alone. Instrument stability, by which is meant the extent to which different tests elicit the same score from the same students, might be the result of avoiding searching questions in all the tests. Examinee reliability, by which is meant constancy on different occasions with the same students, might be the result of chance. Certainly, the high reliability of a particular IQ test does *not* mean that this test is known to be a reliable pointer to intelligence. It means, at best, that the test tends to yield the same results, notwithstanding certain specified variables. That *could* be because it is a trivial or irrelevant test, and it is anyway perfectly consonant with it being a poor test in terms of actually locating intelligence.

Objectivity is a confusing word at the best of times. In the context of evaluation it may become even more misleading as it becomes associated with formal or systematic modes of inquiry. The connotations of 'formal' and 'systematic' themselves may suggest some degree of elimination of human error; but as the terms are used in the context of research they must be interpreted more literally to mean only 'structured in some recognisable way' (formal) and 'structured by some predetermined set of categories' (systematic). Objectivity is a matter of letting the facts speak for themselves rather than overlaying or interpreting the facts with bias or whim. One is relatively objective when one describes the layout of Seattle airport, but becomes more subjective when one describes it as ugly, or when one's description of its layout becomes idiosyncratic thanks to some personal prejudice or obsession. The common mistake of confusing the fact that it is sometimes hard to tell whether a judgement or description is more or less objective, with the false assumption that there is no distinction to be drawn in principle, is to be avoided. There is also a widespread failure to recognise that objectivity does not require the total separation of the individual and his judgement. It merely requires that the individual's judgement should not be formed by, or based upon, individual bias. By definition, all judgements have a subjective element in that they are the personal judgement of somebody. But some of them are objective too, in as much as they are based on relevant considerations rather than personal whim: they transcend the personal bias of the person making the judgement.

The question is why it should be assumed that evaluation procedures that avoid asking for impressionistic opinions should be thought to be necessarily more objective. In the first place, as has just been said, opinions can be objective. In the second place, observation of discrete categories of behaviour can be subjective. In the third place, the interpretation of data collected by direct observation, systematic or not, can be subjective. And in the fourth place highly depersonalised instruments of data collecting can be subjective, because they are designed by individuals who may not be objective. In short, avoiding arbitrary bias and irrelevant considerations, which is the real object of the exercise, is not a matter of *what* procedures one adopts, but of how one makes use of any procedures and of their quality.

There are only three possible reasons for assuming that formal procedures, such as the use of a multiple-choice test or the use of an observation schedule, are necessarily more objective than informal procedures, such as the use of the essay or impressionistic observation. The first is to change the meaning of objective from something like 'free of personal bias, and accurate' to something like 'beyond the interpretative control of the observer'. But to devise tests or observation schedules that are marker- or observer-proof does not do away with the chance of bias and personal idiosyncracy; it merely shifts the source of bias to the test or schedule designer. (And in fact few, if any, observation schedules are entirely observer-proof, despite appearances, as we have seen.) The second is to establish independently that a test or schedule is objective. That might be true of a particular multiple-choice test or observation schedule, but to establish that it was would require further examination and further tests.[3] It would not be a function of the fact that the procedures took this form. The third is that the multiple-choice test or observation schedule should necessarily be more objective than other forms of assessment or evaluation, because they are confined to relatively simple, undemanding and unambiguous matters. A multiple-choice test might be devised to find out only whether children have learnt certain dates, for example, and that would be a more objective test than an essay on the Tudor kings, because it is a great deal easier to assess date learning objectively than it is to assess historical understanding. But in such a case the price of objectivity is relative triviality. And, as far as that goes, relatively trivial essays too may be marked relatively objectively. An essay confined to summarising someone else's argument is easier to mark objectively than an essay inviting poetic self-expression.

The striking features of more formal tests and systems of evaluation and observation are that they involve regularity and predictability. Multiple-choice tests will tend to earn students similar marks from different teachers: it will be predictable that if you award Johnny 75 per cent in the test, I shall too, in a way that is not predictable in the case of the essay. Evaluators constrained to categorise what they observe in one of 100 ways, will produce less variation than evaluators free to call on any category they believe to be appropriate, especially if the former have been trained to use the observation schedule in a specific way. But this is quite simply because in such cases markers and evaluators have a very clear idea of what they are to do. Whether those clear ideas are adequate in terms of getting a hold on complex matters realistically is quite another matter. The regularity to be found here is clearly not the same thing as objectivity, either in the sense of freedom from personal bias or perspective, or in the sense of accuracy of reporting. The multiple-choice question paper may involve bias and idiosyncratic judgement, as well as inaccuracy, precisely to the extent that the complexity of what it is testing invites them, although this subjectivity will be manifested in the construction rather than the marking of the test. The systematic observer still makes personal judgements, and his schedule is based on further personal judgements; the extent to which these judgements are sound and objective will again be a function of the match between the observation schedule and the complexity of the situation, and not of the use of such formal measures.

Some research suggests that teacher judgements are often not objective, in the sense of prompted only by an attempt at rational appraisal of the truth. For instance, there is evidence that teachers are influenced by the attitudes of students when judging their ability (Smith, Meadow and Sisk, 1970), and that schools of education tend to allow their judgements about the quality of prospective teachers to be influenced by factors such as the attractiveness of students (Hore, 1971). But it is a mistake to think that procedures that guard against this kind of subjectivity (i.e. personal predilection based on irrelevant criteria) necessarily lead to better judgements in the sense of wiser or more reliable ones. In the first place, although I do not personally believe it very likely, attractiveness and positive attitudes might conceivably make better students, or correlate with ability. In other words, these seemingly irrelevant criteria might in fact have relevance. In the second place, an objective test of student competence, meaning specifically one that allows no freedom for the introduction of unexpected criteria, may obviously conceivably make worse judgements. What emerges from this is that what matters is not whether the manner of making judgements is personal or impersonal, nor whether it is done according to specified or open criteria, but that the criteria be appropriate, and that there be clarity as to what they are. We require explicit criteria of judgement, but that does not necessitate that we use formal instruments.

What obviously has to be guarded against is any move towards the rule: 'Quantify wherever possible.' First, quantification is sometimes inappropriate; secondly, it is not true that quantification is necessarily more objective in the sense of accurate or free of whim, it is only more inflexible. Quantification works very well when what is being assessed *can*, without distortion, be broken down into quantifiable units — where there is agreement on the significance and worth of the units. But sometimes this cannot be done. Judgements as to how interested people are, or how well they understand complex phenomena, for example, cannot reasonably be based on measures of a number of quantifiable factors. In the absence of any adequate conceptualisation we are not in agreement as to what constitutes being interested in or understanding existentialism, and some at least of what some would argue is part of being interested in or understanding existentialism, such as being intrigued by and grasping the concept of *Angst*, cannot be realistically reduced to observable and measurable signs. Sometimes, though it could be done in principle, any actual breakdown would be highly contentious. This is perhaps the case with essay writing. It *could* be assessed by reference to quantifiable features but, as has been suggested, it is arguable that any such breakdown would miss the essence of what writing essays is all about. The truth is that the more readily susceptible to quantification things are, the more trivial they are likely to be, for the very good reason that the more readily quantifiable they are, the more readily observable they will be and, consequently, the less contentious they are.

Validity is the most general of the three terms. Its meaning in technical circles depends partially on reliability (in its technical sense) and objectivity. As with reliability, validity may be ascribed to different dimensions of the exercise. There is concurrent validity, content validity, definitional and curricular validity. These phrases should be self-explanatory in that they simply pinpoint the focus of the validity. The crucial distinction, as all have recognised, is between *direct* and *indirect* validity. The former refers to the fact that there is a direct link between what is tested and what is produced as a finding. The latter refers to an indirect link between what is tested and what is claimed. An IQ test, if it has any validity at all, has only indirect validity for intelligence, since it does not actually measure intelligence, but is thought to measure something that correlates with intelligent behaviour. It is important to bear in mind that almost all educational research has only indirect validity.

A driving test and an eyesight test have direct validity. I get you to drive a car. I conclude, reasonably enough if you do it successfully, that you can. However, even in this apparently simple case there are problems: you may not be able to drive under different conditions. I am still having to make judgements. (Perhaps you grind the gears a bit, stop rather abruptly and are not very courteous to other drivers. Can you, then, really drive? A conceptual question again and one, therefore, that no *system* of testing can get round.) Furthermore, this direct validity has nothing to do with the man in the street's mistaken, but common, assumption that, being valid, the test's conclusions must be true. A driving test has direct validity, whatever the competence of the examiner and the outcome of the test, because validity refers to its relationship to what it is seeking to establish. It is no guarantee that the test as conducted will be an accurate gauge of the truth. None the less, such direct valid testing is not to be sneezed at. It would be valuable to have directly valid tests of intelligence or the effectiveness of curriculum.

The trouble is that we don't have such tests for such things unless, paradoxically, we are prepared to acknowledge impressionistic judgement, based on clear conceptualisation, as the only way of testing with direct validity. What we have are many procedures and tests that have indirect validity, which means that we infer from past correlations that performance on or at X is a significant indication of Y. This obviously chancy assumption is widely agreed to be just that. 'The history of testing', it has been observed, 'is strewn with the wreckage of supposedly predictive tests' (Pratt, 1980).[4] For the evaluator the question of validity is an offshoot or product of other factors, the key ones that we have noted being objectivity and reliability, but there are also congruence, which is a rating of the test's ability to test what it claims to test, discreteness, which is a rating of its freedom from irrelevant variables (an IQ test that incidentally required knowledge of some technical vocabulary would be low in discreteness), and completeness, which refers to the test's capacity to focus on the whole of its object and not just some aspect of it. But none of this alters the fact that to describe a test as valid is to say no more than that it is thought to be a reasonably accurate measure of X, while competence at X is further thought to be a reasonable indicator of Y. The validity of the test is itself a matter of judgement rather than uncontentious observation. And a test which *is* technically valid may none the less be a poor one.

3. INFORMAL EVALUATION

We thus return to the fundamental point that the trappings of evaluation procedures must not be allowed to beguile us. So-called objective, valid and reliable procedures of evaluation, even when they are what they claim, which is by no means always the case since the claims involve judgement and interpretation, are merely relatively explicit instruments. Whether they are suitable for their tasks is another question, and there is no reason to suppose that they are necessarily more illuminating or more accurate than more informal or impressionistic procedures. A driving test is not necessarily more accurate as a measure of good driving than a bird-watcher's judgement is accurate as a measure of bird behaviour. In the particular case of curriculum evaluation, when what we are after is not simply correlation, but cause and effect which no observation procedures can give us directly, there is no *a priori* reason to assume that any formal evaluation techniques will give us a more accurate picture of what is going on than the informal judgement of an informed observer.

For reasons such as those I have given many contemporary curriculum evaluators have strong doubts about the wisdom of too formal an approach, and have therefore swung away from traditional techniques of evaluation, favouring what are sometimes called holistic or illuminative types of evaluation (e.g. Parlett and Hamilton, 1972; Stake, 1972; MacDonald, 1973). The essence of such alternatives is reliance on human judgement based on informal study or observation of what is going on. The tendency is towards understanding or forming a picture of what is happening rather than assessing it, although there is nothing to stop one drawing conclusions and making policy proposals on the strength of one's observations.

Stenhouse (1975), while favouring this kind of approach, long ago pointed out that one likely consequence was that criteria of worth would tend to get lost. Observers would be inclined to remain on the level of description and to refrain from judgements about the value of what was described. But it is arguable that this would be no bad thing. Questions of worth, after all, are a matter for reasoning about, not for observing. Perhaps we do not want people who happen to be experienced in observing classrooms also smuggling in values and confusing the statement that a curriculum does this or that with the judgement that it is a good curriculum. The situation might be less muddled if we first tried to gain a picture of what our curricula actually involve, then tried to draw reasonable inferences about cause and effect, and finally sat down to reason about their worth. And it does seem to me, although I would expect to see all kinds of different procedures on different occasions, that informal procedures of observation are for the most part to be preferred for these two reasons: the negative one that formal procedures are misleading, in that they do not have merits sometimes supposed; and the positive one that the holistic approach allows one to look at a set of complex interactions as the entirety that they are, and to recognise features that the formalist having failed to anticipate cannot perceive, thanks to the constraints of his instrument of observation.

McIntyre and MacLeod (1978) have said that the issue is not 'whether information is neglected' by formal methods of observation, as opponents of such methods argue, 'but rather how it is determined what information will be neglected'.[5] Their point is that no approach can in fact be other than selective, and some points are bound to be missed by phenomenologist observers and systematic tickers-off of schedules alike. With interaction analysis (just another name for systematic observation), the argument continues, we at least know what we are doing and what is being neglected. That is true indeed, but it is not much of an argument. If I measure the incidence of marital disharmony by reference to divorce statistics, you and I both know what I am doing and the limits of my inquiry. But the rather more important point is that I may get a very inaccurate picture of the extent of marital disharmony. Furthermore, it simply isn't the case, as Galton (1980) would have us believe, that, while informal techniques may generate interesting hypotheses, more formal methods are needed to verify them. It is true that informal observation does not in various respects satisfy the canons of scientific proof. The problem is, as must surely be clear by now, that formal methods in this area don't either. They satisfy the appearance of scientific procedure, but they don't satisfy the canons of scientific demonstration. Since, therefore, nothing is being satisfactorily demonstrated, we would be wise to concentrate on aiming for truth and illumination, rather than verification. Here, informal procedures have the edge because they are more open and do not give a false impression of certainty. Rosenshine and Furst's (1973) suggestion that we should concentrate on large-scale surveys, that could take any form, backed up by occasional small-scale experiments to probe particular suggestions, seems eminently sensible, provided we are aware of the very real obstacles in the way of adequate experimental research in education.

In the preceding pages I have tried to expose the myth that identifies accuracy and certainty with formal procedures. The important questions for curriculum evaluators are: Is the way the curriculum is set out helpful? Does the curriculum deliver the proposed goods? Are the goods worth having? To get reasonable answers to these questions, we need far more emphasis on conceptualisation, experience of schooling and teaching, subtlety of observation and reasoning, and rather less on scientific procedures. We cannot measure whether people are becoming emotionally mature or better educated on a scale of 1-10; but we can assess and estimate impressionistically, provided we have very clear concepts and an eye for the complexity of the classroom. When Jeremy Bentham introduced his felicific calculus, designed to catalogue the considerations of time, intensity, extent and such like that need to be taken into account in estimating an overall quantity of happiness, uncomprehending critics assumed that he meant that these aspects have to be separately measured and then added up for an overall score.[6] That would be an absurd suggestion, and Bentham meant nothing so formal. He meant to indicate the sort of factors that need to be taken into account, granted that the judgements would be impressionistic. In the same way, we need a very precise breakdown of the constituent parts of key educational concepts, but we need the breakdown as a reminder of what to look for, rather than to serve as a list of items to be measured.

It has been said that the issue in evaluation is one of measuring versus valuing, or quantity versus quality. I would rather say that it is a question of shifting emphasis away from calculation and observation by numbers, and towards judgement based on clear conceptualisation.

4. INNOVATION AND EVALUATION

What are we to make of Kelly's (1977) contention that innovation without evaluation is meaningless and probably impossible? It is certainly not impossible, either logically or empirically. We can, and we sometimes do, innovate without evaluating. Nor is it clear that such activity is meaningless, since it is not clear what Kelly means by 'meaningless'. Presumably he feels that it is not worth doing, but that seems debatable. If I have reason to introduce a new curriculum along the lines that there are logical reasons to suppose that A will contribute to B, or empirical grounds for supposing it, then that represents a case for doing it, even if it is further conceded that it cannot be satisfactorily evaluated. If the case is logical, then it doesn't need to be empirically verified and, even if it is empirical, a case may be reasonable without being verifiable. It was, for instance, always reasonable to suppose that encouraging children would in various ways be beneficial, and it is still reasonable to suppose so, even though it has not been conclusively established, probably isn't a law, and could not necessarily be shown to be the case in a particular situation. It is reasonable to suppose that teaching children to write well improves their capacity for thought, but one could not evaluate the success of a curriculum programme geared to extensive writing very easily, partly because the pay-off may be long-term and imperceptible by stages, and partly because, in the absence of proper experimental conditions, there is no way of knowing that it is the emphasis on writing that is the cause of any observable improvement in thinking.

However, it would be strange to object to attempts to evaluate innovation. Evaluation of some sort is certainly logically necessary to any judgement of the success of a curriculum innovation, and thinking people are likely to want to know about such success or lack of it. But the current emphasis on evaluation, particularly if that is taken to mean formal evaluation, seems without reasonable foundation. Formal evaluation exercises are vastly overrated. If half the time and energy expended on them were expended on *thinking* about curriculum, we might be getting somewhere.

9 Teacher Education

1. THE EMPEROR'S CLOTHES

The Emperor was naked. But the populace talked as if he were clothed in full ceremonial pomp. And soon they forgot that he wasn't. They became victims of their own way of talking, until a small boy in his simplicity spoke merely of what he saw. He saw nakedness, and the rhetoric was blown. I believe that the study of education generally, and the study of curriculum in particular, is similarly in danger of being a victim of the way in which we talk. This little boy, for one, thinks that our quasi-technological language covers a fair amount of nakedness.

One theme running through this book has been that we need to take the emphasis off the idea of seeing curriculum study as a form of applied science, and off those aspects of educational research that do have some pretentions to being scientific.[1] It is only a question of emphasis. I do not dispute either the need for, or the possibility of, some research that is conducted in a truly scientific manner and that may yield probabilities as strong as some of those in the natural sciences.[2] But the suggestion is that the growing mound of jargon, models and diagrams, designs, research instruments, standardised tests, styles of teaching, and poorly attested data, combined with an uncritical treatment of this material, not only gives a false picture of what we know and need to do, at least to the unwary, but also serves to promote a misconception of the nature of curriculum inquiry.[3]

Few, if any, diagrams offer anything other than a simplified representation of something that, if it needs to be understood at all, needs to be understood fully, and therefore verbally.[4] (This is not a necessary truth, but how many people can in fact claim to be able to express complex ideas pictorially that they could not express verbally?) Besides being simplified, diagrams give a misleading impression of reification: subtle, qualified and abstract explanations of complex phenomena are being presented on the pattern of mechanical interaction. Likewise, models of and metaphors for teaching which might, when fresh, initially prove illuminating, are becoming ossified in textbooks and courses as actual alternative modes of procedure. They thus stand in the way of our really thinking about what teaching involves. For whether teaching has more in common with gardening, acting or filling an empty vessel, to cite three popular metaphors, it is assuredly not very like any of them; and whether, if pushed, it would be preferable to imitate the model of Socrates, Rousseau or one indirectly derived from Piaget or Taba, it is certain that no teacher should seek to be exactly like any of them, even in particular situations, let alone in general.[5] In the same way, even to think in terms of styles of teaching, be it formal, informal, class-enquirer, habitual-changer or group teacher, with their inevitable package-deal nature, seriously inhibits realisation of the flexibility, responsiveness, understanding and variety that any competent teacher needs to exhibit.[6]

Coining new words and phrases to describe the teaching process or classroom events merely makes educational discourse inaccessible and somewhat pretentious, unless they represent genuine new ideas or categories of thought.[7] This they seldom in fact do,[8] and even when they do it is necessary that the new ideas should be fruitful in terms of understanding the events described, which is by no means always the case. Furthermore, a great deal of the seemingly straightforward language of education begs too many questions for a sensible person's comfort. We hear, for instance, a great deal about skills (basic skills, life skills, reading skills, the skill of critical thinking, creative skills, teaching skills, etc.), but are these things all skills? What is a skill? Are not some of these, at the very least, markedly different kinds of skill? and on what grounds are we assuming that, say, thinking critically is a unitary skill at all?[9]

New instruments of observation are not necessarily improvements. Again, it depends entirely on whether they are adequate to cover the complexities of the situation they describe. Sometimes 'new instruments' are merely new ways of gathering information, as when the researcher uses a videotape recorder to supplement his observation, in which case one can see certain advantages (one can replay the scene) and certain disadvantages (it records only part of what is going on in the classroom); but its value as a research tool depends on the use to which the data it records can be put. Sometimes 'new instruments' refers to new ways of observing that involve focusing on new aspects of the situation, as an observation instrument may be designed with entirely new categories. Then the question becomes whether the new categories are well framed and well chosen, and there is no reason to suppose that more than a

handful of the hundreds of observation instruments recorded have
been particularly well suited to catering for the complexities of the
situations they sought to describe.[10]

Standardised tests may seriously mislead if they are taken as
reliable guides to anything other than the ability to perform on that
test at that time.[11] The relationship between what is claimed is being
tested (e.g. creativity, intelligence, personality type, understanding)
and any adequate conception of these things is usually tenuous and
contentious in the extreme: doing well on a creativity test hardly
matches up with familiar notions of what is involved in being a
creative individual.[12] The predictive value of such tests is in fact, on
the whole, low. A claim about predictive value is in any case usually
based on correlations with achievement on other similarly
questionable tests, or with otherwise questionable measures of
subsequent achievement: for example, the predictive value of an IQ
test may be asserted on the strength of the claim that those who do
well on it subsequently achieve high socioeconomic status. But why
should we assume that the latter has anything to do with intelligence?
Generally, the question of what the precise nature of the relationship
between two measures of achievement that correlate highly may be is
also ignored. Is it, for instance, that having a high IQ leads to high
socioeconomic status, that presumption of a high IQ in students leads
teachers to treat them in ways that indirectly contribute to their
gaining such status, that students are fired by the idea that they have
a high IQ, or what? Furthermore, certain assumptions often built
into such tests, such as the assumption that intelligence is normally
distributed throughout the population (i.e. that the majority of
people are clustered in the middle between a few relatively intelligent
and a few relatively unintelligent people) are questionable in principle
and highly misleading in practice, if it is further assumed that a given
group is a truly representative sample of the overall population
distribution.[13] (Some such assumption has to be made about any
group that one is using to design such a test.[14])

The very idea of an ideal way or even a limited number of
acceptable ways to design a curriculum seems misplaced and
misleading.[15] There are no doubt certain questions that anyone
proposing a particular curriculum ought to have an answer to.[16] But
these are questions relating to why we should teach the subject, item
or material, and in what way we should present it overall, rather than
questions about the detailed procedures required in particular
classrooms, or at particular times. A curriculum proposal certainly
ought to be made in the light of some clear aims or objectives, but
that is not the same thing as saying that it ought to contain

specification of the teacher's lesson objectives, still less that any such objectives should necessarily be couched in directly measurable or observable terms. No satisfactory argument has yet been produced for insisting that a curriculum proposal should always contain detailed accounts of such things as student prerequisites, an inventory of skills and dispositions to be developed, methods of grading, strategies for teaching, a schedule for the programme, and such like. Some of these are indeed things that individual teachers need to think about, but they do not all have to adopt the same answers, and it is absurd to think that the curriculum planner, if he is someone other than the teacher of the course, is necessarily well placed to answer them for others.[17]

In the meantime, preoccupation with the *manner* of curriculum *presentation* in the abstract, especially if it is allowed to serve as a substitute for thinking about what our aims should be and what content is educationally worthwhile, leads to the avoidance of key issues. Emphasis on design, development, implementation and evaluation of curriculum as applied sciences falsely suggests that there are ways of doing these things that can be studied in isolation from studying the nature of the enterprise we are trying to engage in, namely education. Just as many courses in leadership or management misleadingly proceed as if there is a science of leadership divorced from questions about who is trying to lead whom, in what context, and for what purposes. (Most of the bad leaders of men I have known have been conspicuous for having a theory of leadership.) But the only techniques of leadership or management that may be recognised and learnt in the abstract are the basic elements of human communication. These, besides probably being readily perceivable, and artificial if engaged in as a result of a course in management rather than as a natural expression of one's personality, are skills the ability to deploy which is less important than the ability to discern when it is appropriate to do so. I, for example, am extremely irritated by brash executives who, having been taught the value of eye-contact, burrow earnestly and searchingly into my soul while I talk to them about the price of groceries; whereas no doubt that same technique may work wonders with others. Unfortunately nobody teaches executives how to judge between people in this respect.

Furthermore, such skills are seldom necessary to successful and effective leadership, and never sufficient. To lead well, you have to take people in a desirable direction successfully, preserving good feeling amongst them, and remaining respected and popular yourself. Such ability comes not so much from management skills as knowing what one is about, knowing and understanding the people one is dealing with, and having a certain kind of personality. In short, successful management is partly a function of luck and partly a function of understanding the people and the context of a particular job, and it may well be achieved in different ways by different people. In the same way, there are indeed points that all implementers, planners and evaluators of curriculum should bear in mind, but they are relatively obvious things such as to express oneself clearly, to bear in mind the ages of the students for whom the curriculum is intended, and not to offend people. The ability to recognise the need for such things and to proceed accordingly does not require expertise nor the backing of large-scale research. Conversely, what experts in curriculum design and large-scale research into matters theoretically of concern to curriculum have thrown up is, as we have seen, very little indeed.[18] Most of what is useful and interesting in curriculum theory is speculative (notwithstanding the fact that it has sometimes arisen in the context of empirical research).

The heart of the problem we face lies in an endemic confusion of form with substance, or manner with content. People appear to take empirically researched claims seriously, regardless of how poorly attested they may be, because they take a somewhat oversimplified view of the natural sciences as the proper model of reliable inquiry, and they uncritically assume that where they see the trappings of science, truth is being unearthed, rather as some people might imagine that technology makes criminal detection more sure. If we have systematic observation, if we have developed instruments, if we have trained observers, if we analyse the data statistically . . . then surely we must be getting at the truth? Obviously not necessarily, and as we have seen, obviously not in fact.

Sometimes the Emperor just isn't wearing any clothes, despite the smokescreen of hustle, bustle, talk and methodology that insists he is. (Unrepentant empiricists, particularly since they have an empire to lose, will no doubt want me to 'systematically' establish empirically that all is as I suggest. The bulk of what I have to say, to the effect that scientific research into education and treating curriculum as an applied science are inappropriate and not getting us far, is not an issue that requires further empirical backing, and the evidence, reasons and argument for that view have been presented in the foregoing chapters.)

Is this, then, a counsel of despair? Does the message of this book amount to the claim that curriculum study is futile, curriculum theory vain science? Certainly not. It merely suggests that certain emphases and assumptions on the part of some educationalists need to be drastically redrafted. The practicality of the matter (though this is only a contingent fact and might therefore be altered) is that currently public opinion, as represented in newspaper and television editorials and correspondence columns, and government attitudes to education, as represented by policy pronouncements and funding policies, are heavily on the side of the technicians — those who, while very often knowing little about the context in which they are working and who consequently produce 'findings' which are the result of techniques and conceptual moves that cannot hope to give us satisfactory information about *education*, none the less appear to be dealing in hard facts rather than the somewhat suspect exercise of thinking. These are the people, therefore, who currently tend to be funded to a vast extent, to be quoted in newspapers, to gain rapid promotion as *educationalists*(!), to move about the world giving public lectures summarising their 'findings' with no time to dwell on the curious means whereby they arrived at them, and whose style of educational research has long dominated North American teacher preparation and, ironically, just as its hold is beginning to weaken there in the face of telling criticism and faltering faith, is beginning, however slightly, to increase its hold on educational study in Britain.[19]

Now, the correct response to this admittedly dismal picture is not to castigate science (or the social sciences), nor to deny that there is a place for scientific research in education. It is rather to insist (a) that the limits and weakness of most actual educational research to date be understood and acknowledged; (b) that the amount of educational research undertaken be drastically reduced, so that it can confine itself to research that can be profitably undertaken empirically, by those competent to do it; (c) that all such research must be conducted in the light of a better conceptual grip on the matters being researched; and (d) that, more important than anything else, all such research into specific matters should be undertaken only by those who have some clear conceptual grasp of the enterprise of education itself.

To recapitulate the most important points: what is essential for any useful curriculum work is a thorough understanding of the nature of fundamental conceptual questions and of the limits of various types of understanding and research. (This appeal for what might be called the philosophy of education and the philosophy of the social sciences is not to be confused with many courses in research methods currently proliferating, which are surveys of ways of proceeding rather than critical examination of the limits of those ways.) Following this, any specific research, if it is going to be illuminating, must operate in the light of clearly articulated concepts; these, as we have said, are not simply definitions or truncated lists of examples or general indications of how to interpret a term.[20] What are required are coherent, fully explained ideas, with their implications spelled out, that do some justice to the rest of the community's view of the ideas. A more cautious approach to empirical research in the context of this greater understanding could then be usefully linked to the actual experience of practising teachers in a variety of ways. For undoubtedly much of what we as professors of education study is only marginally relevant to the practising teacher, and much of what we research insignificant. Closer links with the concerns of the classroom are certainly desirable.

However, it does not seem to follow that one should necessarily accept the view of those such as Stenhouse (1975) who argue strongly for the teacher as researcher.[21] This idea sometimes has the appearance of having grown out of the unwillingness of teachers to cooperate to any great extent with research or to show any particular interest in research findings. Certainly, there has been that lack of closeness between research and classroom. But this, I suggest, is largely because of the credibility gap between theory and practice. The fact is that the two logically go hand in hand, as has been argued.[22] But bad research and theory, of which we have had plenty, by definition doesn't accord with practice, which gives teachers good reason for seeing the two as divorced; in addition, it must be admitted that some teachers do not fully appreciate the logical connection between good theory and sound practice. This, one feels, may partly account both for the view of some that curriculum should be imposed from without by experts, and for the view that research should involve teachers, who might thereby be more disposed to take it seriously.

I would not wish to suggest that teachers should not or could not be involved in empirical research, but there is no compelling reason for them to be, and sometimes they should not be. The question of who should be involved in carrying out particular pieces of empirical research should be decided by reference to their competence in relation to the exercise, and not by their role. If, for example, we want to find out whether children are mastering quadratic equations by a certain age, then we need a widespread survey coordinated by somebody who is not fully engaged teaching a particular class. If, on the other hand, we are looking into some aspect of teaching literature, then it is essential to have somebody involved who knows something about teaching literature. It is noteworthy that all Stenhouse's examples of curriculum research based on schools are centred upon the question of the internal practicability and efficiency of curriculum proposals in particular schools, rather than the educational value of the changes. Clearly, research into the effects of a change in a particular school is likely to be expedited by researchers who know and understand the school. It is true that he does also say that we should make the school more and more like a research laboratory, experimenting with curriculum, and that ultimately the curriculum that the teacher-researchers create is 'to be judged by whether it advances our knowledge'[23] which might seem to suggest that he regards teachers in general as competent researchers into educational worthwhileness. But in fact this reference to judging advances in our knowledge is ambiguous as between advancing our knowledge of curriculum implementation and advancing our knowledge of education.

The former suggestion is not really acceptable as the way for all educational research to go: we cannot afford the time, trouble and expense involved in turning schools into perpetual workshops concerned only to find out more about the boundaries of being workshops, and there are, besides, other things to be inquired into. But if we are talking of judging the quality of our curriculum experimentation, then ultimately any judges of the success of the experiment will need to stand outside the school, and to consider the nature of knowledge and education (and various other things), as well as what we may happen to know about alternative means of achieving similar ends. One wonders at times whether Stenhouse has not confused the reasonable point that good theory must logically be practicable and useful theory must in fact be practicable, with the false claim that the test of a good curriculum is whether it operates successfully in a school. However that may be, we can say that, while certainly curriculum theory should be practicable and accessible, it does not follow that it has to be school-based. Much of it needs to be undertaken on a wide scale and will be time-consuming and require expertise, all of which will lead to a continued need for full-time experts in educational research. There is certainly no inherent reason why a curriculum theorist or empirical researcher should always be a practising teacher, especially given that we have argued that the manner of implementation of a curriculum should, for several reasons, be left to a large extent to individual practitioners.

A word should be said in passing about a recent school of thought in curriculum theory usually labelled 'reconceptualist'. While much of what individual reconceptualists say (e.g. MacDonald, 1973; Apple, 1979) is as interesting, true and useful as anything anybody else has had to say, it is a mistake to see them as representing a movement that offers a new conception of curriculum inquiry. What unites them and gives rise to the identity of a reconceptualist is rather a particular view of how change occurs both in schooling and through schooling, and of what sort of change should occur. (As a matter of fact it is a largely Marxist viewpoint, and seems to me to have the strengths of many of the individual insights of Marxism in all its shapes and forms, and the weakness of the uncompromising single-minded vision of each of its forms.) The reconceptualists are, in other words, curriculum theorists with a particular view of the nature of curriculum change, and a particular interest in that question. They do not offer a distinctive theory of curriculum theory; they merely have, as we all have, their distinctive theory of curriculum.

It should now be evident that Egan (1982) was entirely correct when he pointed out that Walker (1976) was simply mistaken to say that 'curriculum problems are practical not theoretical ones'.[24] Such a remark takes us back to a simple-minded and false dichotomy between theory and practice. Curriculum problems are many and various (What should we teach? How should we teach it? How should we organise it? When should we teach it? Can we get children to see what we're after? Can we persuade the powers that be to let us adopt this curriculum?), but while each solution, if it can be found, is by definition going to be practical, arriving at any solution, is, equally by definition, largely a theoretical business.

Reason lies at the heart of the educational business. Education itself is centrally concerned with the development of reason.[25] Empirical research must strive to be rationally explicable and defensible in its procedures, based on well-reasoned concepts and related in some way to inquiry into the development of reason. We undoubtedly want rational curriculum planning, in the sense that we want our curriculum practice to answer to rational criteria of judgement. We have to be aware that as a matter of fact educational theorists, not being politicians, education ministers or headteachers, generally make their impact indirectly. At best they are studied and acted on, at worst they sometimes slowly 'change the climate in which policy is made' (Jenkins and Shipman, 1976).[26] But does that necessarily matter? Is it a cause for grave concern, such that we should concentrate on seeking alternative paths to political control, rather than the path of sound deliberate reason? The impact, to take extreme cases, of a Karl Marx or a John Stuart Mill on political life has not been any the less because their influence was not immediate and has come about indirectly from a theoretical base, rather than through their own limited attempts at political intervention. The task of curriculum theorists, if that is what they are to be, as opposed to politicians, remains that of thinking about curriculum, rather than devising strategies for proving effective agents of change. And there never should have been any doubt about what curriculum theory

involves: 'Curriculum theory I see as arriving at the production of
. . . general principles for our practice, the best most rationally
defensible statements of what we ought to do in situations having
certain characteristics . . . we need teachers who can indeed make
rational practical judgements in their own contexts, but that is surely
only possible if there is a body of rational curriculum principles they
can intelligibly employ' (Hirst, 1980).

2. GIVING TEACHING BACK TO TEACHERS

Superficially, there may seem to be something of a paradox in the title
of this book, since I have said little about teachers, and have
specifically disassociated myself from the view that we should adopt
a policy of developing teacher-researchers. My final task is therefore
to explain the sense in which it seems to me imperative that teaching
should be firmly entrusted to teachers — whether it ever was
entrusted to them and hence whether it is strictly speaking a question
of giving it 'back' is not very important — and to draw out the
implications of the argument in the previous chapters that lead to this
conclusion.

There are two main aspects to my view of the centrality of teachers
in the teaching enterprise: first, that the individual teacher's
judgement and decision-making should play, and be acknowledged to
play, a very large part in curriculum decisions relating to particular
classrooms, and by extension that teachers within a school should
play a prominent part in school curriculum planning. Secondly, that,
as a consequence, teachers should be thoroughly initiated into
curriculum theory, but in a specific manner that does not necessarily
closely resemble what goes on in many current teacher preparation or
in-service programmes. As so often this is to some extent merely a
question of shifting emphasis, but whether in particular cases it be
that or a more positive change of direction the argument is that we
need to move away from a situation in which teachers can be readily
distinguished from specialist curriculum experts, and in which
detailed prescriptions for practice are derived from the findings of the
latter and imposed on the former, towards a situation in which
teachers are both expected to, and competent to, make most of their
decisions about what to teach and how to teach themselves.

One would expect a public system of schooling none the less to
subserve some common set of social and educational goals, and I am
not arguing that individual teachers should be free to pursue whatever
aims they choose, although I would argue that they should be more

involved in discussing, arguing about and formulating them than they have generally been. The argument is not, therefore, about whether particular teachers should or should not feel free to opt for indoctrination rather than education, to curb imagination, critical thought and creativity, or to ignore the claims of literacy in favour of developing expertise in automobile engine-stripping. It is a question of whether teachers should not play a far more prominent role in deciding what materials they will use to promote education, critical thought, imagination and literacy, how they will organise their material, how they will organise their students, how they will teach them, how they will assess their progress, how, in short, they will plan their curriculum. It is evident that any increase in individual teacher autonomy has implications for such things as teacher accountability and public examination systems. I do not intend to go into such matters here, beyond remarking that (a) if the argument for a fair degree of teacher autonomy, given certain features of teacher preparation, is strong, then we must surely accept that as an argument against too restrictive forms of accountability and examination; and (b) even if, for the moment, we accept that there will be public examinations that place constraints on teachers' freedom to choose materials and objectives, and forms of accountability that further restrict their freedom, there is still considerable latitude within which the teacher can be encouraged to display more or less autonomy.[27]

The argument for allowing a great deal of scope to individual teacher initiative and judgement, implicit throughout this book, is very simple and is not based on any particular sectarian or idealistic view of teachers. It is, essentially, that we know very little indeed about the best way to proceed in detailed terms, whether we are talking about teaching techniques or the organisation of material, time and content. We do know something about the questions that need to be asked, but we do not have any universally applicable answers of value. We certainly do not have any reason to suppose that there is a 'proper' way to design, develop or implement a curriculum, nor that there are any 'correct' ways to assess children's progress or the success of our curriculum. How a teacher should proceed stems essentially from a view of what the educational enterprise is all about, what the particular subject matter one is dealing with may contribute to that enterprise, and how dealing with it in one way or another may facilitate that contribution. Even if we were not remarkably ignorant in respect of general answers to such questions, there may legitimately be different answers to them, and particular circumstances will often directly yield different answers; therefore, what constitutes good teaching has to be judged by reference to particular contexts. The only constants are likely to be some of the broad criteria whereby we judge success.

It has not been denied that there are certain claims that we can hand on to teachers which it is reasonable to regard as true: children only gradually acquire the ability to handle abstract concepts and to see relationships in the way that we do. (This is almost certainly because these things are *not* matters of simple maturation.) It is inadvisable to adopt one specific style of teaching for all occasions. Pupils may find learning difficult for a wide variety of reasons. Some things can be learned by doing, others only by means of verbal (or some other symbolic form of) understanding. Intelligence is at least partially affected by environmental factors. 'Time spent on reading and numbers is associated with growth in those areas' (Rosenshine, 1976).[28] A coherent curriculum must have some objectives. But such claims, besides being sometimes self-evident (who has ever encountered a young child, and not been aware that it could not handle the concept of democracy as you and I can?), and sometimes bordering on the tautologous (of course a coherent curriculum must have objectives; that is part of what is meant by 'coherent'), are of no practical use. In order to teach successfully, we need to know what conceptual ability this particular child has, what factors are making learning difficult in this case, what things this child can, and can best, learn by doing, how much time to spend on reading, and in what way, with particular children, and what kind of formulation of what kind of objectives is required when.

It is also true that we can, with some degree of plausibility, supplement some of those general but useless claims with more specific information. We can, for example, list some of the factors that may make learning difficult (inability to understand, distraction, lack of motivation) or some of the environmental factors that may affect intelligence (linguistic deprivation, socioeconomic status, anxiety). But such information still does not help us establish why a particular child is finding it difficult to learn, or appears to be relatively unintelligent, and it doesn't tell us what to do, if we knew.

When it comes to attempts to give us practically useful information, we have to recognise more or less total failure. We do not know whether group teaching, in one sense or another, is preferable to didactic instruction, or even whether it much matters whether we adopt either style. The little that we can get out of such research is once again largely tautologous (e.g. group teaching, defined to involve the handling of questions by pupils, gives them some facility in handling questions). We do not know how to combat environmental restraints on intelligence; we do not know how to develop intelligence. We do not know how to enhance learning in general. (At least, we do not know such things from empirical research. There are some truths that we can draw from thinking about what intelligence and learning particular things actually involve.) We do not know how to develop imaginative, creative or critical adults. We do not know how best to teach mathematics to grade 11 students, or how best to teach history to 7-year-olds.

The immediate reason that we do not know such things is that the research into them has been seriously deficient.[29] But it is highly likely that the underlying reason, which also accounts for some of the contradictions and inadequacies in the research, is that there is no single answer to such questions: there is no best way to teach history to a particular age group, and no correct way to develop rationality. Rather, given the enormous number of factors that may make for or mar success in teaching, factors to do with the teacher, the subject-matter, the child and the classroom climate, the best way for a teacher to proceed must depend upon the particular context in which he is operating, his own personality and knowledge, that of his children, and the situation they are all in as individuals and as a group. And even then, there is no *a priori* reason to assume that there is one proper way to proceed rather than several equally efficacious ways. (Some might choose to say that at any rate some empirical research is now beginning to confirm this hypothesis. That, alas, is not strictly speaking true. Some research concludes that there is no best way to teach overall, but in view of the weaknesses in all such research, it can hardly claim to have empirically verified it, notwithstanding the fact that it is almost certainly the case.)

If it is correct to assert that the best we can do is itemise hundreds of factors that in themselves and in a multiplicity of combinations *may* affect the success of the schooling enterprise in one way or another, it surely follows that the judgement of the individual teacher, who is at least in a position to know something about himself, his students and what he is trying to do, must be paramount in deciding how to proceed, rather than the generalised demands of some curriculum design or otherwise imposed rules of educational experts. Nor is there any reason to suppose that the individual teacher's judgement will be other than impaired by any training programme that involves too great an adherence to a necessarily selective number of models of teaching, pieces of research, means of assessment or curriculum designs. Any such approach merely strengthens the myth that there are right and wrong things to do in education, which can be generalised and established without reference to a fully articulated conception of education and particular circumstances. The teacher will have to make his own decisions, and he will have to do so in the light of a general appreciation of factors that may make a difference, combined with a pretty clear idea of what he is doing and why, and some insight into the particular children he encounters.

It may be conceded that some teachers, probably many, are not in fact in a very strong position to exercise such judgement. But if that is so, it is because teacher training, particularly in so far as it is concerned to perpetuate the idea of a science of teaching, has done little to foster a capacity for articulating a coherent view of what one is doing and why, and a capacity for recognising the complexity and subtlety of human interaction. I doubt very much whether we can with much assurance teach prospective teachers to judge the state of mind of individual children well, but we could certainly encourage the exercise of such judgement by refraining from presenting human interaction on the crude mechanistic level that so much research into teacher effectiveness and psychology of education does. And certainly this argument that teachers should be encouraged to exercise a great deal of autonomy has to be accompanied by a demand, supported by precisely the same set of considerations, that teacher-preparation should get its act together — in a phrase, that it should be genuine teacher education rather than teacher training.

If teachers are to make sound judgements about their practice, then they need to have a set of very clear educational concepts, and they need to understand why they have to take the responsibility of autonomy and cannot reasonably rely on directions from 'experts'. This leads inevitably to some kind of teacher preparation course that starts with a rigorous and sustained examination of the question of what schools are for. What purposes do they in fact appear to serve, and what purposes should they serve? This is not simply a matter of combining sociology and philosophy, for what is required is not a detailed sociological perspective on schooling, or a study of educational philosophy for its own sake, still less the training of a sociologist or academic philosopher. What is required therefore is not a detailed study of this particular piece of sociological research and that analysis of the nature of schooling (although any such combination would be preferable to the one-sided courses that some students currently receive), but a more general awareness of the sorts of claim that have been made about the purposes schools actually serve, and a thorough consideration of what the students in question think are the purposes they should serve. This will lead directly to the location of certain central concepts, and these in turn need to be minutely examined.

One would guess that the central concepts would include education itself, socialisation, learning, intelligence, moral development, emotional development, physical development, knowledge, understanding, and possibly, creativity and imagination. Examining such concepts is, of course, technically a philosophical activity, but here again we do not necessarily wish to conceive of a course in philosophy of education as sometimes actually practised. In the first place, we want to be selective in our choice of concepts. We may not want to examine indoctrination and play, for example, because, however philosophically interesting they may be, it may be felt that they are not the central concepts of the enterprise of schooling. We want to know what education is, rather than to produce a fluent account of something that it is not, such as indoctrination. (It may be pedagogically useful to try and get at education by contrasting it with indoctrination, but that is a separate point that does not effect the tenor of this argument.) Play may certainly be an important consideration in relation to some aspects of schooling, but unless somebody actually wants to argue that it is central to the enterprise in some way, it is not a concept that has priority here. It may also be that certain concepts, though felt to be central, do not in fact require too much consideration because they are relatively clear: one might suggest that whereas what constitutes education and knowledge does require some thought, it is actually pretty clear what teaching and learning mean. (This is not to say we know much about them, merely that we know what they are.)

Secondly, although individual instructors might think it helpful to proceed by looking at what various philosophers have said, the point of this exercise is not to study philosophy of education, but to ensure that the students really do articulate full and coherent conceptions of their own. The idea is that they should start their preparation as teachers by acquiring a clear set of central concepts that are individually coherent and mutually compatible. For the strange truth is that whereas most professions centre on an activity based upon a clearly articulated and shared set of concepts, whether we are talking of physicists, footballers or pharmacists, education does not. Educationalists very often actually mean different things by the same words, even when the words are central to their activity. We cannot legislate against this, but we can ensure that every individual is aware of it (aware, for example, that the education that programmed learning is designed to provide is a quite different thing from the education that others seek to provide), and that he himself knows precisely what he is talking about.

Following some such basic course, the prospective teacher needs to think equally hard and long about what his teaching specialism or area of interest actually involves, and why it should be engaged in. What, for example, is music education supposed to be, why should anyone be subjected to it, how does it contribute to any of the central purposes of schooling? How does primary schooling fit into the overall pattern of schooling, what are we trying to achieve in the name of 'reading with understanding', what precisely counts as being numerate, and how important is it that people should be numerate and to what extent? Since it is very easy to give some reason or set of reasons for teaching virtually anything ('I teach cooking, because most people will need to cook in their lives'; 'I teach typing, because it's an economically useful accomplishment'; 'I teach Biblical studies, because the Bible informs much of our literature and way of life'), it is important that students think about the claims of their own specialism in relation to those of others. The question is not whether a case can be mounted for teaching geography, but whether geography is more deserving of limited curriculum time than other things, whether it should be compulsory for all, or an option available to some, and so forth. Therefore consideration of one's curriculum specialism should ideally take place in a setting that brings many different kinds of would-be teachers together.

A most important aspect of this second proposed course must not be overlooked. Our conception of an activity combined with our reasons for engaging in it, tells us a great deal about *how* we ought to engage in it. Even with something as simple as soccer, the question of how one should proceed on the field, not only in terms of what is permissible and what isn't, but also in terms of strategy, is largely answered by understanding what the game is about. One can go further and say that what constitutes a good player is largely determined by the nature of the game. In exactly the same way, what largely determines what is good history teaching or what is good elementary teaching is our understanding of what teaching history or teaching elementary pupils is and what we are doing it for. We are, therefore, at this point directly engaging our students with the vexed question of methodology and style of teaching in what is surely the most appropriate manner. We are providing them with criteria to judge proper ways of proceeding.

What we cannot do by this route is ensure them success or reveal a procedure that is bound to be successful in terms of teaching history to a particular age group for certain purposes, and to fit the special requirements of particular children. Thirdly, therefore, prospective teachers need to consider the broad question of learning, without reference to specialisms. But, in view of what has been said in previous pages, it is surely clear that it is neither reasonable nor sensible to approach this task by courses involving detailed study of developmental theory, learning theory or teacher effectiveness.[30] What is required is a sustained examination of the nature of, and problems in, research into such matters. Let students give critical thought to such questions as what research into mental concepts such as intelligence and creativity is actually like, what it could hope to achieve, what it has achieved, and why one should care. At the same time the most important 'finding' of such research needs to be emphasised, namely the enormously long list of factors, personal, social and contextual that may affect success in the classroom.

Fourthly, and finally, students need to consider, not rules and mechanisms for assessment and evaluation, but the nature of assessment, the problems of assessment, and the different requirements in terms of assessment that different activities may lead to.

Armed with some such thorough understanding of the nature of the enterprise they are involved in, the nature of their own role and its demands on their practice, as well as the constraints on our hopes of improving our knowledge, teachers will be as well placed as they can be to make particular judgements about how to proceed in their classrooms, as well as to evaluate the curriculum proposals of others and to plan their own curriculum.

The question has been raised of how we would be able to assess the quality or efficacy of the teacher judgement that I am arguing has to be central.[31] The question itself betrays a lingering preoccupation with the idea of teaching as a science. 'If we cannot monitor good and bad teacher judgement, how can we allow the educational enterprise to rest upon it?' My response is predictable. It will not be possible for supervisors or inspectors to walk into a classroom and accurately measure the quality of teacher judgement displayed. But then it is not possible now to walk into a classroom and judge the overall quality of a teacher, except by arbitrarily reducing 'quality' to a set of more or less directly observable behaviours that as likely as not have no bearing on the question. We have to face up to the inevitability of it being impossible, except in extreme cases, to estimate confidently the quality of a teacher simply by observing him in action. There are things that are more or less accurately measurable and monitorable, such as whether he talks a lot, whether he asks a lot of questions, whether children stay in their places, whether they stare out of windows, and whether they can spell or do quadratic equations. But some of these things do not matter, and taken together they do not add up to a tenth part of what the enterprise is about. If you are in the business of playing a small part in an operation that overall seeks to promote understanding, conceptual finesse, appreciation, enthusiasm, social cooperativeness, personal adjustment, moral maturity, intellectual rigour, information and imagination, then you are doomed to having to rely much of the time on impressionistic appraisal. But we should not forget that sometimes an attempt to ensure that something is happening, in this case the exercise of sound autonomous teacher judgement, is better served by making the correct preparations beforehand than by imperfect attempts to check success after the event. If you prepare someone well as a runner, a salesman or a doctor it becomes less important to check afterwards that he can run, sell or practise medicine well. In the same way, if we know what we are trying to do and prepare teachers accordingly, we have some reason to suppose that much of what they subsequently do will be sensible.

The current situation in terms of centralisation of education differs considerably in different parts of the world (often differing from province to province or state to state). The degree of change from existing practice that may be involved in what I propose therefore differs enormously from place to place. But, as my concern has been to argue about what there is good reason to do, rather than to claim any particular new insights, that is neither here nor there. What seems clear is that any hope for sound teacher education, and hence a sound educational system, lies in teachers being prepared, in the manner I have outlined, to think about curriculum matters in such a way as to enable them to make detailed judgements about curriculum content and practice for themselves, while emphasis should be taken off the notion of curriculum study as an applied science.

Does this prescription contradict my argument against curriculum design in Chapter 3? Am I not offering a specific curriculum for teacher education? Yes, I am; but there is no contradiction. On the contrary, the curriculum outline is confirmation of my thesis that some fairly specific curriculum points can be made, but that they arise out of a thorough explication of the nature, point and purpose of the enterprise. Beyond that we cannot reasonably go, and therefore I do not offer detailed prescriptions for the organisation, teaching and evaluation of such a curriculum.

Let us prepare teachers for autonomy, and then let us give teaching back to teachers.

Notes

CHAPTER 1

1. Stenhouse (1975), p.3. For some perceptive comments on the place of philosophy and aims see Macdonald-Ross (1975).
2. Jenkins and Shipman (1975), p.4.
3. Kelly (1977), p.10.
4. For a more detailed account of the nature of definition and analysis, see Barrow (1981, 1982 and 1984).
5. On the importance of discrimination, see Barrow (1982). The importance of having specific concepts in order to think about, and conduct empirical research into education is a theme that recurs throughout this book. See particularly, Chapter 6.
6. Ch. 2.s.5.
7. On theory, see further Barrow (1978a 1981a); Tibble (1971) and Hirst and O'Connor (1972).

CHAPTER 2

1. See below, Part III, especially Ch. 7.
2. See also Nigel Wright's useful book, *Progress in Education* (1977).
3. This is to follow Bruner's view. See Lytton (1971), p.3.
4. See below Ch. 5.s.5.
5. See below Ch. 6. ss.6 and 7.
6. Further points are made about intelligence and standardised testing at Ch. 2.s.3; Ch. 6.s.6; Ch. 8.s.2; and Ch. 9.s.1.
7. On (indirect) validity, see Ch. 8.s.2.
8. See references quoted at beginning of Ch. 6.
9. Substantiation for all the claims made in this section, including relatively peripheral ones such as that, when the point about inherent weaknesses is acknowledged, it is sometimes done in 'a curiously disarming manner', will be found in Chs 5, 6 and 8. Ch. 6 in particular provides most of the evidence and argument that lies behind the general view of curriculum theory here advanced.
10. Plato: an Athenian philosopher, 4th century BC. Pupil of Socrates; author of dialogues such as *Republic*. See Barrow, *Plato and Education* (1976). J.J. Rousseau: French philosopher, 18th century. Author of *Social*

Contract and *Emile*. See Barrow, *Radical Education* (1978), Chs 2 and 3. E. Durkheim: Sociologist, 19th century. Author of *Suicide* (1952). See Morrish, *Disciplines of Education* (1967). J. Piaget: Swiss psychologist, 20th century. See Ch. 5. S. Freud: Viennese psychoanalyst, 20th century. See Ch. 5. C. Burt: Prominent British psychologist earlier this century. Recently presumed to have behaved questionably in use of research methods. See Burt (1923 and 1949). A. Jensen: American psychologist who argues for predominance of genetic factors in intelligence. See Jensen (1969). K. Marx: 19th century author of *Capital* (1938), founding father of some versions of Marxism. His influence on educational theory as such has been negligible. However, for a contrary view, see Matthews, *The Marxist Theory of Schooling* (1981).

11. See Barrow (1976).
12. J. Dewey: Considerable influence on North American philosophy of education. See Dewey (1938) and Peters (1977). Paul Hirst: Contemporary British philosopher of education. See Ch. 4. Richard Peters: Contemporary British philosopher of education whose seminal work has had great influence. See Peters (1966). Ivan Illich: Author of *Deschooling Society* (1971) and other works concerned to expose the grip of institutionalisation on modern life. See Barrow, *Radical Education* (1978), Ch. 6.
13. For a more detailed account of such agencies, see e.g. Kelly (1977); Taylor and Richards (1979); and Becher and Maclure (1978).
14. See Ch. 6.
15. See Ch. 6.s.6.
16. Cronbach (1975), p. 119.
17. Snow (1977), p. 12.
18. See Barnes (1976); Bernstein (1971); and Labov (1966). See also Barrow (1982a) for explanation of judgement in text.
19. See Ch. 5.s.3.
20. For a brief comment on this generalisation, see Ch. 5.s.4.
21. See Barrow (1981).
22. Ibid.
23. Tasos Kazepides (1982) says that this use of 'socialisation' is peculiar to me; hence my emphasis on the fact that this at any rate is what I mean by the word.
24. The use of the word 'incorrect' is obviously dangerous in such a context. See Barrow (1984). My concern is that the reader should play fair: regardless of what it implies to talk of correct/incorrect usage, does the reader not in fact agree with what is said in the text? On education, see Peters (1966) and Barrow (1975 and 1981).
25. On conceptual finesse, see Barrow (1981 and 1982).
26. See, e.g. Warnock (1976); Hare (1964); Wilson (1973); and Hospers (1956).
27. See Barrow (1981), Bedford (1964) and Hepburn (1972).

CHAPTER 3

1. Pratt (1980), p. 5.
2. For a useful review of some of the more common design analogies, see Sockett (1976), particularly Chs 1 and 2. For a very useful discussion of the value and limits of metaphor, see Milburn (1983, a, b and c). See also s.5 below and Ch. 9.s.1.
3. Pratt (1980), p. 4.
4. Ibid., Ch. 4.
5. Ibid., p. 80.
6. Ibid., p. 85. See also LaPierre (1934) and Haberman (1966).
7. Pratt (1980), p. 87.
8. Ibid., pp. 81-84.
9. For further discussion of needs, see Dearden (1972) and Barrow (1975).
10. Pratt (1980), p. 91.
11. 'To enable students to use an English dictionary effectively' is Pratt's (1980) example, taken from Appendix IV, p. 469.
12. Pratt (1980), pp. 151, 152.
13. Ibid., p. 148.
14. Ibid., pp. 150, 151.
15. Ibid., p. 198.
16. Ibid., p. 199.
17. Stufflebeam (1968), p. 6. Pratt (1980), p. 207.
18. For Plato and Rousseau, see Ch. 2, n.10. Comenius, 17th century author of e.g. *The School of Infancy* (1957).
19. Taylor (1970), p. 76.
20. Skilbeck (1976); Taylor and Richards (1979), p. 74.
21. See e.g. Taba (1962); Kerr (1968); Rubin (1977); Joyce (1979), Taylor and Richards (1979); and Pratt (1980). For a sensible comment on the situation see Jenkins and Shipman (1975).
22. See e.g. Joyce (1979).
23. Figure 1 from Keating (1982).
24. Figure 2 from Taylor and Richards (1979); Figure 3 from Kerr (1968).
25. The term 'educanto' was coined by James D. Koerner, *The Miseducation of American Teachers*. He sums up the knowledge gained by a graduate in educanto as follows: 'You will know that dynamically reinforced growth of your ideational and cross-fertilized learnings has occurred, hopefully through intravariable autorivalry, enriched need arousal, purposeful goal-orientated behavior, and persistent achievement motivations. Your self-actualization, together with your real-life readiness for situational and refractive testing against Yoakam's Readability Formula, will be concretioned', etc. As Koerner says, educanto, besides masking 'a lack of thought (that) in fact makes thought of any important kind extraordinarily difficult', can also 'reduce any mildly sensitive layman to a state of helpless fury in a matter of minutes.'
26. According to a standard dictionary. According to Pratt's (1980) glossary it means: 'the generation of ideas or solutions to problems involving free-

flowing creative thought and spontaneous non-critical expression of ideas; often conducted in a group.' But what does that mean and how does one come by it?

27. Taylor and Richards (1979), p. 152.
28. Pratt (1980), p. 152.
29. This is not a quotation from Pratt, but from Rugg (1926) quoted by Pratt (1980) p. 32. I presume it represents the latter's view.
30. Pratt (1980), p. 35.
31. Ibid., pp. 70, 71.
32. Bobbit (1918), p. 284; Goodlad (1958), p. 391.

CHAPTER 4

1. For further discussion of elitism and problems concerning quality in art, see Barrow (1975) and Bantock (1963).
2. For a useful discussion of this issue, see Woods and Gregory (1974).
3. See White (1973) and Barrow (1976a).
4. On the use of transcendental arguments, see Brent (1978) and Kleinig (1973).
5. I, for one, have tried to kill it (see 1976a, 1978, 1981 and 1984a).
6. See Ch. 3.s.1; and Pratt (1980), Ch. 4.
7. Pratt (1980), p. 60.
8. Ibid., p. 59.
9. Ibid., p. 69.
10. On interests, see also Wilson (1971); Dearden (1976); and Barrow (1975). On other possible functions of interest as motivation, see Ch. 5.s.4.
11. See further the discussion of A.S. Neill in Barrow (1978).
12. The basic point about transference was clearly seen and stated by Herbart (1904) some hundreds of years ago.
13. For an excellent discussion of critical thinking, see McPeck (1981).
14. On culture, see also Lawton (1975) and Barrow (1975).
15. Bantock has also posited a third sense of culture, in Bantock (1968).
16. See Lawton (1975).
17. Comenius (1957) saw this distinction between encyclopediac knowledge and wisdom well, as Plato (1955) had done and Peters (1966) has done.
18. This explains why I do not examine e.g. Phenix (1964) in the text.
19. Hirst's views have developed since initially presented, as the papers collected in Hirst (1974) indicate. What I say in the text represents the most satisfactory account I can give of his thinking.
20. See e.g. Ayer (1971).
21. For some comments on integration, see Ch. 5.s.3.
22. Kelly (1977), p. 37.
23. On a core curriculum see Barrow (1976a) and 1984b).

CHAPTER 5

1. An important book on this topic is Egan (1983).

2. Lawton (1978), p. 61.
3. Fontana (1981), p. 147; Tomlinson (1981).
4. On the meaning of know, see e.g. Hospers (1956).
5. Fontana (1981), p. 147.
6. See e.g. Gagné (1970).
7. Ibid., p. 207.
8. Sockett (1976), p. 73.
9. Peters (1974), p. 203.
10. Ausubel (1959), p. 245.
11. See Freud (1901, 1938 and 1962).
12. The similarity between Freud's view and Plato's view of the three part soul may be remarked.
13. Brown (1964), p. 12.
14. Morris (1958).
15. Morrish (1967), pp. 171-173.
16. For a good discussion of Kohlberg, see Peters (1974) Chs 15, 16 and 17.
17. See also Piaget (1929 and 1947).
18. Isaacs (1930).
18a. See also M. Cole (1975) 'An ethnographic psychology of cognition' in R.W. Brislin *et al.* (eds) *Cross Cultural Perspectives in Learning* (New York: Sage 1975) commenting on the fact that most Australian Aborigine adults fail Piagetian tests of conservation: 'are we to believe that Aborigine adults will store water in tall thin cans in order to "have more water"?'
19. Stenhouse (1975).
20. John Stuart Mill (1962). But see his autobiography in this connection.
21. A.N. Whitehead (1929). A classic text.
22. Lawton (1978), p. 96.
23. The logical points, if there are any to be made, will need to be discerned by clear thinking. See e.g. Claiborne (1983) on reading.
24. On readiness, see further Barrow (1975).
25. On integration, see also Warwick (1973) and Barrow (1981).
26. Kelly (1977), p. 63.
27. See e.g. Fontana (1981), Ch. 15; and Davidoff (1976) pp. 201-203.
28. See e.g. Peters (1966).
29. Mussen (1979). See Fontana (1981), p. 156.
30. Given the overall argument of this book, especially the following chapter, I am somewhat diffident about referring to this claim as 'well-attested' and accepting the claims of other research as I do in this section. I believe the claims here cited to be more acceptable than those discussed elsewhere because they are more limited in scope and seem more in accord with common sense and personal experience.
31. Pratt (1980), p. 274.
32. Bloom (1976), p. 7.
33. On discovery learning, see also Dearden (1967) and Barrow (1975).
34. See Plato's *Meno* (1956) and Barrow (1976 and 1983).
35. Hamlyn (1967), p. 24.

36. Duchastel and Merrill (1973), p. 63.
37. Bertrand Russell, 20th century British philosopher, peace activist and educationalist. See Russell (1932 and 1967-9).
38. Popham (1977), p. 612.
39. Stenhouse (1975), p. 83.
40. Taylor (1970), p. 76.
41. See Barrow (1984b).
42. See e.g. Pratt's list of such things in his specimen curriculum. Pratt (1980), Appendix IV.

CHAPTER 6

1. Dunkin and Biddle (1974), p. 7.
2. Heath and Nielsen (1974), p. 483.
3. Good, Biddle and Brophy (1975), p. 8.
4. Berliner (1976), p. 12.
5. Dunkin and Biddle (1974), p. 131.
6. Ibid., p. 132.
7. Ibid., p. 80.
8. Ibid., pp. 161, 377.
9. Ibid., p. 135.
10. Ibid., p. 174.
11. Ibid., p. 157.
12. Kounin (1970), p. 8.
13. Ibid., p. 67.
14. Ibid., p. 68.
15. Ibid., p. 85.
16. Dunkin and Biddle (1974), p. 151.
17. Ibid., p. 158.
18. Ibid., p. 375.
19. Ibid., p. 374.
20. Ibid., p. 152.
21. Ibid., pp. 375, 377.
22. Ibid., p. 157.
23. Ibid., p. 153.
24. Ibid., p. 377.
25. Ibid., p. 161.
26. Ibid., p. 377.
27. Ibid., p. 146.
28. Ibid., pp. 161, 374.
29. Flanders (1967), p. 109.
30. Ibid., p. 106.
31. Dunkin and Biddle (1974), p. 112.
32. On teacher directness, see e.g. Perkins (1964); Dahllof and Lundgren (1970); Flanders (1970); Tisher (70). On pupil talk, see e.g. Furst (67b); Lohman (67); Flanders (1970).

33. Hoehn (1954).
34. Hill and Furst (1969).
35. Dunkin and Biddle (1974), p. 116.
36. E.g. Sorber (1967). See also ss. 5 and 6 below.
37. Dunkin and Biddle (1974), p. 116. Herman (1967).
38. See also Ch. 2.ss.2 and 3; and Ch. 6.s.6, Ch. 8.s.2 and Ch. 9.s.1.
39. Amidon and Giammatteo (1967). But cf. contrary conclusion of Hughes (1959).
40. Medley and Hill (1970).
41. Fowler and Soar (n.d.) McGee (1955).
42. Johns (1966) and Mood (1972). But cf. contrary conclusion of Measel (1967). On my comment that the finding seems to accord with common sense, Measel notwithstanding, see further below s.6, comments on the nature of the analytic truth.
43. Dunkin and Biddle (1974), p. 117. Amidon and Flanders (1961); Furst (1967b); Sprague (1971).
44. Dunkin and Biddle (1974), p. 117. Johns (1966); Lohman (1967); Bondi (1969); Rian (1969); Traill (1971). Note that contrary claims are made about correlations between indirect style and pupil response to teacher initiations. E.g. Rian (1969) as compared with Bondi (1969). (This difference is reported by Dunkin and Biddle as the finding that there is a lowering and the finding that there is a raising.) Note also the difficulty in disentangling pupil response to teacher initiation and pupil initiation.
45. Furst (1967a); Hunter (1968); Penny (1969); Flanders (1970).
46. Soar (1966). But on creativity see e.g. ORACLE, s.6 below.
47. Soar (1966).
48. Dunkin and Biddle (1974), p. 117. See above n. 44.
49. For a full list of studies, see Dunkin and Biddle (1974), pp. 106-111, 113-116.
50. Dunkin and Biddle (1974), p. 117. Campbell (1970).
51. E.g. (i) Flanders (1967); Altman (1970); Dahllof and Lundgren (1970); Tisher (1970). (ii) Good *et al.* (1973), Good and Brophy (1972), Silberman (1969). (iii) Rubovits and Maehr (1973). (iv) Rubovits and Maehr (1973). (v) Smith (1965). (vi) Brophy *et al.* (1973). But cf. contrary claim of Altman (1970).
52. E.g. (vii) Wallen (1966); Felsenthal (70); cf. Wright and Nuthall (1970); Soar *et al.* (71). (viii) Flanders (1970).
53. Spaulding (1963).
54. Wallen and Wodtke (1963).
55. Dunkin and Biddle (1974), p. 124. Research behind claim (i) Emmer (1967); (ii) Soar (1966); Flanders (1970). Cf. contrary claim of Perkins (1965). (iii) Soar (1966).
56. E.g. (i) Jackson and Lahaderne (1966); Brophy *et al* (1973); Evertson *et al.* (1973). Cf. contrary claim of Davis and Slobodian (1967). (ii) Brophy *et al.* (1973). Cf. contrary claim of Altman (1970). (iii) Good *et al.* (1973). (iv) Good and Brophy (1972). (v) Campbell (1970). (vii) Spaulding (1963). (viii) Soar (1966). (ix) Soar (1966).

57. Also claimed by ORACLE. See below s.6.
58. Dunkin and Biddle (1974), e.g. p. 117
59. Ibid., e.g. p. 117. See also p. 87.
60. Ibid., e.g. p. 118.
61. Ibid., p. 131. See also pp. 104, 5. cf. Ch. 2.
62. Ibid., pp. 4, 11.
63. Ibid., p. 13 (cf. p. 657).
64. Ibid., p. 59 (for the purposes for which they were designed).
65. Ibid., p. 80.
66. Ibid., pp. 408, 11, 418.
67. Ibid., p. 12.
68. Sanders (1978), p. 186. See Barrow (1984c).
69. Johnston (1975).
70. Cronbach (1975), p. 116.
71. Snow (1977), p. 12.
72. Ibid., my italics.
73. Bennett (1976). Indeed he does, though for the wrong reasons. Bennett has now come to the conclusion that his original statistical work was awry. As should be clear from the text, that is of very little practical significance.
74. See also Barrow (1981).
75. For a more detailed consideration of standardised measures, see Ch.2.ss.2 and 3; Ch.6.s.6; Ch.8.s.2 and Ch.9.s.1.
76. The reason that he gives for initially adopting a wide variety of style categories are similar to those that I have given for avoiding broad concepts.
77. But, if it was something to do with her teaching, we are in no position to know what it is about her teaching that is significant.
78. See e.g. Joyce and Weil (1979).
79. Plowden Report (1967), p. 11.
80. Cox and Dyson (1969).
81. Galton and Simon (1980), p. 18.
82. Ibid., p. 18.
83. Ibid., p. 18. Galton *et al.* (1980), Appendix 1.
84. Galton and Simon (1980), pp. 46-7.
85. Ibid., p. 47. Quoted from the skills classification of the Richmond tests.
86. See e.g. Elliott (1971); White (1972); Barrow (1975). One curious point worth remarking is that Brian Simon is the author of a book that exposes many of the fundamental flaws in standardised tests such as his programme of research employs: *Intelligence Testing and the Comprehensive School.* (Lawrence and Wishart, 1953.)
87. Galton and Simon (1980), p. 113.
88. Galton *et al.* (1980), p. 94.
89. Ibid., pp. 17, 90, 95.
90. Ibid.
91. Ibid., p. 166.
92. Ibid., pp. 1, 155, 156.

93. Ibid., p. 60.
94. Ibid., p. 60.
95. Ibid., p. 62.
96. See above, n. 57.
97. Galton *et al.* (1980), p. 66.
98. E.g. ibid., pp. 23-27. This point is made more than once, but generally ignored when it comes to drawing 'significant' conclusions.
99. Ibid., p. 67.
100. Ibid., p. 69.
101. Ibid., p. 74.
102. Ibid., p. 88.
103. Ibid., p. 90.
104. Galton and Simon (1980), p. 71.
105. Ibid.
106. Dunkin and Biddle (1974), p. 14.
107. Galton and Simon (1980), p. 149.

CHAPTER 7

1. Pratt (1980), p. 425.
2. Kelly (1977), p. 132.
3. Taylor and Richards (1979), p. 92.
4. Orlosky and Smith (1978), p. 329.
5. Or see e.g. Doll (1970); Harris *et al.* (1975); Becher and Maclure (1978).
6. For discussion of an appropriate teacher education, see Ch. 9.s.2.

CHAPTER 8

1. Kelly (1977), p. 143.
2. See Barrow (1981 and 1982a).
3. And, of course, it is imperative that those further tests should themselves be agreed to be free of bias or subjectivity. In point of fact this is seldom the case. A test is judged to be objective on the basis of concurrence with other tests no more certainly objective.
4. Pratt (1980), p. 202.
5. McIntyre (1978), p. 82. Cf. Galton and Simon (1980), Appendix I.
6. Bentham (1948).

CHAPTER 9

1. See especially Chs 3, 5, 6 and 8. Chs 2 and 4 add something about the positive practical value of non-empirical work.
2. See especially Ch. 6.s.4.
3. See especially Chs 3.s.5, 6.s.5, 7.s.2, and Chs 5 and 6 *passim*.

4. See Ch. 3.s.5.
5. For Socrates and Rousseau, see above Ch. 2, n.10. For Piaget see Ch. 5.s.2. For American curriculum design theorist Hilda Taba, see Taba (1962).
6. See Ch. 6.ss.5 and 6.
7. See Ch. 3.s.5.
8. See especially Ch. 6.ss.1, 2 and 3.
9. It certainly isn't. See McPeck (1981), and Ch. 3.s.5.
10. See Simon and Boyer (1967) and Galton (1978); and Ch. 6, above.
11. See Ch. 2.ss.2 and 3; Ch. 6.ss.6 and 8; Ch. 9.s.1.
12. See Barrow (1975) and White (1972).
13. See Ch. 8.s.2.
14. As psychologists acknowledge, e.g. Fontana (1981).
15. See Ch. 3.
16. See Chs 2 and 4.
17. See Ch. 5.ss.3 and 4.
18. Chs 5 and 6.
19. Professor Flew has taken me to task for making similar remarks in a concluding chapter to Barrow (1982) without citing specific media sources. But that failure does not detract from the obvious truth of the claims.
20. Ch. 1.
21. See Ch. 7.s.2.
22. Ch. 1.s.3.
23. Stenhouse (1975), p. 125.
24. Walker (1975); Egan (1978).
25. Ch. 2.s.5 and 4.s.6.
26. Jenkins and Shipman (1976), p. 55.
27. See e.g. Dearden (1972) and Bridges (1979).
28. Rosenshine (1976), p. 345.
29. Ch. 6.
30. Ch. 5.ss.1 and 2; Ch. 6.
31. By Sanders in a private communication.

Bibliography and References

Adelman, C. (1976) Re-thinking case study: notes from the Second Cambridge Conference. *Cambridge Journal of Education,* 7.1.

Altman, H. (1970) Teacher – student interaction in inner-city and advantaged classes using the science curriculum improvement study. *Classroom Interaction Newsletter* 6(1), 5 – 16.

Amidon, E.J. and Flanders, N.A. (1961) The effects of direct and indirect teacher influence on dependent-prone students learning geometry. *Journal of Educational Psychology,* 52(6), 286 – 291.

Amidon, E.J. and Giammatteo, M. (1967) The verbal behavior of superior elementary teachers. In E.J. Amidon and J.B. Hough (Eds), *Interaction Analysis: Theory, Research and Application.* Reading, Mass.: Addison-Wesley.

Anderson, H.H. (1939) The measurement of domination and of socially integrative behaviour in teachers' contacts with children. *Child Development,* 10, 73 – 89.

Anderson, R.C. (1959) Learning in discussions: A resumé of the authoritarian – democratic studies. *Harvard Educational Review,* 29, 201 – 215.

Apple, M.W. (1979) *Ideology and Curriculum.* London: Routledge & Kegan Paul.

Arnold, M. (1932) *Culture and Anarchy,* Ed. J. Dover Wilson, Cambridge: Cambridge University Press.

Ausubel, D.P. (1959) Viewpoints from related disciplines: Human growth and development. *Teachers College Record,* 60, 245 – 254.

Ausubel, D.P. (1968) *Educational Psychology: A Cognitive View.* New York: Holt, Rinehart & Winston.

Ayer, A.J. (1971) *Language, Truth and Logic.* Harmondsworth: Penguin Books.

Baldwin, A.L. (1967) *Theories of Child Development.* New York: John Wiley.

Bantock, G.H. (1963) *Education in an Industrial Society,* London: Faber.

Bantock, G.H. (1965) *Education and Values.* London: Faber.

Bantock, G.H. (1968) *Culture, Industrialisation and Education,* London: Routledge & Kegan Paul.

281

Barnes, B. (1974) *Scientific Knowledge and Sociological Theory.* London: Routledge & Kegan Paul.
Barnes, D. (1976) *From Communication to Curriculum.* Harmondsworth: Penguin Books.
Barrow, R. (with R.G. Woods) (1975) *Introduction to Philosophy of Education.* London: Methuen.
Barrow, R. (1976) *Plato and Education.* London: Routledge & Kegan Paul.
Barrow, R. (1976a) *Common Sense and the Curriculum.* London: Allen & Unwin.
Barrow, R. (1978) *Radical Education.* Oxford: Martin Robertson.
Barrow, R. (1978a) *The Canadian Curriculum.* London, Ont.: University of Western Ontario.
Barrow, R. (1980) *Happiness.* Oxford: Martin Robertson.
Barrow, R. (1981) *The Philosophy of Schooling.* Brighton: Wheatsheaf.
Barrow, R. (1981a) *Educational and Curriculum Theory.* Vancouver: University of British Columbia.
Barrow, R. (1982) *Injustice, Inequality and Ethics.* Brighton: Wheatsheaf.
Barrow, R. (1982a) *Language and Thought.* London, Ont.: University of Western Ontario.
Barrow, R. (1983) There is no conversation. *Hesperiam,* December.
Barrow, R. (1984) Does the question 'What is education?' make sense? *Educational Theory,* 33 (3 & 4).
Barrow, R. (1984a) How married are you, Mary Ann? *Oxford Review of Education,* 10(2).
Barrow, R. (1984b) The non-negotiable curriculum. *Curriculum Inquiry.*
Barrow, R. (1984c) Teacher judgement and teacher effectiveness. *Journal of Educational Thought,* August.
Becher, T. and Maclure, S. (1978) *The Politics of Curriculum Change.* London: Hutchinson.
Bedford, E. (1964 Emotion. In D. Gustafson (ed.), *Essays in Philosophical Psychology.* Garden City, N.Y.: Anchor Books.
Bennett, N. (1976) *Teaching Styles and Pupil Progress.* London: Open Books.
Bentham, J. (1948) *The Principles of Morals and Legislation.* New York: Hafner.
Berliner, D.C. (1976) Impediments to the study of teacher effectiveness. *Journal of Teacher Education,* 27(5).
Bernstein, B. (1971) *Class, Codes and Control,* vol. 1. London: Routledge & Kegan Paul.
Biddle, B.J. and Ellena, W.J. (eds) (1964) *Contemporary Research on Teacher Effectiveness.* New York: Holt, Rinehart & Winston.
Black, M. (1962) *Models and Metaphors: Studies in Language and Philosophy.* Ithaca, N.Y.: Cornell University Press.
Bloom, B. (1976) *Human Characteristics and School Learning.* New York: McGraw-Hill.

Bloom, B. *et al.* (1956) *Taxonomy of Educational Objectives: Handbook 1, Cognitive Domain.* London: Longman.

Bobbit, F. (1918) *The Curriculum.* Boston: Houghton Mifflin.

Boden, M.A. (1979) *Piaget.* Brighton: Harvester.

Bondi, J.C. (1969) The effects of interaction analysis feedback on the verbal behaviour of student teachers. *Educational Leadership,* 26, 794-799.

Boydell, D. (1978) *The Primary Teacher in Action.* London: Open Books.

Bowen, J. (1962) *Soviet Education.* Madison: University of Wisconsin Press.

Bowen, J. (1981) *A History of Western Education,* vol. 3. London: Methuen.

Brent, A. (1978) *Philosophical Foundation for the Curriculum.* London: Allen & Unwin.

Bridges, D. (1979) *Education, Democracy and Discussion.* Slough: NFER.

Brophy, J. *et al.* (1973) *Communication of Teacher Expectations: Fifth Grade* (Report Series No. 93). Research and Development Center for Teacher Education, University of Texas, Austin.

Brown, J.A.C. (1964) *Freud and the Post-Freudians.* Harmondsworth: Penguin Books.

Brown, R.H. (1977) *A Poetic for Sociology: Toward a Logic of Discovery for the Human Sciences.* Cambridge: Cambridge University Press.

Brown, S. *et al.* (1981) *Conceptions of Inquiry.* London: Methuen.

Bruner, J. (1966) *Towards a Theory of Instruction.* Cambridge, Mass.: Harvard University Press.

Bryan, J.F. and Locke, E.A. (1967) Goal-setting as a means of increasing motivation. *Journal of Applied Psychology,* 51, 274-277.

Bryant, P.E. and Trabasso, T. (1971) Transitive inferences and memory in young children. *Nature,* 232, 456-458.

Bullock Report (1975) *A Language for Life.* London: HMSO.

Burt, C. (1923) *Handbook of Tests for Use in Schools.* London: King.

Burt, C. (1949) The structure of the mind. *British Journal of Educational Psychology.*

Byrne, E.M. (1974) *Planning and Educational Inequality.* Slough: NFER.

Campbell, W.J. (1970) Some effects on affective climate on the achievement motivation of pupils. In W.J. Campbell (ed.), *Scholars in Context: The Effects of Environments on Learning.* Sydney: Wiley.

Cashdan, A. and Whitehead, J. (eds) (1971) *Personality Growth and Learning.* London: Longman.

Child, D. (1973) *Psychology and the Teacher.* New York: Holt, Rinehart & Winston.

Chisholm, R. (1966) *Theory of Knowledge.* Englewood Cliffs, N.J.: Prentice-Hall.

284   Bibliography

Claiborne, J. (1983) *Our Marvellous Native Tongue*. New York: Times Books.

Coffman, W.E. (1971) Essay examinations. In R.L. Thorndike (ed), *Educational Measurement*. Washington, D.C.: American Council on Education.

Coleman, J.S. *et al.* (1966) *Equality of Educational Opportunity*. Washington, D.C.: US Government Printing Office.

Comenius, J.A. (1957) *The School of Infancy*, (ed.), E.M. Eller, University of North Carolina Press.

Coopersmith, S. (1968) Studies in self-esteem. *Scientific American*, February.

Cox, C.B. and Dyson, A.E. (1969) *Fight for Education: A Black Paper*. Manchester: Critical Quarterly Society.

Cremin, L.A. (1961) *The Transformation of the School*. New York: Alfred A. Knopf.

Cronbach, L.J. (1975) Beyond the two disciplines of scientific psychology. *American Psychologist*, February, 116-127.

Dahllof, U.S. and Lundgren, U.P. (1970) *Project Compass 23: Macro and micro approaches combined for curriculum process analysis*. Paper presented at the annual meeting of the American Educational Research Association, Minneapolis.

Davidoff, L.L. (1976) *Introduction to Psychology*. New York: McGraw Hill.

Davie, R. *et al.* (1972) *From Birth to Seven*. London: Longman.

Davis, O.L. and Slobodian, J.J. (1967) Teacher behavior towards boys and girls during first grade reading instruction. *American Educational Research Journal*, 4, 261-270.

Dearden, R.F. (1967) Instruction and learning by discovery. In R.S. Peters (ed.), *The Concept of Education*. London: Allen & Unwin.

Dearden, R.F. (1972) Needs in education. In R.F. Dearden *et al.* (eds), *Education and the Development of Reason*. London: Routledge & Kegan Paul.

Dearden, R.F. (1972a) Autonomy and Education. In R.F. Dearden *et al.* (eds), *Education and the Development of Reason*. London: Routledge & Kegan Paul.

Dearden, R.F. (1976) *Problems in Primary Education*. London: Routledge & Kegan Paul.

Degenhardt, M.A.B. (1982) *Education and the Value of Knowledge*. London: Allen & Unwin.

Delamont, S. (1983) *Interaction in the Classroom*. London: Methuen.

Devries, D.L. and Edwards, K.J. (1973) Learning games and student teams: Their effects on classroom processes. *American Educational Research Journal*, 10, 307-318.

Dewey, J. (1938) *Experience and Education*. New York: Collier Macmillan.

Doll, R.C. (1970) The multiple forces affecting curriculum change. *Phi Delta Kappa*, 51, 382-4.

Duchastel, P.C. and Merrill, P.F. (1973) The effects of behavioral objectives on learning: A review of empirical studies. *Review of Educational Research,* 43, 53-68.

Dunkin, M.J. and Biddle, B.J. (1974) *The Study of Teaching.* New York: Holt, Rinehart & Winston.

Durkheim, E. (1952) *Suicide: A Study in Sociology.* London: Routledge & Kegan Paul.

Durkheim, E. (1964) *The Rules of Sociological Method.* New York: Collier Macmillan.

Egan, K. (1978) Some presuppositions that determine curriculum decisions. *Curriculum Studies,* 10(2).

Egan, K. (1979) *Educational Development.* New York: Oxford.

Egan, K. (1982) On the possibility of theories of educational practice. *Journal of Curriculum Studies,* 14(2).

Egan, K. (1983) *Education and Psychology.* New York: Teachers' College Press.

Eisner, E. (1969) Instructional and expressive objectives. In W.J. Popham *et al.* (eds), *Instructional Objectives.* Chicago: Rand McNally.

Eisner, E. (1979) *The Educational Imagination: On the Design and Evaluation of School Programmes.* New York: Macmillan.

Eisner, E. and Vallance, E. (eds) (1974) *Conflicting Conceptions of Curriculum.* Berkeley: McCutchan.

Eliot, T.S. (1949) *Notes Towards the Definition of Culture.* London: Faber.

Elliott, J. (1977) The conditions of public accountability. *Cambridge Journal of Education,* 7.2.

Elliott, R.K. (1971) Versions of creativity. *Proceedings of the Philosophy of Education Society of Great Britain,* (5(2).

Emmer, E.T. (1967) *The effect of teacher use and acceptance of student ideas on student verbal initiation.* Unpublished doctoral dissertation, University of Michigan.

Eraut, M., *et al.* (1975) *The Analysis of Curriculum Materials.* Brighton: University of Sussex Education Area.

Erikson, E. (1965) *Childhood and Society.* London: Hogarth Press.

Evans, E.G.S. (1969) *Modern Educational Psychology.* London: Routledge & Kegan Paul.

Evertson, C.M. *et al.* (1973) *Communication of Teacher Expectations: Second Grade* (Report Series 92). Austin, Texas: University of Texas, Research and Development Center for Teacher Education.

Felsenthal, H. (1970) *Sex Differences in Teacher-Pupil Interaction in First Grade Reading Instruction.* Paper presented at the annual meeting of the American Educational Research Association, Minneapolis.

Fenstermacher, G.D. (1979) A philosophical consideration of recent research on teacher effectiveness. In L. Shulman (ed.), *Review of Research in Education.* Itasca, III.: Peacock.

Flanders, N.A. (1963) *Teacher and Classroom Influences on Individual Learning.* Paper presented at the Seventh Annual Curriculum Research Institute, Eastern Section, Association for Supervision and Curriculum Development.

Flanders, N.A. (1967) Teacher influence in the classroom. In E.J. Amidon and J.B. Hough (eds), *Interaction Analysis: Theory Research and Application.* Reading, Mass.: Addison-Wesley.

Flanders, N.A. (1970) *Analyzing Teacher Behavior.* Reading, Mass.: Addison-Wesley.

Fontana, D. (1981) *Psychology for Teachers.* London: Macmillan.

Fowler, B.D. and Soar, R.S. (no date) *Relation of Teacher Personality Characteristics and Attitudes to Teacher-Pupil Behaviors and Emotional Climate in the Elementary Classroom.* (mimeo), University of South Carolina.

Frankenburg, W.K. and Dodds, J.B. (1967) The Denver developmental screening test. *Journal of Pediatricians,* 71, 181-191.

Freud, S. (1901) *The Psychopathology of Everyday Life.* London: Benn.

Freud, S. (1938) *An Outline of Psycho-Analysis.* London: Hogarth.

Freud, S. (1962) *Two Short Accounts of Psycho-Analysis.* Harmondsworth: Penguin.

Fullan, M. and Pomfret, A. (1975) *Review of Research on Curriculum Implementation.* Toronto: OISE.

Furst, N.F. (1967) *The multiple Languages of the Classroom.* Paper presented at the annual meeting of the American Educational Research Association, New York.

Furst, N.F. (1967a) The effects of training in interaction analysis on the behaviour of student teachers in secondary schools. In E.J. Amidon and J.B. Hough (eds), *Interaction Analysis: Theory, Research and Application.* Reading, Mass.: Addison-Wesley.

Gage, N.L. (1972) *Teacher Effectiveness and Teacher Education.* Palo Alto, Calif.: Pacific Books.

Gage, N.L. (ed.) (1963) *Handbook of Research on Teaching.* Chicago: Rand McNally.

Gagné, R.M. (1970) *Conditions of Learning.* London: Holt, Rinehart & Winston.

Gagné, R.M. (1974) *Essentials of Learning for Instruction.* Hinsdale, Ill.: Dryden Press.

Galton, M. (ed.) (1978) *British Mirrors.* Leicester: School of Education.

Galton, M. (ed.) (1980) *Curriculum Change.* Leicester: University of Leicester Press.

Galton, M. *et al.* (1980) *Inside the Primary Classroom.* London: Routledge & Kegan Paul.

Galton M. and Simon, B. (1980) *Progress and Performance in the Primary Classroom.* London: Routledge & Kegan Paul.

Gesell, A. (1928) *Infancy and Human Growth.* New York: Macmillan.

Gibson, R. (1981) Curriculum criticism: Misconceived theory, ill-advised practice. *Cambridge Journal of Education,* 11.

Godshalk, F.I., Swineford, F. and Coffman, W.E. (1966) *Measurement of Writing Ability*. New York: College Entrance Examination Board.
Golby, M., Greenwald, J. and West, R. (eds) (1975) *Curriculum Design*. London: Croom Helm.
Good, T.L. and Brophy, J.E. (1972) Behavioral expression of teacher attitudes. *Journal of Education Psychology,* 63, 617-624.
Good, T.L., Biddle, B.J. and Brophy, J.E. (1975) *Teachers Make a Difference*. New York: Holt, Rinehart & Winston.
Good, T.L. *et al.* (1973) Effects of teacher sex, student sex and student achievement on classroom interaction. *Journal of Educational Psychology,* 65, 74-87.
Goodlad, J.I. (1958) Toward a conceptual system for curriculum problems. *School Review,* 66, 391-401.
Goodlad, J.I. and Richter, M. (1966) *The Development of a Conceptual System for Dealing with Problems of Curriculum and Instruction*. Los Angeles: University of California.
Gould, S. (1981) *The Mismeasure of Man*. New York: Norton.
Greene, M. (1978) *Landscapes of Learning*. Columbia: Teachers' College Press.
Gress, J.R. (ed.) (1978) *Curriculum: An Introduction to the Field*. Berkeley, California: McCutchan.
Gronlund, N.E. (1970) *Stating Behavioural Objectives for Classroom Instruction*. London: Collier MacMillan.
Haberman, P.W. and Sheinberg, J. (1966) Education reported in interviews: An aspect of survey content error. *Public Opinion Quarterly,* 30, 295-301.
Hamilton, D. (1975) *Curriculum Evaluation*. London: Open Books.
Hamlyn, D. (1967) The logical and psychological aspects of learning. In R.S. Peters (ed.), *The Concept of Education*. London: Allen & Unwin.
Hamlyn, D. (1978) *Experience and the Growth of Understanding*. London: Routledge & Kegan Paul.
Hamner, W.C. (1974) Goal-setting, performance and satisfaction in an interdependent task. *Organisational Behavior and Human Performance,* 12, 217-230.
Hare, R.M. (1964) *Language of Morals*. Oxford: Oxford University Press.
Harris, A., Lawn, M. and Prescott, W. (1975) *Curriculum Innovation*. London: Croom Helm.
Havelock, R.G. (1971) *Planning for Innovation Through the Dissemination and Utilization of Knowledge*. Ann Arbor, Michigan: Center for Research and Utilization of Knowledge.
Heath, R.W. and Nielsen, M.A. (1974) The research basis for performance-based teacher education. *Review of Educational Research,* 44, 463-484.
Hempel, C. (1966) *Philosophy of Natural Science*. Englewood Cliffs, N.J.: Prentice-Hall.
Hepburn, R.W. (1972) The arts and the education of feeling and

emotion. In R.F. Dearden *et al.* (eds) *Education and the Development of Reason.* London: Routledge & Kegan Paul.

Herbart, J.F. (1904) *Outlines of Educational Doctrine,* trans. A.F. Lange, New York: Macmillan.

Herman, W.L. (1967) An analysis of the activities and verbal behaviour of selected fifth grade social studies classes. *Classroom Interaction Newsletter,* 2(2), 27-29.

Hilgard, E.R. (1956) *Theories of Learning.* New York: Appleton-Century-Crofts.

Hill, R.A. and Furst, N.F. (1969) *A comparison of the Role of Teachers in CAI Classrooms and Teachers in Traditional Classrooms.* Paper presented at the American Educational Research Association, Los Angeles.

Hirst, P.H. (1968) The contribution of philosophy to the study of the curriculum. In J.F. Kerr (ed.), *Changing the Curriculum.* London: University of London Press.

Hirst, P.H. (1974) *Knowledge and the Curriculum.* London: Routledge & Kegan Paul.

Hirst, P.H. (1980) The logic of curriculum development. In M. Galton (ed.), *Curriculum Change.* Leicester: University of Leicester.

Hirst, P.H. and O'Connor, D.J. (1972) The nature of educational theory. *Proceedings of the Philosophy of Education Society of Great Britain,* 6(1).

HMI Survey (1978) Department of Education and Science. *Primary Education in England: A Survey by HM Inspectors of Schools.* London: HMSO.

HMI Report (1983) *The Quality of Teaching.* London: HMSO.

Hoehn, A.J. (1954) A study of social status differentiation in the classroom behavior of nineteen third grade teachers. *Journal of Social Psychology,* 39, 269-292.

Hooper, R. (ed.) (1971) *The Curriculum: Content Design and Development.* Edinburgh: Oliver & Boyd.

Hore, T. (1971) Assessment of teaching practice. *British Journal of Educational Psychology,* 41.

Hospers, J. (1956) *An Introduction to Philosophical Analysis.* London: Routledge & Kegan Paul.

House, E.R. (1974) *The Politics of Educational Innovation.* Berkeley, Calif.: McCutchan.

Hughes, M. (1959) *Assessment of the Quality of Teaching in Elementary Schools,* Salt Lake City: University of Utah Press.

Hunter, C.P. (1968) *Classroom Climate and Pupil Characteristics in Special Classes for the Educationally Handicapped.* Unpublished doctoral dissertation, University of Southern California.

Illich, I.D. (1971) *Deschooling Society.* London: Calder.

Isaacs, S. (1930) Intellectual Growth in Young Children. London: Routledge & Kegan Paul.

Jackson, P.W. and Lahaderne, H.M. (1966) Inequalities of teacher-pupil contacts. *Psychology in the Schools,* 4(3), 201-211.

Jencks, C.S. (1969) The Coleman Report: A reappraisal of the most controversial educational document of our time. *New York Times Magazine,* 10 August.

Jenkins, D. and Shipman, M. (1976) *Curriculum: An Introduction.* London: Open Books.

Jensen, A. (1969) How much can we boost IQ and scholastic achievement? *Harvard Educational Review,* 39, 1-123.

Johns, J.P. (1966 *The relationship Between Teacher Behaviors and the Incidence of Thought-provoking Questions by Students in Secondary Schools.* Unpublished doctoral dissertation, University of Michigan.

Johnson, D.W. and Johnson, R.T. (1974) *Learning Together and Alone: Cooperation, Competition and Individualisation.* Englewood Cliffs, N.J.: Prentice Hall.

Johnson, J.R. (1974) *Development and Implementation of a Competency-based Teacher Education Module.* Paper presented at the annual meeting of the American Educational Research Association, Chicago.

Johnson, M. (1967) Definitions and models in curriculum theory. *Educational Theory,* 17, 127-140.

Johnston, M. (1975) Conceptual confusion and premature policies. In R.A. Smith (ed.), *Regaining Educational Leadership.* New York: Wiley.

Joyce, B.R. (1978) *Selecting Learning Experiences: Linking Theory and Practice.* Washington, D.C.: Association for Supervision and Curriculum Development.

Joyce, B.R. and Weil, M. (1979) *Models of Teaching* (2nd edn). Englewood Cliffs, N.J.: Prentice Hall.

Julian, J.W. and Perry, F.A. (1967) Cooperation contrasted with intra-group and inter-group competition. *Sociometry,* 30, 79-90.

Kazepides, T. (1982) Educating, socialising and indoctrinating. *Journal of Philosophy of Education,* 16(2).

Keating, H.,R.F. (ed.) (1982) *Whodunit?* London: Windward.

Kelly, A.V. (1977) *The Curriculum: Theory and Practice.* London: Harper & Row.

Kelly, P.J. (1975) *Curriculum Diffusion Research Project Outline Report.* Centre for Science Education, University of London.

Kerr, J. (ed.) (1968) *Changing the Curriculum.* London: University of London Press.

Kleinig, J. (1973) R.S. Peters' use of transcendental arguments. *Proceedings of Philosophy of Education Society of Great Britain,* 7(2).

Kleinig, J. (1982) *Philosophical Issues in Education.* New York: St Martin's Press.

Kohlberg, L. (1969) Stage and sequence: The cognitive-developmental approach to socialization. In D. Goslin (ed.), *Handbook of Socialization Theory.* Chicago: Rand McNally.

Kounin, J.S. (1970) *Discipline and Group Management in Classrooms.*

New York: Holt, Rinehart & Winston.

Kounin, J.S. and Gump, P.V. (1958) The ripple effect in discipline. *Elementary School Journal,* 35, 158-162.

Kounin, J.S. *et al.* (1966) Managing emotionally disturbed children in regular classrooms. *Journal of Educational Psychology,* 57, 1-13.

Labov, W. (1966) *The Social Stratification of English in New York City.* Washington, D.C.: Center for Applied Linguistics.

Lapierre, R.T. (1934) Attitudes versus actions. *Social Forces,* 13, 230-237.

Lawton, D. (1968) *Social Class, Language and Education.* London: Routledge & Kegan Paul.

Lawton, D. (1975) *Class, Culture and the Curriculum.* London: Routledge & Kegan Paul.

Lawton, D. *et al.* (1978) *Theory and Practice of Curriculum Studies.* London: Routledge & Kegan Paul.

Lewin, K. *et al.* (1939) Patterns of aggressive behavior in experimentally created 'social climates'. *Journal of Social Psychology,* 10, 271-299.

Locke, E.A. *et al.* (1970) Studies of the relationships between satisfaction, goal-setting, and performance. *Organizational Behaviour and Human Performance,* 5, 135-158.

Lohman, E. *et al.* (1967) A study of the effect of pre-service training in interaction analysis on the verbal behavior of student teachers. In E.J. Amidon and J.B. Hough (eds), *Interaction Analysis: Theory, Research and Application.* Reading, Mass.: Addison-Wessley.

Lortie, D.C. (1975) *School Teacher: A Sociological Study.* Chicago: University of Chicago.

Louch, A.R. (1966) *Explanation and Human Action.* Berkeley: University of California Press.

Lytton, H. (1971) *Creativity and Education.* London: Routledge & Kegan Paul.

MacDonald, B. (1973) Innovation and incompetence. In D. Hamingson (ed.), *Towards Judgement: The Publications of the Evaluation Unit of the Humanities Curriculum Project 1970-72,* Occasional Publications No. 1. Norwich: Centre for Applied Research in Education.

MacDonald B. and Walker, R. (1976) *Changing the Curriculum.* London: Open Books.

MacDonald-Ross, M. (1975) Behavioural objectives: A critical review. In M. Golby (ed.), *Curriculum Design.* London: Croom Helm.

McGee, C.S. *et al.* (1977) Children as therapeutic change agents: Reinforcement intervention paradigms. *Review of Educational Research,* 47, 451-477.

McGee, H.M. (1955) Measurement of authoritarianism and its relation to teachers' classroom behavior. *Genetic Psychology Monographs,* 52, 89-146.

McIntyre, D. and MacLeod, G. (1978) The characteristics and uses of systematic classroom observation. In R. McAleese and D. Hamilton (eds), *Understanding Classroom Life.* Slough: NFER.

McNamara, D.R. *et al.* (1977) *Education for Teaching.* London: SRHE.
McPeck, J. (1981) *Critical Thinking.* Oxford: Martin Robertson.
Madsen, M.C. (1971) Developmental and cross-cultural differences in the cooperative and competitive behaviour of young children. *Journal of Cross-Cultural Psychology,* 2, 365-371.
Mager, R.F. (1962) *Preparing Instructional Objectives.* Palo Alto, California: Fearon.
Marx, K. (1938) *Capital: A Critical Analysis of Capitalist Production,* I. London.
Maslow, A.H. (1954) *Motivation and Personality.* New York: Harper.
Matthews, M.R. (1981) *The Marxist Theory of Schooling.* Brighton: Harvester.
Measel, W.W. (1967) *The Relationship Between Teacher Influence and Levels of Thinking of Second Grade Teachers and Pupils.* Unpublished doctoral dissertation, University of Michigan, Ann Arbor.
Medley, D.M. and Hill, R.A. (1970) *Cognitive Factors in Teaching-style.* Paper presented at the annual meeting of the American Educational Research Association, Minneapolis.
Michaelis, J.W. (1977) Classroom reward structures and academic performance. *Review of Educational Research,* 47, 87-98.
Milburn, G. (1983) *On Discipline Stripping: Difficulties in the Application of Humanistic Metaphors to Educational Phenomena.* Paper presented at the meeting of the Canadian Society for the Study of Education, Vancouver.
Milburn, G. (1983a) *Deciphering a Code or Unravelling a Riddle: A Case Study in the Application of Humanistic Metaphor to the Reporting of Social Studies Teaching.* Paper presented at the College and University Faculty Assembly, National Council for the Social Studies, San Francisco.
Milburn, G. (1983b) *Linguistic Madness with a Method: On Humanistic Metaphors and Educational Research.* Unpublished paper.
Mill, J.S. (1962) *Utilitarianism* (ed.) M. Warnock. London: Fontana.
Mill, J.S. (1960) *Autobiography.* New York: Columbia University Press.
Mood, D.W. (1972) Teacher verbal behavior and teacher and pupil thinking in elementary school. *Journal of Educational Research,* 66(3), 99-102.
Morris, B. (1958) Mental health in the classroom. In *Studies in Education,* no. 7. London: Evans.
Morrish, I. (1967) *Disciplines of Education.* London: Allen & Unwin.
Mussen, P.A. *et al.* (1979) *Child Development and Personality* (5th edn). New York: Harper & Row.
Neagley, R.L. and Evans, N.D. (1967) *Handbook for Effective Curriculum Development.* Englewood Cliffs, N.J.: Prentice-Hall.
Orlosky, D.E. and Smith, B.O. (1978) *Curriculum Development: Issues and Insights.* Chicago: Rand McNally.

Parker, J. and Rubin, L. (1966) *Process as Content*. Chicago: Rand McNally.

Parlett, M. and Hamilton, D. (1972) Evaluation as illumination: A new approach to the study of innovatory programmes, *Occasional Paper 9*. Centre for Research in Educational Sciences, University of Edinburgh.

Penny, R.E. (1969) *Presentational Behaviors Related to Success in Teaching*. Unpublished doctoral dissertation, Stanford University.

Perkins, H.V. (1964) A procedure for assessing the classroom behavior of students and teachers. *American Educational Research Journal*, 1(4), 249-260.

Perkins, H.V. (1965) Classroom behavior and underachievement. *American Educational Research Journal*, 2, 1-12.

Peters, R.S. (1966) *Ethics and Education*. London: Allen & Unwin.

Peters, R.S. (ed.) (1967) *The Concept of Education*. London: Allen & Unwin.

Peters, R.S. (ed.) (1969) *Perspectives on Plowden*. London: Routledge & Kegan Paul.

Peters, R.S. (1974) *Psychology and Ethical Development*. London: Allen & Unwin.

Peters, R.S. (ed.) (1977) *John Dewey Reconsidered*. London: Routledge & Kegan Paul.

Phenix, P.H. (1964) *Realms of Meaning*. New York: McGraw Hill.

Phillips, D.C. and Kelly, M.E. (1975) Hierarchical theories of development in education and psychology. *Harvard Educational Review*, 45(3), 351-375.

Piaget, J. (1924) *Language and Thought of the Child*. London: Routledge & Kegan Paul.

Piaget, J. (1929) *The Child's Conception of Physical Causality*. London: Routledge & Kegan Paul.

Piaget, J. (1947) *The Psychology of Intelligence*. London: Routledge & Kegan Paul.

Pinar, W.F. (ed.) (1974) *Heightened Consciousness, Cultural Revolution and Curriculum Theory*. Berkeley, California: McCutchan.

Pinar, W.F. (ed.) 1975) *Curriculum Theorizing: The Reconceptualists*. Berkeley, California: McCutchan.

Plato (1955) *The Republic* Trans. H. Lee. Harmondsworth: Penguin Books.

Plato (1956) *The Meno* Trans. W.K.C. Guthrie. Harmondsworth: Penguin Books.

Plowden Report (1967) *Children and Their Primary Schools* (2 vols.), Report of the Central Advisory Council for Education in England. London: HMSO.

Popham, W.J. (1968) Probing the validity of arguments against behavioural goals. Symposium presented at the Annual American Educational Research Association, Chicago. In R.J. Kibler *et al.* (eds), *Behavioral Objectives and Instruction*. Boston: Allyn & Bacon.

Popham, W.J. (1977) Objectives 72. In L. Rubin (ed.), *Curriculum*

Handbook. Boston: Allyn & Bacon.

Povey, R. and Hill, E. (1975) Can pre-school children form concepts? *Educational Research,* 17, 180-192.

Pratt, D. (1980) *Curriculum: Design and Development.* New York: Harcourt Brace Jovanovich.

Pring, R. (1976) *Knowledge and Schooling.* London: Open Books.

Reid, W.A. (1978) *Thinking about the Curriculum.* London: Routledge & Kegan Paul.

Reid, W. and Walker, D. (eds) (1975) *Case Studies in Curriculum Change: Great Britain and the United States.* London: Routledge & Kegan Paul.

Reynolds, J. and Skilbeck, M. (1976) *Culture and the Classroom.* London: Open Books.

Rian, H. (1969) Teacher leadership and pupil reaction: The authoritarian-democratic dimension revisited. *Scandinavian Journal of Educational Research,* 13, 1-15.

Rosenshine, B. (1976) Classroom instruction. In N.L. Gage (ed.), *The Psychology of Teaching Methods.* Chicago: University of Chicago Press.

Rosenshine, B. and Furst, N. (1973) The use of direct observation to study teaching. In M.W. Travers (ed.), *Second Handbook of Research on Teaching.* Chicago: Rand McNally.

Rousseau, J. (1972) *Emile.* London: Dent.

Rubin, L. (1977) *Curriculum Handbook: The Disciplines, Current Movements and Instructional Methodology.* Boston: Allyn & Bacon.

Rubovits, P.C. and Maehr, M.L. (1973) Pygmalion black and white. *Journal of Personality and Social Psychology,* 25(2), 210-218.

Rudduck, J. (1976) *Dissemination of Innovation: the Humanities Curriculum Project.* London: Evans/Methuen.

Rudner, R.S. (1966) *Philosophy of Social Science.* Englewood Cliffs, N.J.: Prentice Hall

Rugg, H. *et al.* (1926) The foundations of curriculum making. *Twenty-Sixth Yearbook of the National Society for the Study of Education.*

Russell, B. (1932) *On Education.* London: Allen & Unwin.

Russell, B. (1967-9). *Autobiography.* London: Allen & Unwin.

Rutter, M. *et al.* (1979) *Fifteen Thousand Hours.* London: Open Books.

Sanders, J. (1978) Teacher effectiveness: Accepting the null hypothesis. *The Journal of Educational Thought,* 12(3).

Sanders, J. (1981) Teacher effectiveness and the limits of psychological explanation. *McGill Journal of Education.* 16.1.

Scheffler, I. (1976) Basic mathematical skills: some philosophical and practical remarks. *Teachers College Record,* 78.

Schlechty, P.C. (1976) *Teaching and Social Behaviour: Toward an Organisational Theory of Instruction.* Boston: Allyn & Bacon.

Schon, D. (1971) *Beyond the Stable State.* London: Temple Smith.

Schwab, J. (1969) The practical: a language for the curriculum. *School Review,* 78.1.

Scriven, M. (1967) The methodology of evaluation. In R. Tyler, R.
Gagne and M. Scriven, *Perspectives on Curriculum Evaluation*. Chicago:
Rand McNally.

Seymour, W.D. (1937) An experiment showing the superiority of a light
colored 'blackboard'. *British Journal of Educational Psychology*, 7,
259-268.

Silberman, M.L. (1969) Behavior expression of teachers' attitudes
towards elementary school students. *Journal of Educational
Psychology*, 60, 402-407.

Simon, A., and Boyer, E.G. (eds) (1967) *Mirrors for Behaviour*.
Philadelphia: Research for Better Schools.

Skilbeck, M. (1976) School-based curriculum development. In *Open
University Course 203, Unit 26*, 90-102. Milton Keynes: The Open
University Press.

Skinner, B.F. (1969) *Contingencies of Reinforcement: A Theoretical
Analysis*. New York: Appleton-Century-Crofts.

Smedslund, J. (1979) Between the analytic and the arbitrary: A case
study of psychological research. *Scandinavian Journal of Psychology*,
20.

Smith, B., Stanley, W. and Shores, J. (1957) *Fundamentals of
Curriculum Development*. New York: Harcourt, Brace & World.

Smith, M.B. (1965) Interpersonal relationships in the classroom based on
the expected socio-economic status of sixth grade boys. *Teachers'
College Record*, 36. 200-206.

Smith, R.E., Meadow, B.L. and Sisk, T.K. (1970) Attitude similarity,
interpersonal attraction, and evaluative social perception.
Psychonomic Science, 18.

Snow, R.E. (1977) Individual differences and instructional theory.
Educational Researcher, 6(10).

Soar, R.S. (1966) *An Integrative Approach to Classroom Learning*.
Philadelphia: Temple University.

Soar, R.S. *et al.* (1971) *The Validation of an Observation System for
Classroom Management*. Paper presented at the annual meeting of the
American Educational Research Association, New York.

Sockett, H. (1976) *Designing the Curriculum*. London: Open Books.

Sorber, E. (1967) Classroom interaction patterns and personality needs
of traditionally-prepared first year elementary teachers and graduate
teaching interns with degrees from colleges of liberal arts. *Classroom
Interaction Newsletter*, 2(2), 51-55.

Spaulding, R.L. (1963) *Achievement Creativity and Self-concept
Correlates of Teacher-Pupil Transactions in Elementary Schools*,
Cooperative Research Project No. 1352, College of Education,
University of Illinois.

Sprague, N.F. (1971) *Inquiry Dialogue in the Classroom*. Paper
presented at the annual meeting of the American Educational Research
Association, New York.

Stake, R.E. (1972) *Responsive Evaluation* (mimeo). Urbana-Champaign:

University of Illinois.

Starch, D. and Elliot, E.C. (1912) Reliability of grading high school work in English. *School Review,* 20, 442-457.

Starch, D. and Elliott, E.C. (1913) Reliability of grading work in mathematics. *School Review,* 21, 254-259.

Stenhouse, L. (1975) *An Introduction to Curriculum Research and Development.* London: Heinemann.

Stern, G.G. *et al.* (1956) *Methods in Personality Assessment.* Glencoe, Illinois: Free Press.

Stufflebeam, D.L. (1968) Towards a science of educational evaluation. *Educational Technology,* 8, 5-12.

Taba, H. (1962) *Curriculum Development: Theory and Practice.* New York: Harcourt Brace Jovanovich.

Tanner, D. and Tanner, L.N. (1980) *Curriculum Development: Theory into Practice.* New York: Macmillan.

Taylor, P.H. (1970) *How Teachers Plan Their Courses.* Slough: NFER.

Taylor, P.H. and Richards, C. (1979) *An Introduction to Curriculum Studies.* Slough: NFER.

Tibble, J. (ed.) (1971) *An Introduction to the Study of Education.* London: Routledge & Kegan Paul.

Tisher, R.P. (1970) The nature of verbal discourse in classrooms and association between verbal discourse and pupil's understanding in science. In W.J. Campbell (ed.), *Scholars in Context: The Effects of Environment on Learning.* Sydney: J. Wiley Australasia Pty.

Tomlinson, P. (1981) *Understanding Teaching: Interactive Educational Psychology.* New York: McGraw-Hill.

Traill, R.D. (1971) The effects of using interaction analysis as a means of assisting student teachers to analyze teaching behavior. *Australian Journal of Education,* 15(3), 295-304.

Turbayne, C.M. (1962) *The Myth of Metaphor.* New Haven: Yale University Press.

Tyler, R. (1949) *Basic Principles of Curriculum and Instruction.* Chicago: University of Chicago Press.

Walker, D.F. (1975) Straining to lift ourselves. *Curriculum Theory Network,* 5(1).

Walker, D.F. (1976) Toward comprehension of curricular realities. In Lee S. Shulman (ed.), *Review of Research in Education,* 4. Itasca, Illinois: Peacock.

Wallen, N.E. (1966) *Relationships Between Teacher Characteristics and Student Behavior,* Part 3. Salt Lake City: University of Utah Press.

Wallen, N.E. and Wodtke, K.H. (1963). *Relationships Between Teacher Characteristics and Student Behavior.* Part 1. Salt Lake City: Dept of Educational Psychology, University of Utah.

Waller, W. (1938) *The Sociology of Teaching.* New York: Wiley.

Warnock, G. (1976) *The Object of Morality.* London: Methuen.

Warwick, D. (1973) *Integrated Studies in the Secondary School.* London: University of London Press.

Wheeler, D.K. (1967) *Curriculum Process*. London: University of London Press.

White, J.P. (1973) *Towards a Compulsory Curriculum*. London: Routledge & Kegan Paul.

White, J.P. (1972) Creativity and education: A philosophical analysis. In R.F. Dearden, *et al.* (eds), *Education and the Development of Reason*. London: Routledge & Kegan Paul.

Whitehead, A.N. (1929) *The Aims of Education*. New York: MacMillan.

Whitfield, R. (1980) Curriculum objectives: Help or hindrance? In M. Galton (ed.), *Curriculum Change*. Leicester: University of Leicester.

Whitty, G. and Young, M.F.D. (eds) (1976) *Exploration in the Politics of School Knowledge*. Driffield: Nafferton Books.

Wilson, J. (1972) *Philosophy and Educational Research*. Slough: NFER.

Wilson, J. (1973) *The Assessment of Morality*. Slough: NFER.

Wilson, P.S. (1971) *Interest and Discipline in Education*. London: Routledge & Kegan Paul.

Wiseman, S. and Pidgeon, D. (1970) *Curriculum Evaluation*. Slough: NFER.

Withall, J. (1949) The development of a technique for the measurement of socio-emotional climate in classrooms. *Journal of Experimental Education,* 17, 347-361.

Witkin, H.A. *et al.* (1977) Field-dependent and field-independent cognitive styles and their educational implications. *Review of Educational Research,* 47, 1-64.

Woods, R. and Gregory, I. (1974). Valuable in itself. *Educational Philosophy and Theory,* 6(2).

Wright, C.J. and Nuthall, G. (1970) Relationships between teacher behaviors and pupil achievement in three experimental elementary science lessons. *American Educational Research Journal,* 7, 477-491.

Wright, N. (1977) *Progress in Education*. London: Croom Helm.

Yeomans, A. (1983) Collaborative group work in primary and secondary schools: Britain and the USA. *Durham and Newcastle Research Review,* 10(51), 99-106.

Young, M.F.D. (ed.) (1971) *Knowledge and Control*. London: Collier Macmillan.

Zais, R.S. (1976) *Curriculum: Principles and Foundations*. New York: Harper & Row.

Index